Written under the auspices of the
John M. Olin Institute for Strategic Studies
Center for International Affairs
Harvard University

THE POLITICAL ECONOMY
OF
NATIONAL SECURITY

A Global Perspective

THE POLITICAL ECONOMY OF NATIONAL SECURITY

A Global Perspective

Ethan Barnaby Kapstein

John M. Olin Institute for Strategic Studies
Harvard University
and
Department of Politics
Brandeis University

UNIVERSITY OF SOUTH CAROLINA PRESS

THE POLITICAL ECONOMY OF NATIONAL SECURITY
A Global Perspective

Clothbound edition published in Columbia, South Carolina, by the University of South Carolina Press.

1 2 3 4 5 6 7 8 9 0   DOC DOC   9 0 9 8 7 6 5 4 3 2 1

ISBN 0-87249-815-8

This book was set in Palatino by General Graphic Services, Inc.
The editors were Bertrand W. Lummus and Fred H. Burns;
the production supervisor was Annette Mayeski.
The cover was designed by Nicholas Krenitsky.
The photo editor was Barbara Salz.
R. R. Donnelley & Sons Company was printer and binder.

Library of Congress Cataloging-in-Publication Data

Kapstein, Ethan B.
    The political economy of national security: A global perspective /
    Ethan B. Kapstein.
          p.   cm.
    Includes bibliographical references and index.
    ISBN 0-87249-815-8
    1. National security—Economic aspects.   2. Defense industries.
    3. Military-industrial complex.   I. Title.
    HC79.D4K37   1992
    338.4'76233—dc20   91-23566

About the Author

Ethan Barnaby Kapstein is director of the economics and national security program in the John M. Olin Institute for Strategic Studies, Harvard University, and assistant professor of international relations at Brandeis University. He is the author of *The Insecure Alliance: Energy Crises and Western Politics since 1944* (New York: Oxford University Press, 1990) and many articles dealing with the political economy of national security.

To my students

CONTENTS

LIST OF FIGURES

LIST OF TABLES

PREFACE

Writing in 1941, Edward Mead Earle argued that "in modern times . . . we have constantly been confronted with the interrelation of commercial, financial, and industrial strength on the one hand, and political and military strength on the other. This interrelationship is one of the most critical and absorbing problems of statesmanship."[1] It is that interrelationship which forms the subject matter of this book.

The international system is characterized by anarchy, by the absence of central authority. Within that anarchic world, states must pursue the twin goals of security and prosperity. While states are increasingly adopting the logic of economic liberalism and the global division of labor in their pursuit of wealth, public officials charged with defense policy remain preoccupied with achieving autonomy in foreign affairs and military superiority over all possible rivals. There is thus an underlying tension between nationalistic conceptions of security and the globalization of economic activity. The exploration of that tension provides one of the major themes of this book, and it justifies the need for a new text in the political economy of national security, a text that treats the problem of defense economics in the context of the "open" rather than "closed" nation-state.

Providing for defense is one of the costliest economic activities of every state. But despite the influence of the defense sector on economic performance, industrial policy, and international economic relations, students and policymakers have gone a generation without a book that examines these and other critical policy issues. This work was written to fill that gap.

In preparing the text, I have consciously borrowed from many of the classic works in defense economics of the postwar era.[2] These studies, written mainly during the period 1950–1960, made manifest contemporary concerns about the political and economic implications of a large peacetime "military-industrial complex." It should be recalled that this was a period of awesome change in the international system, characterized by the enormous work of postwar recovery, the threat of U.S.–Soviet tensions leading to nuclear holocaust, and regional conflict throughout the third world. The economic burdens of defending democracy around the globe weighed heavily on American and western leaders. As we would only discover in recent years, the burdens of defense were even greater for Soviet rulers.

In the early 1980s, with the renewal of cold war tensions and a massive defense buildup in the United States and other western countries, public concern over the malign effects of defense spending became prominent once more. Scholars like Paul Kennedy of Yale suggested that the mismatch between defense commitments and economic capabilities had doomed one great power after another throughout history, with important lessons for the United States and, even more pointedly, the Soviet Union.[3] A great debate raged in scholarly journals and the popular press over the relationship between defense spending and economic performance, and the decline of at least one superpower—the Soviet Union—seemed causally related to the high levels of defense spending it had maintained since World War II.

Public concern with issues at the interface of economics and national security was not limited to the potentially malign effects of defense spending. One of the most troubling developments of the emerging new world order is the proliferation of advanced weaponry. States like Iraq were able to amass powerful arsenals on the basis of the arms trade and the globalization of defense-related industries. High on the policy agenda of the United States and other powers in the 1990s is the question of how to control and contain the spread of such weaponry.

Despite the renewed public interest in the economic dimension of national security, students have been without courses and textbooks that explored this issue area. In most universities the study of international relations has become bifurcated, with political economy representing one distinct subfield and security studies another. The teaching of economics has become increasingly theoretical and mathematical, with relatively little attention paid to applied problems. But, clearly, these academic offerings leave a curricular void. If students are to be prepared for the real world of the national security official and industry executive, they should be knowledgeable about both the politics *and* economics of defense issues.

Fortunately, the void is slowly being filled. Thanks to the support of such organizations as the John M. Olin Foundation, the Pew Charitable Trusts, and the Ford Foundation, a number of academic programs in economics and national security have been established at universities around the country, including Harvard, Columbia, Chicago, Duke, Maryland, and UCLA. These programs, which bring together political scientists, economists, and other scholars, are shedding light on such issues as, *inter alia,* weapons procurement, the economic effects of defense spending, the arms trade, and the role of defense industries in the domestic and international economies. In addition to offering new courses in defense economics, professors at these and other universities are expanding existing courses in political economy, security studies, public policy, economics, and history to include material drawn from the defense sector. It is hoped that this book will support their efforts.

As codirector with Professor Raymond Vernon of the Economics and National Security Program in the John M. Olin Institute for Strategic Studies at Harvard, and as a professor of international relations at Brandeis, I have felt compelled to write a new text in the political economy of national security. A book such as this, however, provides at best a snapshot of a field of study at a particular period of time. I have not written the work with the anticipation that it represents the "last word"; if anything, it's more the "first word," given the paucity of recent books on the subject. The selection of topics and the range of coverage represent my subjective estimation of the important issues in economics and national security, and I am aware that other scholars would have made different choices.

The book begins with an introduction that provides a brief overview of the major theoretical approaches to the political economy of national security—namely, liberalism, neo-mercantilism/realism, and Marxism/Leninism. These three traditions, well known to social scientists, have all sought to describe the search by states for security and prosperity in the international environment. Each provides unique analytical and prescriptive insights regarding the defense economy, which will reemerge in the substantive chapters of the book.

The next chapter explores defense economics in historical perspective. This brief review suggests that many of the macroeconomic, microeconomic, and international economic issues that occupy public officials today have long historical roots. Such issues as defense spending, industrial policy, dependence of foreign suppliers, and economic warfare have concerned statesmen for hundreds of years. From a historical perspective, defense has been among the most prominent economic problems of rulers.

The book is then organized into parts that focus, respectively, on "macro," "micro," and "international" issues. The "macro" chapters deal with defense spending and budgeting and with mobilization and war. The "micro" chapters are occupied with the defense-industrial base and weapons procurement. The international chapters examine the economic relations of military allies, the arms trade, and the problem of providing national security in a global economy. The concluding chapter discusses policy implications and provides suggestions for future research.

One of the major points the book tries to make is that national security is and always has been embedded in the international economy. Thus, at the macro level, defense financing has often been provided by foreign countries, while at the micro level states have sought men and materiel overseas. In each chapter, the international dimension is stressed.

The book, in fact, has a global and comparative focus that its predecessors generally lacked. The chapter on the defense-industrial base, for example, includes discussions on the Soviet Union, Japan, Europe, and the developing countries. The chapter on national security and the global economy examines the diffusion of advanced technology around the world and the challenges that presents for policymakers. The defense economy is not a "closed," national system, but it is an integral part of the world economy. If students gain an understanding of this "globalization" of the defense economy, my objectives for the book will have been largely fulfilled.

The reader will note that each chapter contains a selected bibliography and a large number of footnotes. In addition, a complete bibliography appears at the back. This reflects my philosophy of what a good book should do, and that is to stimulate the reader to engage in further study and research.

The large number of notes also reflects the fact that this book has been written on the shoulders of hundreds of scholars, past and present. I am grateful to my colleagues at Brandeis, Harvard, and other universities for the tremendous support they have provided during the writing of this book. I would also like to express my appreciation to the many government officials and industry executives who have given freely of their time in support of this and other projects completed under the auspices of the Economics and National Security Program. One of the great pleasures of being an academic is interacting with stimulating colleagues, and I have written friends an endless stream of IOUs in the process of researching and writing. In extending my thanks, a special word is owed to four scholars who have done so much to support my work in economics and national security: Robert Art, Seyom Brown, Samuel Huntington, and Raymond Vernon. I would also like to thank the scholars who reviewed part or all of the text and made useful comments, including Michael Barnett, Steve Chan, David Haglund, Michael Mastanduno, David Rosenberg, and Kamal Shehadi.

The book, however, is dedicated to my students. They were early supporters of this project, and I wrote the book with them in mind. I thank them all, and hope the final product justifies their interest and support.

Ethan Barnaby Kapstein

Notes

1. Edward Mead Earle, "Adam Smith, Alexander Hamilton, Friedrich List: The Economic Foundations of Military Power," reprinted in Peter Paret, ed., *Makers of Modern Strategy* (Princeton, N.J.: Princeton University Press, 1986).
2. These include James Schlesinger, *The Political Economy of National Security* (New York: Praeger, 1960); Charles Hitch and Ronald McKean, *The Economics of Defense in the Nuclear Age* (Cambridge, Mass.: Harvard University Press, 1960); Klaus Knorr, *The War Potential of Nations* (Princeton, N.J.: Princeton University Press, 1956); George Lincoln, *Economics of National Security* (Englewood Cliffs, N.J.: Prentice-Hall, 1954); Jules Backman et al., *War and Defense Economics* (New York: Rinehart & Co., 1952); Lester Chandler and Donald Wallace, *Economic Mobilization and Stabilization* (New York: Henry Holt and Co., 1951); and Horst Mendershausen, *The Economics of War* (New York: Prentice-Hall, 1943).
3. Paul Kennedy, *The Rise and Fall of the Great Powers* (New York: Random House, 1987).

The Political Economy of National Security
A Global Perspective

Introduction: Theoretical Approaches to Defense Economics

"... national wealth is increased and secured by national power,
as national power is increased and secured by national wealth."
——*Friedrich List (1789–1846)*

States must seek both security and prosperity in an anarchic international environment. Few states in history have been autarkic, or enjoyed complete self-sufficiency; most have had to rely on the world economy to provide the money and materiel needed for defense and war. The purpose of this introduction is to elaborate some of the theories that have analyzed the policies pursued by states as they seek to achieve wealth and power in the international system.

The relationship between economics and national security has been subject to a long and rich theoretical tradition. Here, three of the most prominent paradigms are briefly discussed: neo-mercantilism/realism, Marxism/Leninism, and liberalism.[1] The theories are well known to social scientists, but few scholars in recent years have consciously applied them to issues in the defense economy.[2] Of course, other ideologies, such as fascism, have also explicitly linked economics and security; indeed, it was Nazi minister Hermann Göring who made famous the phrase that Germany aimed at making "guns, not butter." The influence of fascism and other ideologies on social science scholarship and policymaking in the contemporary world is, however, muted.

NEO-MERCANTILISM/REALISM

Mercantilism, the economic doctrine most closely associated with defense economics, dominated international thought from the sixteenth to eighteenth centuries. In the words of one of its great students, Edward Mead Earle, it "was a system of power politics." The object of mercantilism in domestic politics was to strengthen the state vis-à-vis society, while in international politics it was to increase the state's relative power. These goals were unified through government policies aimed at developing the state's "commercial, financial, military, and naval resources." To this end, the state intervened in the domestic and international economies to further its political and military objectives.[3]

Mercantilists held that in the pursuit of wealth and power, countries must possess large reserves of gold—gold that would be needed, among other things, to finance warfare. Since gold was used to pay for goods and services in international trade, this meant that states should seek to run balance-of-trade surpluses. Thus, it was through trade that states achieved wealth and, by extension, security. Contrary to popular conception, mercantilism is not synonymous with autarky, though it did hold that states should promote domestic defense-related industries.

Indeed, mercantilism's promotion of "infant industries" is one of its most prominent legacies. In his famous "Report on Manufactures," presented to the U.S. Congress in 1791, Secretary of the Treasury Alexander Hamilton articulated one of the most nuanced conceptualizations of mercantilist doctrine. Hamilton argued that "not only the wealth but the independence and security of a country appear to be materially connected with the prosperity of manufactures." He said that many of the "embarrassments" suffered by the colonies in their struggle with England were due to dependence on foreign suppliers for defense materiel. A fuller discussion of early mercantilist views appears in the following chapter, which treats defense economics in historical perspective.

Aspects of mercantilist doctrine have enjoyed a renaissance in recent years, through neo-mercantilist and political realist interpretations of international relations.[4] Political realists believe that the most important observation that can be made about the international system is that it is anarchic, that there is no sovereign to enforce agreements between states or maintain world peace. War breaks out because no authority can stop it. International relations is a "zero-sum" game where one state becomes more powerful only at the expense of another. Accordingly, international politics is a "self-help" system in which states can look only to themselves for survival.

A fundamental proposition of the realist tradition is that a powerful state must possess a strong economy. Such an economy is characterized by a relatively high level of gross national product, advanced technology, and a foundation of rich human and natural resources. For the realist/neo-mercantilist, state intervention *is* appropriate to advance national security objectives. On a purely material basis, realists would perceive the United States and the Soviet Union as exceptionally powerful countries, given their relative self-sufficiency. Japan and Germany would be viewed as having severe constraints on their ability to exercise independent action in world politics since they are heavily dependent on foreign sources of supply for raw materials and other resources.

It is crucial to point out that, for the realist, the international economy is no less a zero-sum game than the international system as a whole. In the international economy, states jockey with one another to enhance their relative prosperity—prosperity that someday can be transformed into military power. As they enter into economic agreements, states must concern themselves with the problem of "relative gains," and calculate whether one party to an agreement reaps disproportionate economic benefits.[5]

For the realist/neo-mercantilist, international trade based on the liberal principles of comparative advantage and the division of labor does not just occur through the actions of a global "invisible hand." Instead, economic openness only arises in the presence of a *hegemonic power*, a state willing and able to provide the world with the collective goods of economic stability and international security. A state will only adopt the leadership role of hegemon when it is in its national interest to do so. In short, the theory of hegemonic stability rests on two fundamental propositions: (1) order in world politics is typically created by a single dominant power, and (2) the maintenance of order requires continued hegemony.[6]

Scholars of hegemonic stability cite two examples in support of these propositions: the Pax Britannica, which endured from the end of the Napoleonic wars until 1914, and the Pax Americana, which emerged in 1945 but saw signs of strain beginning in the early 1970s. During both these periods, international economic relations were relatively positive-sum, with the liberal ideal of free trade and investment flows ascendant. The world economy was afforded military protection by the hegemon against all challengers. Since the hegemon was both the major market for the output of the system and the principal military power, small states were provided with positive incentives to cooperate. Over time, however, hegemons lose their relative power. Other actors gain economically and politically at the hegemon's expense. As a result, states begin to "defect" from the hegemon, and systemic fragmentation occurs. Depression, conflict, and war follow.[7]

Hegemonic stability theory, with its emphasis on national resources as the foundation of international power, has a long pedigree in realist thought. Recognizing the economic dimension of military power, the influential geographer N. J. Spykman wrote in 1942 that

> the relative power of states depends not only on military forces but on many other factors—size of territory, nature of frontiers, size of population, absence or presence of raw materials, economic and technical development, financial strength . . . they have value in themselves, and they are means to power.

Modern warfare, Spykman argued, "can be fought successfully only on the basis of a rich supply of strategic raw materials and an enormous industrial output."[8] He recognized that the prosecution of a great-power war would demand the "full participation" of the national economy.

Writing thirty years later, James Schlesinger echoed a similar theme in his work on the political economy of defense. He asserted that states must build an adequate "mobilization base" to produce materiel for war, taking into account the "scarcity of real resources. . . ." This scarcity demanded that the use of economic resources "be coordinated and synchronized in accordance with an overall plan of production." [9] Such plans should be prepared in peacetime, not in the heat of battle. Schlesinger argued that the efficient use of economic capabilities could provide the critical margin needed for victory.

The most noted realist thinker, Hans Morgenthau, was also sensitive to the economic dimension of national power. Morgenthau suggested that geography, natural resources, industrial capacity, and population all influence military capability. He noted:

> The technology of modern warfare and communications has made overall development of heavy industries an indispensable element of national power . . . it is inevitable that the leading industrial nations should be identical with the great powers, and a change in industrial rank, for better or for worse, should be accompanied or followed by a corresponding change in the hierarchy of power.[10]

For the early postwar generation of realists and defense economists, who were writing at the peak of U.S. power, there was no question regarding the supremacy of America's defense industrial base. The United States possessed human, material, and financial capital in abundance, far outstripping any rival. While Soviet advances in atomic weapons and rocketry during the 1950s shook American complacency, it was clear that the arsenal of democracy could beat any foe in a global context. Realists like Schlesinger and Morgenthau saw the United States as autarkic for military purposes, and indeed capable of meeting alliance needs during wartime. The concept of "dependence" on overseas suppliers for critical military inputs, which in recent years has emerged as a policy issue in the United States, was foreign indeed.

It is here that the realist tradition has recently been amplified. While recognizing that military power remains the key currency in international politics, two systemic forces have worked to alter the postwar American defense economy: the end of the cold war and sharper economic competition. With the erosion of the Soviet threat, challenges to American supremacy are coming not only from such regional powers as Iraq, but also from economic competitors like Japan and the newly industrializing countries.

This economic competition is taking place at a time when America's foreign commitments remain widespread. Political scientist David Denoon has put the problem succinctly, arguing that debates over defense spending in the United States have developed from the unsettling recognition that there is an "imbalance between strategy and . . . capabilities." [11] While the United States claims a declining share of the industrial world's economic output, it remains the big spender in defense when compared with its major economic competitors.

Drawing on the realist tradition, Yale historian Paul Kennedy made this observation one of the central themes of his sweeping best-seller, *The Rise and Fall of the Great Powers.*[12] Kennedy assessed the *"interaction* between economics and strategy as each of the leading states in the international system strove to enhance its wealth and its power, to become (or to remain) rich and strong."[13] Beginning with the Hapsburg Empire in the sixteenth century, he argued that the challenge that has faced all great powers has been to match capabilities with commitments. "Imperial overstretch" and increasing military expenditures have doomed all those who would create and maintain a Holy Roman Empire or One Thousand Year Reich; even the Pax Americana could suffer this fate if it does not adjust to the changing distribution of economic capabilities.

Political realism, then, sees a powerful role for the state in the national and international economies. State intervention in the domestic economy is required in order to achieve autonomy and superiority in defense, and in the international economy a hegemon is required to achieve cooperative commercial relations. In the absence of a hegemon, the realist sees the distribution of economic no less than military power as a zero-sum game.

LIBERALISM

It may surprise some readers to learn that liberalism is no less concerned with national security than mercantilism. But liberals view laissez faire doctrine and the international division of labor as better means for achieving prosperity and security. Domestically, as states increase their wealth, the relative burdens of defense will weigh less heavily on overall economic activity. Internationally, as commercial and financial flows become global, economic incentives to engage in hostilities will be reduced, paving the way for a peacful world order. Liberalism, then, offers a powerful alternative to mercantilism as a way of achieving the two most prominent goals of statecraft.

For the greatest of liberal writers, Adam Smith, market-based economies promised greater efficiency, growth, and political and social welfare than was possible in state-directed systems. As economic activity was freed from onerous regulations at home, consumers would have a wider range of goods available to them, and owing to competition, would pay cheaper prices. The overall prosperity of society would increase as individuals and firms allocated scarce resources to their most profitable uses.[14]

At the microeconomic level, however, a fundamental tension existed between laissez faire and national security doctrines. What happened if markets did not provide the resources required for national security in adequate amounts? Adam Smith recognized the possibility of "market failure," and argued that state intervention was justified to enhance national security; as Smith said, "Defense is more important than opulence." National security was a "public good," a good that would not be provided by a profit-seeking private sector. It therefore fell upon the government to raise and outfit the armed forces. National defense thus fell outside Smith's laissez faire framework.

It is of interest to note that Smith and his contemporaries in eighteenth-century Europe nonetheless expressed grave concern about the economic damage wrought by military spending—more on this in Chapter 2. He stressed that defense spending was "unproductive" and sapped the economic vitality of a state. From a philosophical standpoint, he viewed a large standing army as antithetical to economic and political liberties. For the mercantilist, of course, the preeminent problem for every state was survival; political and economic liberties were a secondary concern.[15]

Liberal views also clashed with mercantilist ideology in the realm of international trade. Through Adam Smith, David Ricardo, and such modern authors as Bertil Ohlin and Paul Samuelson, liberalism has expounded the concept of "comparative advantage," meaning that states should produce and export those goods that make intensive use of relatively abundant local factors of production. By the same token, states should give up inefficient domestic production in order to maximize social welfare. Clearly, the maintenance of state-subsidized defense industries on national soil stood in opposition to the dictates of comparative advantage and the international division of labor.

From the perspective of international security, liberals argued that the globalization of economic activity actually promoted world peace. This must be so because the costs imposed by war would increase as states became intertwined and interdependent. In the words of the French philosopher Montesquieu, writing in 1748,

> The natural effect of commerce is to bring about peace. Two nations which trade together, render themselves reciprocally dependent; if the one has an interest in buying, the other has an interest in selling; and all unions are based on mutual needs.[16]

This belief in the peaceful consequences of international trade is among the most enduring and politically significant legacies of liberalism. It has had a major ideological influence on such U.S. Presidents as Woodrow Wilson and Franklin Roosevelt, and indeed has shaped U.S. foreign economic policy since the end of World War II. As Roosevelt's secretary of state, Cordell Hull, wrote in his *Memoirs*, "unhampered trade dovetailed with peace; high tariffs, trade barriers, and unfair economic competition, with war. . . . I reasoned that, if we could get a freer flow of trade . . . so that one country would not be deadly jealous of another . . . we might have a chance for lasting peace." [17] Rather than use its political and economic power after World War II to rebuild the British Empire and the regional trading "blocs" in Asia, central Europe, and the western hemisphere that had characterized the conflictual, "zero-sum" world economy of the interwar years, the United States led in the creation of new international regimes to promote world trade and financial flows, including the General Agreement on Tariffs and Trade and the International Monetary Fund. The United States adopted a liberal approach to the global economy, and it sought to convince its (noncommunist) wartime allies that trade and finance were positive-sum games.

In recent years, liberalism has also begun to exercise greater authority in terms of domestic defense economics. One of the fundamental tenets of neoclassical ideology, competition, has played an increasing role in the complex decisions associated with weapons procurement, notably in Great Britain and, to a lesser extent, the United States. The Reagan administration dovetailed its defense buildup with a call for greater competition among defense industries, and former Secretary of Defense Caspar Weinberger, writing in the Pentagon's 1987 *Annual Report to Congress*, stated that "the most powerful force for efficiency in (defense) production is competition."[18]

Reflecting the degree to which liberal internationalism had embedded itself in the modern defense economy, defense industries in the 1980s and early 1990s were also mirroring their commercial counterparts by becoming increasingly global in their scope of operations. Foreign sourcing of military-related components had become widespread, while more military (and commercial) research was "dual use" in character, meaning that civil and military technologies (like integrated circuits and precision optics) were rapidly becoming indistinguishable. These trends suggested that the defense and commercial economies were becoming increasingly intertwined, and that liberal ideas could be profitably applied to defense-economic decision making.[19]

In sum, liberalism offers a powerful prescriptive alternative to neo-mercantilism in the area of defense economics. Security and prosperity may be achieved, the liberal argues, by promoting free trade internationally and competition domestically. Despite Adam Smith's basically mercantilist approach to the domestic defense economy, neoclassical ideas have profitably been applied to weapons acquisition, especially in Britain. Indeed, liberalism has proved surprisingly durable in facing its hardest test, national security.

MARXISM[20]

A third view of the relationship between economics and national security is provided by the theoretical corpus known as Marxism/Leninism. Like liberalism and neo-mercantilism, Marxism also purports to explain the nature of the defense economy within capitalist states, and the international economic relations such states pursue to achieve wealth and power. Like neo-mercantilism, Marxism takes a fundamentally conflictual, zero-sum view of the international system. Because of the conflicts and contradictions that are endemic to capitalist societies, the ruling class must use force both domestically and globally to maintain its position and suppress the proletariat. Thus, defense spending and the "military-industrial complex" assume a prominent role in the political economy.

Marxism rests on five fundamental tenets.[21] The first is that the historical process is driven by changes in technology, production, and economic activity. The second is that the relationship between workers and those who own the means of production is contradictory and conflictual. Marxist history is concerned with the way in which these contradictions work themselves out over time. The third is that capitalism contains the seeds of its own destruction. The fourth is that society consists solely of classes. States are epiphenomenal, meaning that they are only reflections of a deeper reality, with no independent existence. For the Marxist, the state is nothing more than the "executive committee" of the ruling class. Finally, Marxists believe that socialism represents the "end of history," as workers finally achieve ownership of all means of production.

In terms of defense issues, "Marxists and Communists have always been ardent champions of peace." [22] The security problem for the Marxist is "the aggressive and adventurist nature of capital and imperialism." [23] In Marxist doctrine, "militarism and the arms race" are "embedded in the economic and class character of capitalism." [24] Capitalism pursues an internationally expansive logic as industrial states accumulate surplus production; indeed, one of the major contradictions in capitalism is that industries always produce more than exploited workers are able to buy. According to Marxist accounts of history, by the late 1800s the growing crisis caused by economic surplus led to intense competition among industrial states for unexploited markets overseas and ultimately to the "new imperialism." This phase of capitalism exploded in World Wars I and II.[25]

Following World War II, capitalism entered a new phase. Having defeated all its economic rivals, the United States now led a capitalist coalition against the socialist and third world countries. The arms race of the postwar years was due to the "common class interests of monopolies" and "anticommunism." The ruling classes of capitalist states "use armed forces to safeguard the power of monopoly capital" and to preserve "reactionary regimes and dictatorships." [26]

The quotes offered above suggest that Marxism, unlike liberalism, views militarism and large defense expenditures as inherent to capitalist economies, and indeed necessary to the survival of the ruling class. Further, Marxists (like neo-mercantilists) view the international economic relations of capitalist states as competitive, conflictual, exploitative, and zero-sum. From a normative standpoint, the endgame must be a global, socialist workers' paradise; other-wise, the capitalist arms race will lead to the destruction of the human race. It is not surprising that the Soviet Union has always championed "disarmament" as one of its favorite international causes.

For the Marxist, defense spending decisions in capitalist economies are not taken in response to external threats; instead, decisions are manipulated by the special-interest groups that make up the "military-industrial complex," defined as the "alliance of military-industrial monopolies, the military, and the state bureaucracy." Defense firms are represented in government and the military by sympathetic agents, who agitate for higher levels of weapons procurement and research and development. Organizations like the Council on Foreign Relations (publisher of the prestigious journal *Foreign Affairs*) and the Trilateral Commission (an organization of prominent businesspeople and public officials from Japan, western Europe, and the United States, founded by David Rockefeller) provide the convenient meeting grounds for the ruling-class members of the complex.[27] According to one Soviet observer, "The ruling circles of capitalist countries use military expenditures as a means of state monopoly control of economic development." [28] The "free market" of entrepreneurs and small industrial firms is a myth in Marxist ideology; instead, capitalist economies are characterized by monopolies that exercise control over economic activity. Among these monopolies, none is so important as defense firms.

Marxism, of course, has much more sophisticated variants that cannot be treated in detail here. In recent years, for example, Marxists have explored the concept of "cultural dominance," or the means by which "dominant cultures" transmit their ideologies globally. Unlike traditional Marxists, who focus on economic and political means of exploitation, those who examine cultural domination take a more nuanced look at such socializing mechanisms as education. In terms of defense economics, this approach would account for the spread of militarization in the third world as largely due to the education of military officers from developing countries in the armed forces training programs provided by advanced industrial states. In these programs, military officers from developing countries incorporate "first world" attitudes toward strategic doctrine and technologically advanced weapons systems. Thus, rather than simply spreading through the mechanism of direct economic exploitation, capitalist preferences are globally diffused in a more subtle way.[29]

With the collapse of communism and the end of the cold war, it is tempting to argue that Marxism/Leninism is now only of historical interest as a theoretical construct. This would be an inaccurate assertion. Around the world, many scholars and public officials still accept the fundamental tenets of Marxism, with its emphasis on the contradictions of capitalism and its malign view of international economic relations. Further, the insights of Marxism/Leninism and its contribution to social science theory should not be overlooked. Among other things, Marxism remains unique in its attempt to account for historical *change*. Marxist theorists also continue to draw illuminating connections between apparently discrete phenomena in the political economy. For students of defense economics, Marxism still provides a useful function as an alternative paradigm for explaining military expenditure decisions domestically and the pursuit of wealth and power at the systemic level.

CONCLUSION

Defense economics has failed to capture the attention of many economists and political scientists in recent years. On its face, this is surprising, "given the enormous size and substantial influences of the defense sector in many national economies; given the importance of this sector for the national and international economy, for output and employment, and for international stability. . . ."[30] The relationship between economics and national security has been left in a theoretical vacuum.

This chapter has sought to show that such has not always been the case. Three of the great traditions in modern social science—mercantilism, liberalism, and Marxism—have all been concerned with the problem of how states might achieve security and prosperity in the international system. While they all provide fundamentally different answers, each provides unique insights.

An important policy question, of course, is which one gives public officials the best guidance as they seek national security in a global economy? The perspective that this book takes might be seen as a blend of liberalism and neo-mercantilism. Liberalism is a philosophy of political economy that encourages competition, entrepreneurship, and trade on the basis of comparative advantage. In subsequent chapters it will be seen that all these are of value, in the defense no less than the commercial economy.

National security critics of liberalism often assert that free markets cannot ensure the military goals of autonomy and superiority. Indeed, inherent in the concept of comparative advantage is the fact that states must accept the condition of dependence on foreign countries for a wide range of goods and services. The idea of military superiority is a purely zero-sum, nationalistic one that would seem to have no place in liberal discourse.

There is some truth to mercantilist critiques of liberal theory. But liberal solutions may be found to many national security dilemmas. The problem of economic dependence on foreign suppliers, for example, may be solved by diversifying or by searching for substitutes for defense-related goods (for more on this problem, see Chapter 8, on national security and the global economy). The issue of superiority, the liberal might say, is intimately related to the creation of domestic and international economic conditions that encourage investment and trade. By failing to create such conditions, countries must be doomed to economic failure; witness the Soviet Union.

Yet liberals admit that market failure exists and that state intervention is often required to provide collective goods. On the international level, a hegemon may be needed to provide such collective goods as economic stability and military security. On the domestic level, the liberal would agree that the provision of national security is the foremost goal of the state, and that in order to fulfill this goal the state may have to intervene in certain instances in order to mobilize capital, labor, and natural resources.

The normative implication of this view is that when confronted with a problem in defense economics, policymakers should first explore whether a liberal solution exists. The official should recognize that even within the defense economy, the principles of competition, entrepreneurship, and free trade have a prominent place. But "defense is more important than opulence," and public officials must be prepared to articulate the case for state intervention when such is required on national security grounds. It is not enough for officials to mimic, like parrots, the phrase "the magic of the marketplace." Unfortunately, the marketplace cannot always be relied upon when it comes to the defense economy.

It is not the foremost task of this textbook, however, to convince the reader of the rectitude of one as opposed to another theoretical perspective. Instead, the book's job is to present in an informed and comprehensive way the most important topics in the area of defense economics and to suggest the variety of theoretical approaches that exist for conceptualizing complex problems. Having been introduced to three theoretical traditions, the reader can now weigh the arguments of each as the substantive topics are examined. Out of this process, readers may find that one is particularly compelling, or perhaps they will develop new theoretical perspectives of their own.

Selected Bibliography

Baldwin, David, *Economic Statecraft* (Princeton, N.J.: Princeton University Press, 1985). Chapter 5, "Economic Statecraft in International Thought," provides a useful introduction to a variety of theoretical traditions.

Earle, Edward Mead, "Adam Smith, Alexander Hamilton, Friedrich List: The Economic Foundations of Military Power," in Peter Paret, ed., *Makers of Modern Strategy* (Princeton, N.J.: Princeton University Press, 1986). This is a classic article; "must" reading for the student of defense economics.

Gilpin, Robert, *The Political Economy of International Relations* (Princeton, N.J.: Princeton University Press, 1987). This book provides useful introductions to Marxist, liberal, and neo-mercantilist thought as each applies to international political economy.

Notes

1. For an alternative formulation, see Michael Barnett, "High Politics Is Low Politics: The Domestic and Systemic Sources of Israeli Security Policy, 1967–1977," *World Politics* 42 (July 1990): 529–562. Barnett's three ideologies are power politics, economic nationalism, and Marxism.

2. For two prominent exceptions, see David Baldwin, *Economic Statecraft* (Princeton, N.J.: Princeton University Press, 1985), and Stephen Krasner, *Defending the National Interest* (Princeton, N.J.: Princeton University Press, 1978).

3. See Edward Mead Earle, "Adam Smith, Alexander Hamilton, Friedrich List: The Economic Foundations of Military Power," in Peter Paret, ed., *Makers of Modern Strategy* (Princeton, N.J.: Princeton University Press, 1986).

4. Examples include Robert Gilpin, *The Political Economy of International Relations* (Princeton, N.J.: Princeton University Press, 1987); Paul Kennedy, *The Rise and Fall of the Great Powers* (New York: Random House, 1987); and Ethan B. Kapstein, *The Insecure Alliance: Energy Crises and Western Politics since 1944* (New York: Oxford University Press, 1990).

5. See Joseph Grieco, *Cooperation among Nations* (Ithaca, N.Y.: Cornell University Press, 1990); and Grieco, "Anarchy and the Limits of Cooperation," *International Organization* 42 (Summer 1988): 486–507.

6. On hegemonic stability theory see Charles P. Kindleberger, *The World in Depression: 1929–1939* (Berkeley: University of California Press, 1973); Robert Keohane, *After Hegemony* (Princeton, N.J.: Princeton University Press, 1984); and Gilpin, *Political Economy of International Relations*.

7. For a test of hegemonic stability theory, see Kapstein, *The Insecure Alliance*.

8. N. J. Spykman, *America's Strategy in World Politics* (New York: Harcourt, Brace, 1942), p. 18.

9. James Schlesinger, *The Political Economy of National Security* (New York: Praeger, 1960), p. 76.

10. Hans Morgenthau, *Politics among Nations* (New York: Knopf, 1968), p. 113.

11. David B. Denoon, ed., *Constraints on Strategy* (McLean, Va.: Pergamon-Brassey, 1986), p. 2.

12. Kennedy, *The Rise and Fall of the Great Powers*.

13. Ibid., p. xv.

14. Adam Smith, *An Inquiry into the Nature and Causes of the Wealth of Nations* (Chicago: University of Chicago Press, 1976).

15. See Peter Minowitz, "Invisible Hand, Invisible Death: Adam Smith on War and Socio-Economic Development," *Journal of Political and Military Sociology* 17 (Winter 1989): 305–315.

16. Cited in Baldwin, *Economic Statecraft*, p. 78.

17. Cordell Hull, *Memoirs* (New York: Macmillan, 1948), p. 81.

18. Secretary of Defense, *Annual Report to the Congress: Fiscal Year 1987* (Washington, D.C.: February 5, 1986), p. 23.

19. For an overview of the changes in the defense economy, see Jacques Gansler, *Affording Defense* (Cambridge, Mass.: MIT Press, 1989).

20. This brief overview cannot do justice to the many forms of Marxism; it focuses on what political scientists have labeled "instrumental Marxism" and on the views of Soviet ideologues toward the defense economy.

21. For a good introduction, see Robert Heilbroner, *Marxism: For and Against* (New York: Norton, 1980).

22. Grigori Vodolazov, *Marxism's Revolutionary Ideas Are Not Just History* (Moscow: Novosti, 1988), p. 53.

23. Ibid.

24. Ibid.

25. See V. I. Lenin, *Imperialism: The Highest Stage of Capitalism* (New York: International Publishers, 1939). See also R. Faramazyan, *Disarmament and the Economy* (Moscow: Progress Publishers, 1981), p. 10.

26. Ibid.

27. For one process tracing of the "ruling class," see Michael Parenti, *The Sword and the Dollar* (New York: St. Martin's, 1989).

28. Ibid.

29. See R. Luckham, "Of Arms and Culture," *Current Research on Peace and Violence* 7 (1984): 1–64; and Alexander Wendt and Michael Barnett, "Systemic Dominance Structures and Third World Militarization," unpublished manuscript, June 1990.

30. Michael D. Intrilligator, "On the Nature and Scope of Defence Economics," *Defence Economics* 1 (1990): 3–11.

1

Defense Economics in Historical Perspective

"Coin is the sinews of war." ——*Rabelais (1494–1553)*
"Nothing depends as much on economic conditions as do the
army and navy." ——*F. Engels, Anti-Dühring (1820–1895)*

The objective of this chapter is to provide what could be called a "suggestive" rather than "definitive" history of defense economics. It gives neither a complete description of earlier economists' views on national security nor a comprehensive history of military production; readers looking for this level of detail may find it elsewhere.[1]

Instead, the chapter is used to "raise the historical consciousness" of students of defense economics and to provide sources for those who wish to probe the issues further. The point stressed is that defense economics is among the oldest branches of political economy, and has traditionally been a primary concern of rulers. The microeconomics, macroeconomics, and international economics of defense have all posed problems of considerable complexity for statesmen, and many of the issues faced centuries ago still resonate today. Further, defense economics has always been embedded in the deeper global economic issues of the day. States and private-sector actors have always depended upon the world economy for military financing, labor, and materiel.

The chapter thus provides a brief overview of the history of defense economics. It begins by introducing a framework for analysis and argues that the most useful framework is provided by looking at defense economics through the conventional labels of microeconomic, macroeconomic, and international economic activity. It then turns to each of these economic issues, examining defense financing, military production, and foreign trade and national security. It also treats aspects of the relationship between national security and economic development in the third world; unfortunately, students of economic development have done relatively little research in this area. The history provides us with a rich menu of issues and themes, which reemerge frequently in the ensuing chapters that focus on defense economics in the post-World War II period.

A FRAMEWORK FOR ANALYSIS

States are entities that, among other things, provide their citizens with collective goods. Among these goods, none is deemed so vital to society as security from external attack and domestic instability. States have devoted substantial resources since ancient times to military and police activities.

Not surprisingly, research on defense economics (unlike microeconomics, which focuses on the behavior of firms and households) has tended to emphasize the role of "the state" in all aspects of military preparation, including the financing of national defense and war, weapons production, and research and development. Private-sector actors, and the international economy more broadly, have been treated as tangential to that effort. But the defense economy should be viewed as an open rather than a closed system, and the *problematique* of defense mobilization and financing is deeply embedded in the international system.

The emphasis on state intervention, however, does provide a useful reminder of one of the most significant characteristics of the defense economy. States, according to Aaron Friedberg, have done

> three things in their efforts to generate military power. First, they extract resources from the societies over which they rule. Second . . . they organize and support the production of arms and equipment. And third, they oversee the conduct of scientific research aimed at developing new technologies that will increase the military capabilities of their armed forces.[2]

The separation of the state's war-making capabilities into three categories is helpful in looking at the complex problem of defense economics. Following such scholars as Charles Tilly, William McNeill, and Alexander Gerschenkron, Friedberg suggests that states have had to "extract" labor and money, mobilize production, and provide support for science and technology in an effort to increase their ability to wage war.

And yet this framework presents us with limitations that impede its utility when employed on a stand-alone basis. First, the categories are by no means clear-cut. It is difficult to distinguish between the state's "extractive activities" (defined as its ability to tax and to draft manpower) and its ability to extract such activities as scientific research. The line between these activities is by no means obvious, and the question arises, Why draw it here?

Second, the framework is excessively focused on the state and its *domestic* capabilities. In this chapter, and throughout the book, the perspective adopted is that defense economics has always been, and remains, an *international activity*. States have relied on individuals, firms, and governments in foreign lands for finance and for materiel; few states in recorded history have waged war from a position of autarky. Trade has been used strategically by states to bolster their own military capabilities on the one hand, while denying vital imports to enemies on the other.

Third, the framework lacks resonance from an economist's perspective. Keeping in mind Karl Polanyi's warning that "nothing obscures our social vision as effectively as the economistic prejudice," it is nonetheless useful to apply, where appropriate, standard categories that illuminate important issues.[3] Economists separate the world into microeconomics, macroeconomics, and international economics. Microeconomics focuses on the activities of individuals, households, and firms. Macroeconomics is concerned with the state's economic activities, especially its monetary and fiscal policies. International economics examines intercountry patterns of trade and investment. While economic distinctions may sometimes obscure reality, there is considerable merit in using a framework whose terms are widely agreed upon and understood by the vast majority of social scientists.

DEFENSE AND THE MACROECONOMY

Historically, the most significant economic activity of states has been the provision of national security and the prosecution of war. War costs could disrupt national strategy no less than enemy forces. As Fernand Braudel wrote of sixteenth-century Europe:

> The expense of war crippled states. . . . The inglorious and costly Irish wars ruined Elizabeth's finances toward the end of her brilliant reign and, more than any other single factor, prepared the way for the truce of 1604. The cost of war in the Mediterranean was so great that bankruptcy often followed . . . war fleets devoured money and supplies.[4]

The heavy price tag presented by national defense and war fighting somehow had to be financed if troops and weapons were to be maintained and improved. The methods that rulers have chosen to finance military spending have been a political as much as an economic decision, and the choice has depended upon such factors as the relative strength of the government vis-à-vis its society, the popularity of the war cause, and the natural resources of the state. Over the centuries, rulers have been constrained by their citizens from imposing undue levels of taxation in order to fund military obligations, and have had to seek alternative sources of funds, prominently through the issuance of debt. Of interest, the international economy has been an important source of funds for states doing battle, as governments attempted to borrow abroad. Both opportunities for, and constraints on, debt financing have been presented to state actors by the domestic and international economies.

Military spending has also had severe effects on the overall macroeconomy, and historically the most pernicious effect has been inflation. Again, this inflationary impact has made economic agents wary of military adventurism and excessive defense outlays. In this section we will deal with both the financing of national security and the effects of defense spending on the macroeconomy.

Financing Defense: Taxation

National security has always been a costly undertaking, one that dwarfed other economic activities. That undertaking had to be financed, primarily through taxation and borrowing. Both of these methods of financing have presented rulers with severe challenges, and indeed it can be argued that militarily successful states have been those that, among other things, were able to sustain the heavy financial burdens of war.[5]

In medieval Europe, "the most acceptable justification for taxation" was war.[6] Even preparation for war, however, did not make tax collection easy. Until at least the fourteenth century, "the notion of the realm was lacking," and rulers found that their pleas for taxes were frequently rejected.[7] Nonetheless, war was in many cases the *only* excuse for levying taxes, and scholars have demonstrated that the British and French taxation acts of this period were entirely justified in military terms.

Historian Paul Kennedy of Yale University corroborates this view in the case of Spain. He points out that in Spain "the crown's fiscal rights were in fact very limited."[8] Each of the three realms (Aragon, Catalonia, and Valencia) had separate systems of taxation, and the crown only received a reliable cash flow from royal lands. Indeed, "until the flow of American silver brought massive additional revenue . . . the Habsburg war effort principally rested upon the backs of . . . peasants and merchants. . . ."[9]

During the sixteenth and seventeenth centuries, Europe underwent what has since become known as the "military revolution."[10] Armies and navies grew substantially, and more lethal and expensive weapons, including firearms, were adopted. Between 1590 and 1650, for example, the size of Britain's standing army more than doubled, to reach 70,000 troops.[11] Fitting out and paying for such an armed force required new sources of finance, and rulers sought to increase the amounts extracted from society through direct and indirect taxation.

In Britain, the main forms of taxation used to finance the military revolution were customs taxes (again, highlighting the importance of international trade in war preparation), excise taxes, especially on alcohol, and property tax. The collection of the excise and property taxes was farmed out to private business interests, owing to the absence of a formal state revenue infrastructure. Despite the problems inherent in the farming out of tax collection, customs, property, and excise taxes provided "approximately 90 percent of the state's revenue in the century after the Glorious Revolution."[12]

Historians now believe that the relatively efficient British system of revenue collection gave it important *strategic* advantages over its major continental rivals. According to Kennedy, the French relied much more on such taxes as internal tolls, "which so irritated French merchants and were a disincentive to domestic commerce. . . ."[13] In comparison, the excise and property taxes were relatively "invisible" and failed to hurt particular economic activities.

Assured of cash flow from its tax collection, Britain was then able to refine a system of public credit and foreign borrowing that gave it access to larger pools of capital. As Margaret Levi rightly argues, there is a "crucial link" between taxation and debt financing. Lenders require confidence that their borrowers can make loan and interest payments. The British tax system "provided the confidence." [14]

But even the British Crown confronted the limits of taxation, at least in the colonies. As the American Revolution suggests, British tax policies created deep resentment, and they delegitimized the government in the eyes of some of its subjects. Indeed, Britain's imperial policies came under sharp attack from Adam Smith, whose *Inquiry into the Wealth of Nations* was published in 1776.

With each major war, new methods of taxation have been developed by needy governments. Thus, World War I saw the introduction of the income tax in the United States, and World War II the withholding tax to speed revenue collection. Of interest, during World War II the income tax in Britain and the United States "became more progressive . . . out of a desire to mitigate social inequalities." [15] Tax policy also reveals sharp differences between governments that perceived themselves to be strong vis-à-vis their societies and those that felt themselves to be weaker. The tottering Popular Front government in France before World War II "was in no position to increase taxation," [16] and even Franklin Roosevelt was hesitant to place most of the costs of rearmament and war on the incomes of working people. In Britain and Canada, in contrast, governments were able to pay for the largest part of their military programs out of tax revenues.

But taxes were insufficient to pay for the growing costs of war that buried Europe from the Napoleonic era onward; indeed, they had never been sufficient. In the early colonial period, monarchs had supplemented their finances by the importation of gold and silver, particularly from the new world. Other funds were derived by selling offices or royal land. All these modes of financing provided uncertain cash flows. New methods were needed to ensure the cash required for armaments, for men, and for war.

Financing Defense: Debt Instruments

The expansion of conflict in Europe, and the rising need for cash fueled by the military revolution, led to what has been called the "financial revolution" of the late seventeenth and early eighteenth centuries. [17] During this period, European countries developed their nascent banking and credit markets. These institutions channeled savings into a public sector made voracious by defense requirements.

The primary mechanism for raising public funds to fight wars was the bond market. The bond market depended on two critical variables: first, the existence of a system to market the loans; second, a borrower with creditworthiness. The Netherlands, a rich trading state populated with sophisticated financiers, took the lead in developing this market in eighteenth-century Europe.

It is important to stress for our purposes that Amsterdam became the spoke of finance not just for the States General of the Netherlands, *but for other European countries as well*. As Paul Kennedy writes:

> So successfully did Amsterdam become a center of Dutch "surplus
> capital" that it soon was able to invest in the stock of foreign companies and,
> most important of all, to subscribe to a whole variety of loans floated by for-
> eign governments, especially in wartime.[18]

Ultimately, however, it was in Britain where financial markets were
perfected. Indeed, historian John Brewer speaks of the development of a "fiscal-
military" state beginning in eighteenth-century Britain. This state was characterized by a centralized government, deep credit markets, and an awesome military
apparatus. It was this fiscal-military state that dominated world politics for a
century following Napoleon's defeat at Waterloo.

Even before the Napoleonic wars, Britain had developed a *relatively*
sophisticated financial machine. In fact, it could be said that Britain ultimately
outfinanced rather than outfought its leading competitor, France. It has been
estimated that by the time of the French Revolution in 1789, "75 to 85 percent of
British government expenditures went to pay for the military or to service debts
incurred during earlier wars." [19] If the military machine was to continue operating, a way had to be found to service the debt.

British short-term debt

> consisted of exchequer bills, navy, transport, and victualling bills and ordnance
> debentures. Exchequer bills, which gradually became the chief means of rais-
> ing short-term loans, were interest-bearing bills redeemable on demand and
> managed by the Bank of England. The other bills were issued by spending de-
> partments to pay for the everyday running costs of war.[20]

But even Britain faced financial crises. During wartime the short-term debt
of the British government ballooned. According to Brewer, "Sometimes . . . its
growth became unmanageable. . . . In short, every war created a credit crisis,
and the longer the war went on, the more severe it became." [21]

The solution to the financial crisis was to turn short-term debt into long-
term debt—a practice, incidentally, widely used by bankers today when companies (or developing countries) enter or draw near bankruptcy. This practice
stretched out the payment schedule, even if it raised long-term interest rates.
Oftentimes, the debt stretch-out had to be accompanied by short-term increases
in taxes to meet the immediate cash crunch.

Domestic and international constraints on public-sector spending have
forced states to limit their defense expenditures—sometimes imprudently.
Finance has provided states with opportunities for expansion, but it has set limits
as well. As Aaron Friedberg points out, the critical issue is how public officials
have *perceived* their state's financial position in the international system. Writing
about Britain in the late nineteenth and early twentieth centuries, he suggests
that Conservative party leaders made stringent assumptions about "what the
economic and political traffic would bear," and these assumptions led them to
large-scale reductions of military spending. In Friedberg's words, "The danger
of military disaster overseas seemed preferable to certain electoral defeat at
home." [22]

Nonetheless, by the nineteenth century most of the great powers had developed sophisticated systems of revenue collection. Through the employment of a variety of taxes and bonds, public officials were *capable*—certainly when compared with their fifteenth-century predecessors—of raising the funds needed for defense and war. The awesome ability of the state to claim needed funds was borne out by the experience of World War I. At the cost of increases in inflation, the belligerents financed the war through a combination of increased taxes and borrowings from domestic *and foreign* sources. In Britain, for example, nearly one-third of the war's costs was paid by increases in tax revenue; 57 percent was paid for through domestic bond issues, while the remainder—14 percent—was paid for by foreign borrowings. In France, a smaller number was raised by additions to tax revenues; borrowings at home and abroad largely financed the war. The pattern for Russia was similar to that of France, while the United States and Germany relied almost exclusively on domestic funds.[23]

During the Second World War, the importance of bond financing again became apparent, as states sought to limit the burden of taxation for political reasons. The governments of the United States, Great Britain, and Nazi Germany developed sophisticated advertising campaigns to sell war bonds. In the United States, "Liberty" and "Victory" bonds were sold through radio and newspaper campaigns and in public meetings at which war heroes were honored. Citizens were also asked by employers to allocate a share of their salaries to bond purchases, and the amounts would be automatically withheld; incidentally, this form of "compulsory savings" was originated in Great Britain by John Maynard Keynes.[24]

Few wars have been fought with such overwhelming public support as World War II. This made the task of extracting funds from society relatively easy, although the financing of the war itself remained an immensely complicated task. But when wars were less popular, governments had to seek more nuanced methods to pay for them. Notably, as will be seen in Chapter 3, the Vietnam conflict was financed largely by U.S. government deficit spending rather than through direct taxation. This reflected a political as opposed to an economic choice, and suggested the fragile nature of public support for the war. It was a choice that Adam Smith would have disapproved of; he believed that wars should be paid for out of direct taxation, since the willingness of citizens to be taxed provided the greatest test of public support for war.

Although one of the great objectives of war finance is to moderate civilian purchasing power and thus the amount of currency available for consumption, states involved in military buildups and wars have faced enormous macroeconomic problems. The scourges of inflation and recession, the drop in foreign trade, and the crowding-out of private-sector investment have been among the traditional concerns of great powers. It is to some of these that we now turn.

Economic Effects of Military Spending

As early as the eighteenth century, economists recognized that rising defense expenditures and war fighting would lead to financial crisis and inflation. They saw this as an outcome because, as mentioned above, the meeting of wartime obligations called for an enormous expansion in public debt and in the money supply. In the words of historian John Brewer, "The cumulative effect of short-term borrowing was inflationary, becoming more and more visible toward the end of long and expensive wars." [25]

Wars led to increases not only in the money supply, but in commodity prices as well. The threat of higher taxes and a tendency of frightened populations to hoard supplies during wartime led to the rapid rise in the price of staples and even industrial goods. Of course, in wartime, "goods imported from overseas . . . were vulnerable to destruction and capture by enemy naval ships or privateers." [26] This led to higher insurance and shipping rates, which in turn raised prices for imported goods.

In more contemporary renderings of economic history, warfare has been held by some to be the driving force behind business and economic cycles. A school of "long-wave" theorists, for example, "holds that recurrent major wars are central to economic long waves." [27] The Russian theorist Kondratieff, who originated long-wave theory in the early twentieth century, argued that the three major economic waves he had discovered in modern history were all centered upon major wars. [28]

The position held by these theorists is that while wartime conditions fuel a cycle of high demand, over time warfare inevitably leads to a decline in output owing to shortages of the various factors of production. The result is that "during war periods consumption rises and production falls, leading to a higher ratio of demand to supply and hence to higher prices." [29]

Again, for our purposes it is significant to note that wave theorists emphasize the *global* impact of war on economic behavior. Inflationary jolts, they argue, become globalized during periods of prolonged war, as trade patterns and investment flows become disrupted. Statistical analysis of wheat prices in Europe and America over the period 1400–1942 indicates "that periods of sharp price increases have historically accompanied periods of war. . . ." [30]

A historic correlation between sudden increases in defense spending and inflation has also been posited by the Congressional Budget Office (CBO) for the United States economy. The CBO argues that "at no time in its history has the United States increased defense spending . . . without encountering, at about the same time, a substantial increase in inflationary pressures. . . . Speculative surges in prices occurred at the beginning of U.S. involvement in World War I, World War II, and the Korean conflict." [31] We will discuss this experience in greater detail in Chapter 2.

In terms of economic performance, then, it has long been argued that defense preparation and warfare, while perhaps providing what would now be called a "Keynesian" spending boost to economies over the short term, have had detrimental effects over a longer time horizon. The absence of private-sector investment, the disruption of trade, the increase in the money supply, and the allocation of the factors of production to war have all served to undermine economic growth. The contemporary debate about the impact of defense spending on economic performance thus has a substantial pedigree.

Curiously, however, those who have examined the interaction between the military and the microeconomy present a somewhat more ambiguous story. Many social scientists have argued that national security concerns have *promoted* economic development, spurred innovations in production, and invigorated scientific research and the introduction of new technology. While it is recognized that military expenditures have come at the expense of spending for consumer needs, it is rarely argued by scholars that defense spending has been wholly without benefits to the real economy and to the process of industrialization. Thus, the malign macroeconomic view of defense spending is not generally supported by the more benign microeconomic view, as will be seen in the following section.

DEFENSE AND THE MICROECONOMY

The fighting of wars requires special tools and equipment and the manpower trained to use weapons and move materiel. There is nothing inherent in warfare that deems these requirements must be provided from *national* soil. So long as states are capable of raising the funds needed to prosecute warfare, in theory they could purchase the labor and materiel needed on international markets.

But states have had an ambivalent relationship with the international economy when it comes to matters of national security. With the development of the state system in the seventeenth century, and the military revolution that coincided with it, rulers increasingly felt the need to maintain in their grasp at least some war-fighting capability. This meant having a pool of trained men, along with industries capable of defense production, within the borders of the state or its imperial reach.

Perhaps the boldest effort in early modern history to create a self-sufficient domestic defense-industrial base was that associated with Louis XIV's one-man braintrust, Jean-Baptiste Colbert (1619–1683). Colbert was the quintessential mercantilist, and so powerful was his legacy that until recent times "Colbertism" was often used interchangeably with "mercantilism," particularly in Europe. Colbert instituted a wide-ranging scheme of subsidies and bounties for the promotion of domestic industries, and he brought foreign technicians to French soil. He built state-owned arsenals and shipyards and provided incentives to private-sector entrepreneurs to enter into the businesses of producing gunpowder and small arms. In the end, however, "most Colbertist projects ended in disappointment. Even in shipbuilding, France remained dependent on imports of both raw materials and finished ships." [32]

In few states, however, did security objectives translate into the Colbertist doctrine of defense self-sufficiency within a state's frontiers. Indeed, even in mercantilist thought autarky was at odds with, rather than supportive of, the objective of increasing the state's power. Foreign trade provided a number of positive benefits to the state's security position, only one of which was bringing to local shores needed goods and services. In addition, trade bolstered the navy, and it kept seafarers employed. The maintenance of a mercantile marine, and a large fishery, was viewed not solely in economic terms by seventeenth- and eighteenth-century public officials, but in security terms as well. For mercantilists, "the aim of increased national power . . . and the aim of increased wealth . . . were brought into complete harmony by the balance of trade doctrine. . . ." [33] As Machiavelli pointed out, gold stocks, which increased with trade surpluses, were an important source of military power, since gold could be used to buy professional soldiers. [34]

Nonetheless, states actively, if haphazardly, intervened in their domestic economies to protect or develop industries that were important to the army and navy, and export controls were used on defense-related technology. Early in the sixteenth century, for example, the English forbade the export of various copper alloys. Later proclamations were aimed at preventing the export of cannons and other munitions. [35]

In terms of industrial development, particular attention was given during the Elizabethan period to the saltpeter industry, which was the basis for gunpowder manufacture. According to economist Eli Heckscher, "The eagerness to secure this for military purposes occasioned many conflicts" in the English political economy. [36] Individuals were given privileges to control saltpeter production, and political strains were produced in the process. Indeed, in 1623–1624, James I exempted saltpeter and gunpowder production, as well as artillery and munition works, from the prohibitions against monopoly. However, this did not end the political-economic dispute. In later years, common law judges ruled that anyone should be allowed to produce saltpeter; the government responded by instituting yet new monopoly regulations.

Despite state intervention to support defense-related industries, in Britain these firms were largely held in the private sector. In other states, however, defense industries were state-owned; to understand why this was the case, it is useful to employ Alexander Gerschenkron's notion of "early" versus "late" industrializers. In the archetypal early industrializer, Great Britain, private industry led the way in promoting not only the "civilian" industrial revolution, but also the military revolution. Even English shipping policy—so critical to the state's economic and military power position—"sought support for its military aims in normal, private economic activity." [37] As the examples above suggest, private entrepreneurs played a crucial role in arms-related production. While the state used economic policy (broadly defined to include macroeconomic, microeconomic, and international economic interventions) to advance specific goals, the instruments of policy were largely private-sector actors.

This model would not be replicated in the late industrializers, notably France, Germany, Russia, and Japan. In these countries, the state not only formulated defense and economic policies but, at least initially, engaged in actual production as well. Given the capital and technological requirements of the arms industry by the nineteenth century—the barriers to entry—only the state could mobilize the money and laborers needed to create new industries. Thus, relations between the public and private sectors in different nation-states owe their variance at least in part to the timing of the state's entrance into the world economy. [38]

(Library of Congress)

"Liberty Bonds": Modern warfare required new
methods of financing.

The case of Japan provides an example of a late industrializer that moved
quickly from dependence on the outside world for materiel to near-autarkic
production. During the early nineteenth century, the Japanese gave "little
thought" to the problem of military production. There was no need to, since "in
every war waged since 1815 neutral powers had supplied the belligerents with
the necessary financing and materials." [39] The role of the state was focused on
drafting war plans and ensuring the mobilization of "money, guns and horses."

Of course, the entrance of Japan into the international economy during the
Meiji Restoration changed this world view. The state's slogan became "rich
country, strong army," and it mobilized society to produce materiel for war. The
Yokohama Iron Works turned out ships of the line, while the Imperial Army
acquired its own arms factories. In the words of historian Michael Barnhart, the
army and navy "directed the growth of a military industry that, by the close of
the Russo-Japanese War, was capable of maintaining an army over a million
strong and a navy that had decisively defeated the tsar's finest fleet." [40]

In continental Europe, meanwhile, arms production was entering a period of "privatization." According to Andrew Moravcsik, "With increasing technological sophistication, procurement from concentrated private concerns appeared increasingly attractive for both financial and technological reasons." [41] The great defense industries, like Krupp in Germany and Vickers in Britain, arose in the mid- to late nineteenth century, supplanting state-owned and -operated arsenals. At the same time, these defense industries looked to foreign markets in order to extend production runs and to achieve economies of scale. The late nineteenth and early twentieth centuries were, ironically, the heyday of free trade in armaments.

World War I marked a decisive change in state policy toward military industrialization and arms exports. Despite the spotty history of economic intervention to promote defense-related production, and the rise of some large, private arms manufacturers, the industrial revolution still remained largely a civil and commercial-oriented phenomenon at the turn of the century. The American Civil War notwithstanding, which demonstrated the strategic importance of railroads and industrial superiority in the prosecution of long wars, the European conflicts of the late nineteenth century, including the Franco-Prussian War of 1870–1871, were not fought with sophisticated technology. A distinguished military historian, Martin van Creveld, has written:

> As industrialization metamorphosed the countryside and shifted entire populations, one aspect could be identified in the national lives of most countries that remained curiously exempt from the changes taking place: the armed forces, or more particularly the land forces. As a famous German soldier and military author . . . put it, war would lead to a return "to the simpler circumstances of our ancestors. . . ." [42]

The "Great War" made a cruel hoax of European atavism. Tactical defense ground offenses to a halt, and troops were forced to settle into trenches for long, grinding periods of death, disease, and suffering. Trench warfare, which ate up men and materiel at alarming rates, made industrial mobilization absolutely necessary. Suddenly, soldiers and statesmen were confronted with a long war that would demand unprecedented quantities of money and supplies.

In the process of industrial mobilization, many states were gradually transformed into command economies, with the industrial revolution converted to military production. By 1916, all the major belligerents "were now engaged in essentially the same type of industrial warfare. . . ." [43] The military, which before the war had consumed in the area of 4 percent of gross national product for the major belligerents, now consumed one-quarter to one-third of total output. [44]

The horrific experience of World War I left few postwar statesmen willing to maintain huge military-industrial complexes in its aftermath, and the postwar economic boom enjoyed in the United States and Europe facilitated conversion of most industry back to civilian pursuits. Germany was punished for its actions and given huge reparations to pay; the long-term implications of this policy from the standpoint of European security were clear to only a few clear-eyed observers, among them John Maynard Keynes. The League of Nations launched an investigation into the role of arms trafficking before and during the war, and found that arms manufacturers had fanned the flames of conflict. Nonetheless, states did little to rein in national firms, since domestic demand for weapons declined and foreign sales were viewed as necessary for industrial survival.[45]

One area where the state maintained a modest presence after World War I was in military research and development. Indeed, "even the most ardent economic critics of warfare frequently concede that in one respect war brings economic benefits, in its tendency to promote technological and scientific innovation."[46] As historian A. Hunter Dupree has written, "World War I had profound effects on every part of American science," and the same could be said of Britain, France, and Germany.[47] In the United States, inventor Thomas Edison had been brought to Washington to lead scientific research during the war, and he created an "inventor's bureau" that sought new ideas from the nation's entrepreneurs (a model that the scientific manager of World War II, Vannevar Bush of MIT, would reject). After the war, and despite a trend among scientists to turn away from military research, the armed forces promoted basic research and further development of such weapons as fighter aircraft, bombers, ships, aircraft carriers, and tanks. Further, states investigated electrical communications, anti-submarine warfare detection, navigational improvements, and the development of radar. Many of the revolutionary military technologies of the Second World

Trench Warfare: World War I demanded complete industrial mobilization.

(National Archives)

War—like the aircraft carrier—were largely perfected during the 1920s and 1930s.[48] While state support of these activities was certainly modest, the critical change was the idea that the state had to be constantly involved in the research and development process. It could no longer leave R&D strictly to the market-place.[49]

The "militarization" of science and technology after World War I also had a global dimension that was important for several reasons. First, scientists relied increasingly on research efforts in foreign centers to support or refute their own projects; a classic case is provided by early atomic research, where leading discoveries were made in France, Germany, Italy, and the United States. Second, there was a substantial degree of mobility among the scientific community; even before the German exodus caused by Hitler, scientists were working in centers outside their homeland. It was commonplace for American science students, for example, to spend extended periods of time in European laboratories. Finally, military establishments of necessity had to be aware of ongoing developments occurring in other countries, and intelligence services devoted substantial energy to collecting information on the latest breakthroughs in defense-related R&D.

The great scientific war was, of course, World War II. The war saw the development of radar, computers, the jet engine, and, most dramatically, atomic power. But perhaps the most interesting aspect of the scientific war was its organization. Unlike World War I, where solitary inventors and firms were simply encouraged to develop defense-related technology, the scientific effort became highly directed. In Washington, MIT's Vannevar Bush and Harvard president James Conant created an Office of Scientific Research, and they had direct access to President Roosevelt. Using the best human and capital resources that could be found in universities, industries, and government, they focused the research effort on technologies that appeared to be of particular military importance. Two of the earliest programs focused on radar and atomic power, each involving the "best and brightest" of a scientific generation. So powerful was the scientific arsenal created by Bush and Conant that it endures today, through the Office of Science and Technology Policy in the White House and the National Science Foundation. The governance of science and technology in the United States is in large part a legacy of World War II, and in few areas of the economy has the imprint of state intervention been so powerfully etched.[50]

Overall, however, the history of state intervention in the domestic economy to encourage defense-related production leaves today's policymakers with an ambiguous legacy. While state support has been a commonplace for centuries, that support has usually been haphazard and inconsistent. It has been hard for rulers to justify state support for armaments research, development, and production during prolonged periods of peace, a historical lesson that is of relevance today, with the end of the cold war. Further, since subsidization of domestic military industries removes resources from the civilian economy, trade-offs must be made between economic growth and the national security goals of autonomy and superiority.

NATIONAL SECURITY AND FOREIGN TRADE

*". . . trade causes perpetual strife both in time of war and in time
of peace between all the nations. . . ." ——Colbert*[51]
"The natural effect of commerce is to bring about peace."
——Montesquieu[52]

Defense economics is deeply embedded in the international economy. As demonstrated in the previous discussion, states have depended upon friends, allies, and neutrals for materiel, money, and labor. States have also sought to deny their enemies these goods, and "economic warfare" aimed at shipping has been a long-standing military tactic. As Horst Mendershausen has written:

> The foreign trade of a nation at war is an instrument of war policy. It serves
> four ends: (1) it supplies the domestic war economy with essential products;
> (2) it supports the military effort of allied powers; (3) it satisfies the economic
> needs of friendly neutrals; and (4) it disrupts the trade of the enemy with his
> allies or with neutral countries.[53]

In this section, the relationship between national security and international trade is explored, with a focus on trade during periods of war.

Since ancient times, civilizations have traded goods and services. Not only did trade increase the range of products available to societies, but it provided precious metals and, later, currency that enriched government and private coffers. Further, tariffs—taxes on imports—provided vital sources of revenues. In the words of a twelfth-century Chinese emperor, "The profits from maritime commerce are very great. If properly managed they can be millions. Is it not better than taxing the people?"[54]

In mercantilist doctrine, there was a distinct relationship between wealth and power. States had to maximize their gold stocks in order to have the funds needed for war. This gold could only be earned through trade. Accordingly, states had to maximize their international commerce, consistent with the protection of certain domestic industries crucial to armaments production.

The quintessential expressions of this dual mercantilist objective were the English Navigation Acts, first promulgated in 1660 in response to the rise of the Dutch merchant fleet. These acts were aimed at promoting Britain's shipping and its supply of seafarers. They did so through several policy measures. First, the acts dictated that all overseas commerce be conducted on British ships. Second, they required that vessels over a certain size be built within Britain. Finally, sailors—especially officers—were to be drawn to the extent possible from native stock.[55]

This mercantilist system "was more or less common to all Europe."[56] It was found in thirteenth-century Aragon, and it came to England as early as the fourteenth century. France adopted navigation act policies in the seventeenth century, and the Scandinavian countries adopted similar approaches in the 1700s. "Mastery of the sea"—for reasons of both wealth and power—had become a central concern of European rulers.

In addition to support of the navy and mercantile marines, European governments also bolstered their fisheries. The fishery was viewed as an exemplary training ground for sailors, and indeed few maritime tasks have ever been more demanding than fishing off sailboats. Regulations were emplaced in countries that subjects "eat fish on Fridays" and during Lent. In the Netherlands, and later in Britain, extensive state intervention was directed toward the maintenance and improvement of national fisheries.[57]

This goal of ocean mastery did not change as free-market ideology began its slow global spread beginning in the late eighteenth century. To be sure, Adam Smith and David Ricardo had challenged the mercantilist notion of a zero-sum world economy in which states must compete for a larger share of a fixed pie. By allowing the "invisible hand" to work at home, and comparative advantage to exercise its logic internationally, social welfare for *all* countries might increase. As countries became increasingly interdependent, so the chances of war might diminish. In short, free trade leads to peace. Still, trade could only occur when sea-lanes were protected from pirates and hostile regimes; thus naval power was of no less concern for liberals than for mercantilists.

By the late nineteenth century, Europe was engaged in a period that historians have labeled the "new imperialism." The scramble for colonies—which some scholars have viewed as the transfer of conflict from the European core to the developing periphery—strengthened the link between naval might and commerce. Further, as naval technology changed with the advent of steam power, the need for a far-flung set of coaling bases arose. These factors combined to exempt ocean commerce from free-market logic.

With the publication of Alfred Thayer Mahan's *The Influence of Sea Power upon History, 1660–1783* in 1890, the new mercantilists found their intellectual underpinning.[58] Mahan, a naval officer serving as a professor at the U.S. Naval War College in Newport, Rhode Island, promoted the concept of the superiority of "sea power" over land power and developed what has since been termed a "navalist" view of strategy. Among his many arguments, perhaps his most influential and enduring was that Napoleon had been beaten on the sea as a result of the Royal Navy's economic strangulation of the European continent. The navy, Mahan proclaimed, had destroyed Napoleon's "Continental System," and with it any pretense of French hegemony. As will be seen below, this view would endure in British thinking through the First and Second World Wars.

Mahan's view of the centrality of naval power to wealth and security "seemed well justified by post-1500 economic and political trends."[59] The growth of commerce in the Atlantic and in Asia made all the great powers "aware of the importance of maritime trade and ready to pay for a large war fleet."[60] In the United States, navalists like Theodore Roosevelt built their political careers in tandem with the growth of a "Great White Fleet." In Paul Kennedy's words, "trade, colonies and the navy . . . formed a 'virtuous triangle. . . .'"[61]

The implications of Mahanian beliefs for naval spending were, of course, consequential for all the great powers. In the United States, the Cleveland administration had been determined to reduce naval spending. But a senior official read the book in 1893; and soon after, the administration "persuaded Congress to supply funds for five more battleships." [62] Some states, however, were in a stronger position to bear these costs than others. For Great Britain, the political economy of naval rebuilding became a divisive topic in the late nineteenth century, with extensive debate over the Naval Defense Act, a five-year construction program that carried a price tag of 23 million pounds sterling. This act notwithstanding, by the turn of the century many in Britain were unwilling to shoulder the costs associated with naval supremacy and sought instead to develop a policy of alliances in which the burdens of secure commerce were shared among friends. [63]

The principal threat to British security came from the industrial upstart in the east, Germany. German industrial production blossomed in the late nineteenth century after political unification under Bismarck, and with the levying of substantial tariff barriers on industrial imports. German steel production was larger than that of Britain, France, and Russia by the eve of World War I, and Germany took the lead in the promotion of "new" science-based industries like chemicals and electricity.

At the same time, German exports boomed; by 1913 the country was second to Britain as the world's leading exporter, and its merchant marine also trailed only Britain's. The German Navy League called for a rapid naval building program, and between the years 1900 and 1913 the fleet grew from the sixth largest in the world to "being second only to the Royal Navy." More important, however, was the fact that German ships incorporated the newest technology, including superior armor and firepower provided by the Krupp Works. Comparing the British and German naval fleets, Paul Kennedy concludes that the latter was "pound for pound superior." [64]

The United States went through a similar evolution during this period. In 1890, naval expenditures totaled some 22 million dollars, or less than 7 percent of the total federal budget. By 1914 the figure had climbed to 20 percent of the budget, and the U.S. Navy had become the world's third largest. As in Germany, the growth in waterborne commerce and the creation of an overseas empire after the Spanish-American War were important factors in this naval buildup. At the same time, the ideology of navalism spread from its birthplace at the Naval War College. Mahan's beliefs won substantial political and intellectual support from such members of the American elite as Brooks Adams and Theodore Roosevelt. [65]

World War I provided a great test of the new navalism, and Allied governments emphasized the strategic importance of economic warfare, or the disruption and strangulation of the German economy. Germany in many ways seemed to be the perfect target for economic denial. It lacked many important raw materials, especially petroleum, and its sea-lanes could easily be choked by a superior force. Despite its size, it was unlikely that the German navy would wish to seek out and destroy the British (and later the American) fleet, and this gave Royal Navy planners a strategic advantage in determining how their ships of the line could best be employed. The British utilized essentially the same strategy of economic warfare that had served them so well during the Napoleonic era: choke the enemy's trade and force its collapse. [66]

(Credit to come)

"The Great White Fleet": Mahan's ideas about the role of sea power influenced the American elite, including President Theodore Roosevelt.

The efficacy of this strategy during the First World War may be doubted, as the conflict dragged on for four years. But by the end of the war, the Germans were in fact facing severe shortages of food and fuel. Further, the deterioration of Germany's external trade and financial position made it impossible for the country to purchase goods from neutral powers for other than "cash on the barrelhead" terms. In any event, as the blockade against Germany strengthened, particularly after America's entrance into the war in 1917, neutrals were less interested in selling to it.

The lessons taught by Germany's trade dependence were lost on neither Hitler nor the Allies at the outbreak of World War II. Even before the war, Hitler made preparations for the economic blockade that must occur if conflict began, and indeed war preparation colored his entire economic policy. At home, strategic stockpiles were built up of energy and raw materials. Abroad, trade agreements were struck with neutrals, especially Sweden and Switzerland, to ensure access to such vital goods as iron ore, ball bearings, and precision optics.[67]

Nowhere was the mercantilist nature of Hitler's foreign economic policy more evident than in eastern Europe. During the 1930s, Hitler launched a foreign trade offensive in the region that aimed at making it dependent on Nazi Germany for markets, in the process breaking long-standing economic ties with Britain and France. The Germans engaged in preemptive buying of eastern European agricultural goods and raw materials; that is, they would purchase certain quantities at a fixed price before such goods could be competitively offered in the international marketplace. In turn, they would sell manufactured goods and armaments at preferential prices. The Germans also established preferential tariff agreements with the eastern Europeans. By the outbreak of World War II, eastern Europe had fallen into Germany's sphere of influence. Germany's Axis partner, Japan, had adopted similar strategies in east Asia.[68]

According to the great student of Nazi trade policy, Albert Hirschman, Hitler saw that foreign economic policy had a *supply effect* and an *influence effect*. The former simply referred to the ability of a country to obtain through trade a wide range of goods at competitive prices, freeing scarce domestic resources for more productive purposes. In essence, this was the liberal argument for trade. The influence effect was more distinctive, and this entailed fashioning a trade policy that made a region dependent on its major trading partner. The influence effect was established not only through such positive measures as preemptive buying and preferential tariffs, but also through the coercive threat of disrupting existing trade patterns if country X did not follow country Y's instructions on economic or political matters.[69]

Despite Germany's preparations for war, Hitler believed in 1939 that his country was not ready either economically or psychologically for a prolonged conflict—thus the emphasis on the blitzkrieg, or lightning war, strategy. Hitler hoped that quick victories would establish his hegemony on the continent, forcing his remaining adversaries to sue for peace. Apparently, the Japanese held a similar view, thinking that rapid victories in the Pacific would force the United States and Britain to come to terms.

The Allies, however, saw neither Hitler nor Tojo as being any better prepared than Napoleon to withstand an economic blockade; in this regard the island nation of Japan appeared particularly vulnerable. As a result, economic warfare assumed critical strategic importance in the early days of World War II. A Ministry of Economic Warfare was established in London, and the United States established its counterpart upon entering the war in 1941. Indeed, given the invention of long-range bombers, and the fact that the current war would be even more energy-intensive than its predecessor (nowhere was Hitler more dependent than for his oil supplies), the Allies thought that economic warfare would be especially decisive against the Axis powers.[70]

In this they were disappointed. As Alan Milward writes, "Economic warfare did have its tactical successes and played its role in the Allied victory. But it fell far short of the extravagant hopes placed on it and a study of its effect is more a study of failure."[71] The Axis powers proved adept at developing substitutes for imports, notably the German effort to produce petroleum from coal. Further, the Axis powers had been able in the early days of the war to expand into regions that provided needed defense inputs. By 1941, Germany had won the oil fields of Rumania and Russia, and the Japanese had gained the oil of

Indonesia. Of course, after four years of pounding by Allied bombers and the wholesale sinking of merchant fleets, the war potential of all the Axis nations had been greatly reduced. Indeed, the Allies themselves thought that economic warfare had been critical to victory, and control of the sea-lanes remained a key American strategic aim until the war's end. But it is rare in the annals of military history that economic warfare alone has led to capitulation of an enemy force.

In conclusion, in every great power economics and security have met at the waterfront. The growth of trade and the need for foreign funds created an inextricable link between commerce and military power. Liberalism may have begun to supplant other economic ideas on land, but even after World War II, mercantilism still ruled the waves.

ECONOMIC DEVELOPMENT AND NATIONAL SECURITY

Before concluding this historical introduction, one final issue might appropriately be raised, and that concerns the relationship between national security and economic development. According to the "pure" theories of laissez faire or neoclassical economics, states maximize social welfare by specializing in the production of goods and services in which they hold comparative advantage. States that are favored with a relative abundance of capital would do well to produce capital-intensive goods, while states with a substantial labor pool would do better to focus on labor-intensive production. In the theory of international trade, it is sensible for states that hold particular natural resources to trade those resources with states that produce manufactured goods.[72]

Economists have noted for some time that the empirical data on trade diverge from the predictions of pure theory.[73] For a number of reasons, states have failed to follow economic arguments and have pursued the production of a wide range of goods and services. Many producers of primary products, for example, have accepted the *structuralist* argument that they inevitably face declining terms of trade, and in response they have sought economic diversification.

Here we emphasize the national security factor in economic development. Surprisingly, few traditional works on economic development explicitly address national security issues. The academic literature tends to reflect what political scientist Robert Gilpin has labeled a "liberal bias." As Gilpin has written, "For the liberal, the goal of economic activity is the optimum or efficient use of the world's scarce resources and the maximization of world welfare."[74] National security simply has not been perceived by modern economists as a major goal of economic policy. The result is that economic development has been treated by the contemporary literature as if it has occurred without reference to internal and external threats.

In this section it is argued that national security concerns have influenced the scope, timing, and direction of economic development policies. National security has also figured in such microeconomic decisions as geographical location, ownership (public versus private sector), and the choice of technology employed in capital-intensive projects. Indeed, in certain cases, such as South Korea and authoritarian Latin America (especially the Latin America of the first half of the twentieth century), "national security" has even been used as an *ideology of economic development*, supplanting economic nationalism, liberalism, and other contending philosophies. This ideology identified communism as the greatest threat to national economic progress, and it called for the creation of "statist" regimes in which a combination of public enterprise, multinational direct investment, and local private economic activity provided for sustained growth and the development of an indigenous military-industrial complex. Further, by placing national security concerns along the east-west axis, third world countries were able to solicit superpower economic support for their development programs.

To illustrate these points, let us examine the case of Brazil. Until the mid-twentieth century, little in the way of industrialization had occurred in this country. The economy reflected comparative advantage, in that it focused on exportation of coffee and other raw materials in exchange for imports of capital-intensive goods.

The outbreak of World War I caused a sea change in traditional trade patterns. Owing to domestic demand in the belligerent countries and to wartime disruption of trade routes, Brazil (and other developing countries) lost access to imported capital goods, as well as to export markets. In Brazil, along with much of Latin America, the war led to the development of light industry, and industrial production tripled during the conflict.[75]

The experience of the First World War contained many economic lessons for officials in the developing world. Above all, the war had been an industrial conflict calling for total mobilization of economic resources. Steel and oil emerged as strategic commodities, in the absence of which a nation was doomed. State support for the steel and fuel industries had, in fact, become a component of national security policy throughout Europe.

In the developing world, the military incorporated these lessons and it began to play a larger role in economic policymaking. The Brazilian armed forces saw to it that the constitution of 1891 was amended to read that "mines and mineral deposits necessary for national security and the land in which they are found cannot be transferred to foreigners." As Europe again headed toward conflict in the 1930s, the Brazilian military urged that the country build an industrial base that could withstand "war or blockade."

The depression years and the Second World War that followed provided another major spur to Brazilian economic development. The military's economic project was focused on the creation of domestic steel and oil industries, but now the country's efforts were aided by its wartime alliance with the United States. The United States sent a special economic mission to Brazil "with a view toward influencing the direction of its growth." Owing to common security concerns, the United States assisted in the development of an economy that could provide war materiel, with only partial consideration of the laws of comparative advantage. Most notably, the war resulted in the construction of Volta Redonda, a great modern steel-manufacturing complex.[76]

The crucial point to make here is that external political-military factors catalyzed Brazil's economic development and shaped its trajectory. The steel plant at Volta Redonda was built during the war because of its promised military contribution. It was located inland, away from the coast, in order to be out of range of naval gunfire (it would have been more economic to place the plant near the coast, to lessen transportation costs of such inputs as coal and shipment of the final steel product to consumers). The plant was owned by the Brazilian government; the military was opposed to allowing the private sector or foreign interests to own strategic industries. Further, the plant was designed to utilize Brazilian coal, even though its heat value was lower than American or European coal. As historian John Wirth has noted, "Thus, in the event of war, continuous steel production . . . would be assured; the primary military goal of self-sufficiency was attainable." [77]

To summarize, the experience of war and concerns with national security have significantly shaped third world economic development, and indeed the development of all countries. This aspect of economic policymaking has been significantly absent from most contemporary treatments of the topic. But history suggests that economic development policy has responded to more than just "market" forces, or the forces of "particular" interest groups; it has also responded to systemic political-military crises.

CONCLUSION

Just as warfare is, by definition, an international activity, so too is defense economics embedded in the international economy. Manipulation of foreign trade, borrowing from foreign lenders, purchase of foreign materiel, and hiring of foreign labor have all been instruments of state policy for purposes of defense and war fighting. The state may be the instigator in matters of national security, but few states in history have been autarkic. Indeed, the notion of a self-sufficient "national security state" is a relatively modern one.

This chapter has provided a "suggestive" history of defense economics. It demonstrates that many of the issues confronting public officials today have their antecedents deep in centuries past. Financing defense, subsidizing military research, development, and production, and striking a balance between autarky and trade have been traditional concerns of statesmen. Further, officials have worried about the economic impact of defense spending on civilian sectors, and have attempted to minimize its malign macroeconomic aspects while promoting its positive microeconomic spinoffs. These themes all seem familiar to us today.

Selected Bibliography

Earle Edward Mead, "Adam Smith, Alexander Hamilton, Friedrich List: The Economic Foundations of Military Power," in Peter Paret, ed., *Makers of Modern Strategy* (Princeton, N.J.: Princeton University Press, 1986). This article remains the best single introduction to defense economics in historical perspective.

Kennedy, Paul, *The Rise and Fall of the Great Powers: Economic Change and Military Conflict from 1500 to 2000* (New York: Random House, 1987). This best-seller provides a provocative, well-written account of the relationship between economic and military power. The citations are a rich resource for those who seek to do research in the history of defense economics.

McNeill, William H., *The Pursuit of Power: Technology, Armed Forces, and Society since A.D. 1000* (Chicago: University of Chicago Press, 1982). McNeill is the master of "macro-history." An excellent introduction.

Milward, Alan S., *War, Economy and Society: 1939–1945* (Berkeley: University of California Press, 1979). This is the unsurpassed economic history of World War II, beautifully written; a classic.

van Creveld, Martin, *Supplying War: Logistics from Wallenstein to Patton* (London: Cambridge University Press, 1977), and *Technology and War* (New York: Free Press, 1989). Van Creveld is one of the great historians of defense economics.

Notes

1. On economic thought, see Edward Mead Earle, "Adam Smith, Alexander Hamilton, Friedrich List: The Economic Foundations of Military Power," in Peter Paret, ed., *Makers of Modern Strategy* (Princeton, N.J.: Princeton University Press, 1986); on economic statecraft more broadly, see David Baldwin, *Economic Statecraft* (Princeton, N.J.: Princeton University Press, 1985). For a review article on the economic thought of the "realists," see Ethan B. Kapstein, "Economics and Military Power," *Naval War College Review* (Summer 1989). On military technology, see William H. McNeill, *The Pursuit of Power* (Chicago: University of Chicago Press, 1982), and Martin van Creveld, *Technology and War* (New York: Free Press, 1989). For a magisterial overview of economics and security, see Paul Kennedy, *The Rise and Fall of the Great Powers: Economic Change and Military Conflict from 1500 to 2000* (New York: Random House, 1987).

2. Aaron Friedberg, "States as Creators of Military Power," paper presented at the 1989 Annual Meeting of the APSA, September 1989.

3. Karl Polanyi, *The Great Transformation* (Boston: Beacon Press, 1944), p. 159.

4. Fernand Braudel, *The Mediterranean and the Mediterranean World in the Age of Philip II* (New York: Harper & Row, 1973), vol. 2., p. 840.

5. See Kennedy, *Rise and Fall*.

6. Margaret Levi, *Of Rule and Revenue* (Berkeley: University of California Press, 1988), p. 105.

7. Ibid.

8. Kennedy, *Rise and Fall*, p. 53.

9. Ibid.

10. For good overviews, see Gunther Rothenberg, "Maurice of Nassau, Gustavus Adolphus, Raimondo Montecuccoli, and the 'Military Revolution' of the Seventeenth Century," in Paret, ed., *Makers of Modern Strategy*; and Michael Howard, *War in European History* (Oxford: Oxford University Press, 1976).

11. John Brewer, *The Sinews of Power* (New York: Knopf, 1989), p. 8; Kennedy, *Rise and Fall*, p. 56.

12. Brewer, *Sinews*, pp. 90–95.

13. Kennedy, *Rise and Fall*, p. 79.

14. Levi, *Of Rule*, p. 126.

15. See Alan Milward, *War, Economy and Society* (Berkeley: University of California Press, 1977), pp. 44–107.

16. Ibid., p. 44.

17. For a detailed account of the financial revolution, see Kennedy, *Rise and Fall*, pp. 76–86.

18. Ibid., p. 78.

19. Levi, *Of Rule*, p. 126.

20. Brewer, *Sinews*, p. 116.

21. Ibid.

22. Aaron Friedberg, *The Weary Titan* (Princeton, N.J.: Princeton University Press, 1988), p. 134.

23. Horst Mendershausen, *The Economics of War* (New York: Prentice-Hall, 1943), p. 360.

24. Ibid.

25. Brewer, *Sinews*, p. 193.

26. Ibid.

27. Joshua S. Goldstein, *Long Cycles* (New Haven, Conn.: Yale University Press, 1988), p. 33.

28. Cited in ibid., p. 33.

29. Ibid.

30. Ibid., p. 35.

31. *Defense Spending and the Economy* (Washington, D.C.: Congressional Budget Office, February 1983), p. 4.

32. Andrew Moravcsik, "Arms and Autarky: The Internationalization of the European Defense Industry in Historical Perspective," unpublished manuscript, Economics and National Security Program, Harvard University, October 1990. On Colbert, see the classic two-volume history by Charles Cole, *Colbert and a Century of French Mercantilism* (New York: Columbia University Press, 1939).

33. Albert Hirschman, *National Power and the Structure of Foreign Trade* (Berkeley: University of California Press, 1945), p. 4.

34. I thank Kamal Shehadi for raising this point. See Felix Gilbert, "Machiavelli: The Renaissance of the Art of War," in Paret, ed., *Makers of Modern Strategy*.

35. Eli F. Heckscher, *Mercantilism* (New York: Macmillan, 1955), vol. 2, pp. 32–33.

36. Ibid.

37. Ibid., p. 35.

38. Alexander Gerschenkron, *Economic Backwardness in Historical Perspective* (Cambridge, Mass.: Harvard University Press, 1962).

39. Michael Barnhart, *Japan Prepares for Total War* (Ithaca, N.Y.: Cornell University Press, 1987), p. 22.
40. Ibid.
41. Moravcsik, "Arms and Autarky."
42. Martin van Creveld, "The Origins and Development of Mobilization Warfare," in Gordon H. McCormick and Richard E. Bissell, eds., *Strategic Dimensions of Economic Behavior* (New York: Praeger, 1984), p. 27.
43. Ibid., p. 30.
44. Kennedy, *Rise and Fall*, p. 262.
45. John Maynard Keynes, *The Economic Consequences of the Peace* (New York: Harcourt, Brace and Howe, 1920).
46. Milward, *War, Economy and Society*, p. 169.
47. A. Hunter Dupree, *Science in the Federal Government* (Cambridge, Mass.: Harvard University Press, 1957), p. 323.
48. Kennedy, *Rise and Fall*, pp. 295–296.
49. For an excellent history of military technology, see McNeill, *The Pursuit of Power*; see also van Creveld, *Technology and War*.
50. See Dupree, *Science in the Federal Government*; and Don Price, *The Scientific Estate* (Cambridge, Mass.: Harvard University Press, 1965).
51. Quoted in Heckscher, *Mercantilism*, p. 27.
52. Cited in David Baldwin, *Economic Statecraft*, p. 78.
53. Mendershausen, *Economics of War*, p. 279.
54. Quoted in McNeill, *Pursuit of Power*, p. 41.
55. Heckscher, *Mercantilism*, p. 35.
56. Ibid.
57. See Ethan B. Kapstein, "The Improvement of the West Highlands Fisheries: 1785–1800," *Journal of the Royal Nautical Society* (May 1980).
58. For a good introduction to Mahan, see Philip Crowl, "Alfred Thayer Mahan: The Naval Historian," in Paret, ed., *Makers of Modern Strategy*. For the original text, see Mahan, *The Influence of Sea Power upon History, 1660–1783* (New York: Hill and Wang, 1957).
59. See Kennedy, *Rise and Fall*, pp. 96–97; and Friedberg, *Weary Titan*, pp. 140–141.
60. Ibid.
61. Ibid.
62. Crowl, "Mahan," p. 471.
63. On the British debate, see Friedberg, *Weary Titan*.
64. Kennedy, *Rise and Fall*, pp. 211–212.
65. Ibid., pp. 247–248.
66. Milward, *War, Economy and Society*, p. 295.
67. See Milward, *War, Economy and Society*; Mendershausen, *Economics of War*; and Burton Klein, *Germany's Economic Preparations for War* (Cambridge, Mass.: Harvard University Press, 1959).
68. The classic account of German trade policy is Hirschman's *National Power and the Structure of Foreign Trade*.
69. Ibid.
70. For the classic account, see W. N. Medlicott, *The Economic Blockade*, 2 vols. (London: HMSO, 1952, 1959).
71. Milward, *War, Economy and Society*, p. 298.

72. Except where noted, this section is derived from Ethan B. Kapstein, "Economic Development and National Security," in Edward Azar and Chung-In Moon, eds., *Third World National Security* (London: Elgar, 1988).

73. See Richard Caves and Ronald Jones, *World Trade and Payments* (Boston: Little, Brown, 1981), pp. 144–151.

74. Robert Gilpin, *U.S. Power and the Multinational Corporation* (New York: Basic Books, 1975), p. 25.

75. For the classic study, see Werner Baer, *Industrialization and Economic Development in Brazil* (Homewood, Ill.: Richard D. Irwin, 1965).

76. Ibid.

77. John Wirth, *The Politics of Brazilian Development, 1930–1954* (Stanford, Calif.: Stanford University Press, 1954), p. 125.

PART ONE

Macro Issues

2

Defense Spending and Budgeting

"The cost of one modern heavy bomber is this: a modern brick
school in more than 30 cities. It is two electric power plants, each
serving a town of 60,000 population. It is two fine, fully
equipped hospitals. It is some 50 miles of concrete highway."
——*President Dwight David Eisenhower*

National security is a *public good*. That is, it is a good that is enjoyed by all
residents, whether they have paid for it or not, and it is a good whose enjoyment
cannot be denied to any resident. Once it has been provided by a government,
everyone on the country's soil benefits.

And yet, in recent years, some critics have claimed that *defense spending*—as
opposed to national security—is a *public bad*, that it has widespread negative
effects on the domestic, and indeed the international, economy. Defense spending, it is said, is unproductive and inflationary. Even worse, while the United
States has been spending billions on defense, its allies—notably Japan—have
invested instead in civilian industries. The net result is that U.S. industry has
become increasingly uncompetitive.

In this chapter, we will examine some of the critical questions associated
with defense spending and budgeting. These include: What is the impact of
defense spending on economic performance? How does the United States
measure the defense spending of its adversaries? How are defense budgets
established? What are the international effects of defense spending? While we
cannot provide definitive answers to all these questions, it is hoped we can build
a framework for analysis.

By way of introduction, it will be useful to review what is meant when we
say that national security is a public good. Public goods have two prominent
characteristics: *first*, nonexcludability; *second*, jointness of supply. Once a nation
provides itself with a military capability, every person benefits from the security

that capability provides, whether he or she paid for it or not. Further, the consumption of defense by one citizen does not diminish the enjoyment of that good by additional citizens. To state the issue differently, public goods "have two critical properties: the first is that it is not *feasible* to ration their use. The second is that it is not *desirable* to ration their use."[1]

The clearest example of a good for which rationing by market means is not possible is nuclear deterrence. So long as America's policy of nuclear deterrence prevents the Soviet Union (or other state) from launching a strategic first strike, then everyone resident on U.S. soil will benefit. Private goods, in contrast, are *exclusive.* Once an ice cream cone is consumed, nobody else can enjoy it. Further, any effort to share the ice cream cone means that someone has to consume less than he or she otherwise would wish. The benefits of private goods are readily captured by those who purchase them.

This discussion should make it clear why the private sector cannot be relied upon to provide national defense. As stated above, once nuclear deterrence is provided, all can enjoy it, whether or not they have paid for it. There is simply no economic incentive for a private actor to provide the good, since he or she cannot collect payment for the service rendered. As a result, we are coerced by the government into paying for nuclear deterrence (and other government services) through the mechanism of taxation. If we were asked to "purchase" it on a voluntary basis, it is unlikely that sufficient revenues would be generated.

People who do not pay for goods that they nonetheless consume are called *free riders;* they are benefiting from a good that somebody else has purchased or provided. You might "free-ride" on the wonderful odor provided by the neighborhood French bakery, or on the morning newspaper of a colleague. This free riding becomes an interesting economic problem when actors attempt to collect rents on the goods they are providing, e.g., if your colleague tries to charge you for looking at the front page of her *New York Times.*

The free-riding problem is important in the context of western alliance relations, and will be discussed fully in Chapter 7. Briefly, it has been said that the western allies are free riders on the U.S. defense budget, and this is why they are able to devote a smaller percentage of their gross national product to defense than we do.[2] Since the United States unilaterally provides nuclear deterrence, the small allies have no economic incentive to contribute to that good; it has already been provided without their assistance. Debates over defense *burden sharing*—or the distribution of costs associated with alliance military spending—really represent efforts to mitigate the free-rider problem in the alliance framework.

DEFENSE SPENDING AND ECONOMIC PERFORMANCE

This section discusses the political economy of defense spending, focusing on the debate over its impact on economic performance.[3] In recent years, exorbitant defense spending has been targeted by some critics as a major contributor to America's (and more pointedly the Soviet Union's) economic decline. An alternative view, however, is that the massive American military buildup of the

1980s served as an economic stimulant while the economy was mired in its deepest recession since the 1930s (some strategists would also argue that the defense buildup broke the economic back of the Soviet Union, leading to the collapse of communism). Although the long-term effects of heavy defense burdens are difficult to assess, it is nonetheless appropriate to take stock of the defense spending debate and the evidence that has been marshaled by the various parties to it.[4]

To cite a leading student of global military expenditures, Steve Chan of the University of Colorado, "Whether we use the term 'impact,' 'consequence,' or 'effect,' the analytical challenge is to arrive at a valid causal inference: Whether and how a change in defense spending causes a change in economic performance."[5] Measurement of such change poses a significant challenge for social scientists for several reasons. First, there is the quality and comparability of data. What is defense spending? Different countries incorporate different elements in defense reporting. Thus, in some countries, veterans' benefits are counted as defense spending, while other countries count police and customs activities. Further, national income accounting is more reliable in some countries than others. Throughout the developing world, defense spending numbers remain unreliable.

There are methodological ways of coping with these difficulties. Several data sets exist on military expenditures, published by such organizations as the U.S. Arms Control and Disarmament Agency (ACDA), the United Nations, and the Stockholm International Peace Research Institute (SIPRI). Among these, the most useful at the aggregate level is probably the annual ACDA series, entitled *World Military Expenditures and Arms Transfers*, which relies on "all source" information gathering. The data are then "massaged" in order to ensure cross-country comparability.[6]

A second measurement problem concerns timing. When questions are posed concerning the impact of X on Y, it is important to specify the time frame under consideration. All things being equal, over the short term, boosts in defense (or other government) spending will almost certainly increase economic growth. Over a longer time horizon, however, the detrimental effects of defense spending may become apparent, as inflation sets into an economy and as private-sector investment is "crowded out."[7]

A number of studies employing statistical and econometric models have been conducted by social scientists that purport to demonstrate the relationship between defense spending and economic growth.[8] One of the simplest and most cited is the rank correlation analysis employed by Robert DeGrasse.[9] Rank correlation analysis involves a comparison between two variables, such as military expenditures and investment, or military expenditures and gross national product. DeGrasse suggested that, in general, countries that spend more on defense invest less in capital and other productive goods and, as a result, experience lower rates of economic growth.

More sophisticated econometric techniques have been employed by such scholars as Steve Cahn, Bruce Russett, Karen Rasler, William Thompson, and Ron Smith.[10] In his widely cited study of defense spending and economic performance in the major industrial countries, Smith employed a regression analysis, testing the ratio of investment to gross national product against the GNP growth rate, unemployment, and military expenditure as a percentage of GNP. He found a powerful correlation between defense spending increases and investment spending declines, contributing to the theory of a trade-off between defense and economic growth.

Other scholars, however, have expressed doubts that such a trade-off exists. Given the ability of modern industrial states to finance their myriad activities, there is no consistent support for the thesis that budgetary choices are, in effect, a zero-sum game. One sophisticated and oft-cited study of the advanced industrial countries over the period 1948–1978 found no evidence of a trade-off between defense and social spending, since states were willing both to raise taxes and to use deficit spending to increase government budgets.[11]

While developing countries are more constrained in their budgetary activities, even here we have a wide range of findings. In the case of Taiwan, for example, Chan found that despite "a heavy defense burden in both dollars and manpower," its economy had achieved one of the world's fastest rates of economic growth.[12] Similarly, Chung-In Moon and In-Taek Hyun have argued that despite continued external threats and heavy defense spending, "South Korea's performance in economic growth and social welfare has remained impressive, posing an interesting anomaly to the theories on the trade-offs between guns and butter."[13]

Concern with defense spending in the United States, which now consumes one-third of the federal budget, is evidently linked to "widespread concern about the effect of the overall Federal budget deficits. . . ."[14] From 1981 to 1988, the United States spent 2 trillion dollars on defense, and the military's share of the economy over that period grew from 5 to over 6 percent (see Table 2-1). By helping to fuel the budget deficit, the Pentagon has been accused of contributing to other systemic economic problems as well, including high interest rates that have buoyed the dollar and propelled large trade deficits.

Indeed, such scholars as political scientist David Calleo have causally linked American military strategy with high defense budgets that in turn have created the huge deficits of recent years. According to Calleo, the roots of America's contemporary economic problems (meaning the budget and trade deficits and suppressed inflation) go back to the Kennedy administration's decision to back a strategy of flexible response. This meant a dramatic improvement in the quality and quantity of conventional forces, especially in the European theater. In order to equip this strategy, defense budgets had to rise over time. This trend, coupled with the Vietnam war and the proliferation of social programs during the Johnson administration's "Great Society" and afterward, has made budget deficits a systemic part of American economic life. Over the past three decades, the United States has had a budget deficit every year since 1961, with the exception of 1969.[15]

Most countries in the world would be prevented from executing this type of fiscal policy, since budget deficits normally create inflationary pressures that must inevitably undermine the performance of the economy; think of such

Table 2-1 Defense Spending and the Economy, 1965–1990

Fiscal Year	DoD Outlays as % of GNP	DoD as % of Labor Force
1965	6.8	7.8
1970	7.8	8.1
1975	5.6	5.3
1980	5.0	4.7
1985	6.2	5.5
1990	5.4	5.4*

*1988 statistic.

Source: Department of Defense, *Annual Report to the Congress: Fiscal Year 1990* (Washington, D.C.: Government Printing Office, 1989), p. 221.

countries as Brazil and Argentina, which are plagued by large federal budget deficits and external debts. These countries have only survived on the basis of extraordinary loans from the first world, which permit them to continue importing essential goods and to pay dividends on existing investment.

Calleo would argue that the United States has been able to pursue economically irresponsible policies, however, because of its hegemonic domination over the world economy. The dollar is the world's key currency, and the United States remains the largest market for the world's output. During the 1960s, this enabled it to "export inflation" to western Europe; basically, Europeans bought dollars whose value was rapidly depreciating. This practice came to an end when President Charles de Gaulle of France demanded gold for dollars, which America refused to exchange. In August 1971, President Nixon closed the gold window, and the postwar regime of fixed exchange rates came to an end.

Since that time, the United States has had to find new ways of financing its deficit. The Reagan administration's approach was to maintain high real interest rates, which sucked in capital from such trading partners as western Europe and Japan. But Calleo would assert that this policy must ultimately come to an end, as foreign investors begin to worry about the value of their financial assets like treasury bonds. Indeed, already a trend is evident of massive foreign direct investment in the United States; foreigners are purchasing real as opposed to financial assets. Over the ten-year period 1978–1987, foreigners purchased nearly 2000 U.S. companies; 220 of these were purchased in 1987 alone (for more on this phenomenon, see Chapter 8).[16]

Calleo has argued that the cure for America's economic disease is straightforward: the United States must cut defense spending, particularly its spending for European defense. The NATO partners and Japan must contribute more to their own defense; they must share more of the collective burden. Calleo has recommended large withdrawals of U.S. troops from Europe, leaving the Europeans themselves to make up for any strategic gaps that remain.

Calleo's alliance argument will be discussed in Chapter 7; here we wish to ask: What about his economic argument, that defense spending has undermined American economic performance? In thinking about the impact of defense spending on performance, it's useful to consider macroeconomic and microeconomic effects in turn.

Let us first consider the argument that defense spending has produced government budget deficits. As political scientist Aaron Friedberg reminds us, "Budgetary outcomes are . . . never the result of any one thing. They are, instead, a *resultant* of several sets of decisions taken simultaneously—about expenditures, on the one hand, and about appropriate levels of taxation, on the other."[17] It is nonsensical to blame defense for budget deficits without examining other contributory factors.

Between 1960 and 1980, the connection between defense and deficits was "extremely weak." Although military outlays increased in terms of absolute, current dollars, they did not grow nearly as quickly as total government spending or the economy as a whole. During this period, defense spending actually fell as a percentage of total government outlays (from 50 percent in 1960 to 23 percent in 1980) and of gross national product (from slightly over 9 percent of GNP to 5 percent.

As defense spending went down in relative terms, nondefense spending rose dramatically from the mid-sixties on. Between 1965 and 1980, nondefense expenditures (not including interest payments on the national debt) increased from 50 to 68 percent of government outlays and from 9.5 to 17 percent of GNP. In the nondefense category, so-called entitlement programs (mostly social security, medicare, and pensions) expanded most rapidly.[18]

While government expenditures on defense and nondefense programs continued to grow, federal tax revenues stayed constant as a percentage of GNP.

The Pentagon: Does the United States spend too much on defense?

(Department of Defense)

This naturally led to the production of budget deficits; until the late 1970s, however, these were small relative to other developed economies, averaging less than 2 percent of GNP.

During the Reagan administration, the federal budget deficit mushroomed. Defense increased its share of GNP, but at the expense of social welfare programs. Of greatest importance, Reagan proceeded with his military buildup while cutting taxes. Tax receipts fell, deficits climbed, and the national debt expanded substantially.

Still, there is nothing inherent in defense spending that causes it as opposed to other programs to produce deficits. The deficits were created by the math of subtracting revenues from expenditures and having a large balance left to finance. To be sure, had the Reagan administration *not* chosen to build the nation's defenses, the deficits would have been smaller. But once the decision was taken, other methods, such as direct taxation, could have been used to pay for it.[19]

Even if we linked defense spending and deficits, however, we must ask whether the sorts of remedy proposed by scholars like Calleo would make a material difference. If we assume an annual deficit of about 150 billion dollars, Department of Defense outlays of some 300 billion dollars must be virtually halved in order to eliminate the deficit. Analysts have pointed out that Calleo's formula of removing half of the American ground troops from Europe and putting them on reserve status at home would save some 67 billion dollars; that makes it at best a contribution, a "peace dividend," rather than a solution, to the deficit problem.

It is of interest to note that polling data from 1990 suggest that while most Americans would like to see defense spending reduced now that the cold war is over, relatively few suggest that the peace dividend be used to lower the deficit. Instead, myriad problems call for public attention, and Americans want more money spent on AIDS research, shelter for the homeless, and so forth. Controlling the deficit does not appear to be the first item of business for most of the public.

When the Reagan defense program was announced in 1980, along with the tax cuts, economists feared that the resulting deficits would lead to high levels of inflation, or increases in the price level. At no time in history had the United States embarked on such a sustained military program without substantial increases in inflation rates (see Table 2-2). On the basis of this history, economists warned that the Reagan defense budget would fuel inflation.[20]

In considering whether defense spending will contribute to inflation, one must consider the overall economic environment. In 1980, Reagan administration economists were facing a deep recession. Macroeconomic forecasts for the period 1983–1985 foresaw slow rates of growth and relatively depressed utilization of manufacturing capacity. Resource utilization in 1982 stood at its lowest point since the Second World War; manufacturing plants were operating at 70 percent capacity, while the unemployment rate hovered above 10 percent. At the same time, restrictive monetary policies by the Federal Reserve Bank under Paul Volcker kept interest rates high and inflationary expectations low.[21]

TABLE 2-2 Wars and Prices

War	Percent Prices Rose
Revolutionary War 1775–1783	201
War of 1812 1812–1815	39
Mexican War 1846–1848	8
Civil War 1861–1865	
Price rise in the Union	117
Price rise in the Confederacy	9,210
Spanish-American War 1898	8
World War I 1917–1918	126
World War II 1941–1945	108
Korean War 1950–1953	2
Vietnam War 1964–1973	69

Source: Claudia Goldin, Harvard University, cited in *New York Times,* March 10, 1991, p. 24.

Inflation, of course, has two manifestations: demand-pull and cost-push. Defense spending may cause demand-pull inflation because it raises national income without increasing the supply of goods and services available for civilian consumption. Increases in demand may lead to price hikes as manufacturing capacity reaches full utilization and, concurrently, unemployment decreases.

Cost-push inflation, in contrast, results from the rising prices associated with military procurement. Defense production does not take place in a competitive environment; it occurs among a small number of firms that are dealing with the Pentagon, which is a *monopsonist,* or single buyer. Inefficiencies and the incorporation of technological changes over time lead to increased prices for weaponry, which can ripple through the economy to inflate prices more generally—more on this in Chapter 5, on weapons procurement.

Has defense spending contributed to inflation in the United States in recent years? The evidence for a causal link is very weak. Indeed, "rising defense expenditures since 1980 have been accompanied by declining inflation rates. . . ."[22]

This does not mean that the inflationary problem has been licked. Had the defense buildup continued, then inflationary pressures would surely have built over time, in the absence of nondefense spending cuts and increased taxation. To be sure, inflation could be controlled by high interest rates, but at a potentially severe cost to economic growth.

The balancing act is to maintain a situation in which federal spending continues to meet legitimate collective needs without crowding out private-sector investment. The inflationary danger comes as manufacturing reaches capacity and the labor market becomes tight. The natural response of the Federal Reserve Board is to raise interest rates, turning money away from consumption and into savings; the danger, however, is that high interest rates will discourage borrowing. Inflationary conditions began to emerge in the United States in the mid-1980s, and indeed real interest rates have been at historically very high levels for nearly a decade.[23]

Defense spending has been further criticized for diverting scarce resources to essentially nonproductive assets and investments.[24] Tanks and fighter aircraft have limited use in the civilian economy, nor can the plants that produce these things easily be converted to civilian use (for more on this, see the section on conversion that appears in Chapter 3).[25] Indeed, one of the telling critiques of the "war economy" or "Pentagon capitalism" is that it traps policymakers into pouring continued amounts of money into defense, since the defense-industrial base must be maintained despite the cost to the larger economy.

From a macroeconomic perspective, national income is represented by the equation $Y = C + I + G + (X - M)$, where Y = GNP, C = consumption, I = investment, G = government spending, X = exports, and M = imports. Let us assume for the moment that $X - M$ is a relatively small number, and focus on the other components.

For political economists interested in defense, a crucial macroeconomic question is whether or not government spending and private consumption have risen at the expense of private-sector investment. According to economist Richard DuBoff, the *major* change in the U.S. economy that has occurred between the 1930s and the 1980s is the "much larger volume of government spending in relation to GNP."[26] Some economists argue that the result has been a crowding-out of private-sector investment. Since defense spending (G) rose quickly in the 1980s, and investment (I) fell, it is suggested that a one-to-one trade-off exists.

Supporters of this view state that positive rates of economic growth are correlated with high rates of investment. Countries that choose to spend relatively large amounts on defense at the expense of private investment risk paying for that choice with slow economic growth. If one contrasts the experience of such countries as Japan with that of the United States, there is cause for concern about the impact of a sustained defense expansion.[27]

But there are important exceptions. South Korea and Taiwan, for example, both have relatively high levels of defense expenditure, but both have enjoyed high rates of economic growth. For that matter, the United States during the Reagan administration increased its defense spending and its rate of growth.

Once again, it is critical to locate defense spending within the context of the broader domestic and international economic environment. The fear that government spending would crowd out private investment, for example, has been partly mitigated by the inflow of foreign direct investment into the United States. If defense spending hurts the domestic economy, why would foreigners invest here?

Further, at least some defense spending does constitute productive investment. Military financial support for research and development and for procurement, not to mention military construction projects (housing, infrastructure), has resulted in spin-offs and spillover into the civilian economy. This is not to argue that the Pentagon is an efficient allocator of scarce resources; it only means that a portion of Department of Defense spending must be counted as having "investmentlike" qualities even though the numbers are not captured by national accounts.[28]

The evidence purporting to show that defense spending causes a decrease in investment and, by extension, a decrease in economic growth is thus circumstantial at best. To be sure, it would not be wise for any state to spend excessive amounts on defense over an extended period of time; states like Israel and the Soviet Union show the malign consequences of a heavy defense burden on economic performance. But it is not clear that defense spending has negatively impacted American economic performance, at least in the short run. The longer-term effects, however, are less clear, and microeconomic analysis suggests some reasons for concern.

From a microeconomic standpoint, defense spending is troublesome because it takes resources from other, more productive sectors. Some analysts believe that the use of resources by the Pentagon depletes productivity growth in the economy; others contend that defense spending reduces employment since such spending is not an efficient generator of jobs. As the Congressional Budget Office (CBO) has written, "Both issues concern the particular pattern of resource demand that derives from defense spending."[29]

Defense spending potentially has both adverse and beneficial effects on private-sector productivity. Defense production employs much of the nation's scarce scientific and engineering talent and considerable capital that could otherwise contribute to productivity growth in the civilian sector. By competing for these resources, defense spending could well restrict private-sector efforts to improve productivity. On the other hand, R&D efforts sponsored by the Pentagon have yielded knowledge that ultimately proves useful to the civilian sector. The computer and semiconductor industries provide dramatic examples of technologies fostered by military R&D that have contributed to private-sector productivity.[30]

Assessing the net effect of these opposing influences is extremely difficult. The major contributors to productivity growth in an economy are investment, research and development, and education and training. Some analysts have claimed that defense spending contributes to economic growth because it plays an important role in technical training for young people.[31] This may be true, but it has yet to be demonstrated that the military is an efficient educator.

The empirical data on the subject provide mixed results. Some studies do suggest that high defense spending is correlated with low productivity growth (but remember the difference between correlation and causation). The industrial countries with the highest productivity growth since World War II, Japan and West Germany, have also spent relatively little on defense. Countries that have traditionally spent more, like the United States and Great Britain, have had lower rates of productivity growth. But once again the evidence is inconclusive; productivity growth in the United States also slowed during periods of declining defense spending.[32]

Nonetheless, there is reason to be concerned about the claim of the Defense Department on the scientific and engineering talent of the United States. The Department of Defense "spends a significant share of US R&D dollars" and "it is responsible for the employment of between one-third and one-fourth of the nation's scientists and engineers." Specifically, about one-half of the R&D in aerospace and about one-third of the R&D in electronics are funded by the Department of Defense. Further, since the Department of Defense is less concerned about cost than commercial customers, the R&D is not necessarily geared to efficient and competitive production of civilian products. Because the United States is no longer the low-cost producer in many technologies that have both civilian and military uses (like numerically controlled machine tools), foreign suppliers have been able to export their product to American customers in civilian sectors.[33]

What about the role of the Department of Defense as job generator? According to Jacques Gansler, "A defense budget of about $300 billion supports, directly and indirectly, between 7 and 8.5 million jobs in the public and private sectors."[34] Each 1 billion dollars added to the defense budget creates between 25,000 and 35,000 jobs. Alternatively, when defense budgets are cut, the impact on regional economies can be significant.

Do other sectors of the economy generate more jobs per dollar? To be sure, other sectors are more labor-intensive. But it has been argued that defense is a better stimulus, because it is more capital-intensive and thus creates a greater economic multiplier for the dollars invested. Analysts in the CBO have found that defense and nondefense federal spending have roughly the same job-creation capability. Others say that since defense relies most heavily on skilled labor, it does nothing for the chronically unemployed and the unskilled. Indeed, defense does draw its labor mainly from such specialists as engineers, computer scientists, and the skilled trades (welders, machinists, etc.).

Defense potentially contributes to the economy in yet another way—through exports. The defense industry exported some 14 billion dollars' worth of goods in 1988, about half of which came from military aerospace. Since U.S. exports totaled approximately 220 billion dollars that year, the contribution of defense was on the order of 5 percent. The sectoral importance to aerospace, of course, was of much greater importance than the gross numbers suggest.[35]

In conclusion, defense spending obviously *does* have a significant impact on economic performance. Yet whether that impact is benign or malign, and how to quantify it, remains subject to scholarly debate, as this section has suggested. To be sure, defense spending is helpful—indeed vital—to particular sectors. But whether those benefits have come at the cost of productivity increases in other sectors is unclear. Economics need not be a zero-sum game in which the gains of one sector mean that another sector loses an equal amount. But to the extent that resources are allocated to inefficient users, then the overall economy is the loser. And in cases where heavy defense burdens are borne for extended periods of time, it does appear that productive investment and sustained growth suffer as a result. For a case in point, let us turn to the Soviet Union.

MEASURING SOVIET DEFENSE SPENDING

As of 1990, President Mikhail Gorbachev appeared to be making serious efforts to reduce defense spending. The Soviet economy is in crisis, with the government running budget deficits that are estimated to be as high as 20 percent of gross national product! By pumping rubles into the economy, the government has fueled hyperinflation, eroding all confidence in the value of the currency.

At the same time, it has been argued that excessive defense spending on the part of Moscow has gutted the consumer economy, exacerbating the chronic shortages of goods and services that have always been part of the Soviet economic scene. Many Soviet economists have placed the blame for their country's economic and political devolution squarely on the shoulders of military spending. Taking a page from such critics of excessive defense spending as Paul Kennedy and David Calleo, they argue that Soviet military expansion has overburdended the economy—that military commitments have outstripped economic capabilities.

Specifically, critics of Soviet defense spending argue that defense expenditures have been unproductive from a societal perspective, and that the military has gotten "the best of everything—brains, skills and materials. . . ."[36] Ironically, nowhere is the military-industrial complex under stronger attack than in the Soviet Union. According to one estimate, some 70 percent of all scientists and engineers in the country work on weapons production. In addition, it has been argued that the military-industrial complex has been allowed to "raid" civilian factories on a regular basis whenever it needs supplies, as if the country were always in a state of conflict.[37] Decline has been the inevitable result of Moscow's effort to maintain a war economy.[38]

For most of postwar history, Moscow had refused to release defense budget figures, saying they were a "state secret." But in the spring of 1989, for the first time in memory, the Soviet Union made an official announcement concerning its level of defense spending. According to government spokespeople, including President Gorbachev himself, the Soviet Union had a defense budget of 77.3 billion rubles for the year. This announcement shocked foreign observers for two reasons: first, because of the precedent it represented; second, because the actual number announced was out of line with intelligence community estimates of Soviet defense spending, which believed the actual number to be much higher (see Table 2-3).

How *do* we estimate the defense spending of foreign nations? The issue is surprisingly complex. In some cases, like the Soviet Union, we have problems comparing economic systems, including prices, resource allocation, productive efficiency, and so forth. We are further hampered by a lack of information. In other cases, problems arise out of comparing exchange rates, calculating the subsidization of military production, determining the opportunity costs associated with low-wage military personnel, etc. Military spending estimates are, as a result, partly art, partly science.

The U.S. Central Intelligence Agency (CIA) and Defense Intelligence Agency (DIA) use, broadly speaking, two methodologies for assessing foreign defense spending: first, *local currency* valuations; second, *dollar costing* of defense activities.[39] Let us examine the advantages and disadvantages associated with each methodology.

The simplest way of calculating defense spending is to use local currencies; in the Soviet case, this would be the ruble. The most straightforward calculation uses current ruble values of defense costs. Intelligence analysts use Soviet and other sources in making an estimate of the actual amount of rubles spent on defense in a given year. Thus, if an intelligence analyst discovered that a Soviet tank cost 1 million rubles to build and that the Soviets built 500 tanks in the year under study, he or she would know what the Soviet tank budget for the year was 500 million rubles. Similarly, if an analyst knew the wage scale for the Soviet armed forces and knew the number of soldiers and sailors, an estimate of salaries paid could be prepared. Clearly, it is a major intelligence challenge to get reliable local currency costs of all the many elements that constitute a country's total defense budget.

When an analyst wishes to study defense spending trends in a country over a period of time, some estimate must be made of the amount of inflation that the country has experienced during that period. One year must be selected as the base year, and the subsequent years can then be adjusted to reflect inflationary trends. In order to reflect the impact of inflation, it is necessary to calculate defense spending in terms of *constant* rubles, yen, or whatever currency is under study. In Table 2-3, Soviet defense spending is presented in terms of constant 1982 rubles; that is, 1982 is taken as the base year, and defense spending in the other years is adjusted to 1982 ruble values.

For analytical purposes, however, local currency valuations have limited utility. To be sure, the intelligence community can provide the President and Congress with estimates of foreign defense burdens as a percentage of gross national product; that burden can then be compared with our own (indeed, it is the issue of *relative burden* in terms of gross national product that has fueled the debate over alliance defense spending, or *burden sharing*). Yet local currency

Table 2-3 Soviet Defense Spending, 1970–1985[a] (billion 1982 rubles)

	1970	1975	1980	1985	1988
GNP	481.4	561.3	624.0	684.7	NA
Defense spending	80.0	95.0	105.0	110.0	NA
As % of GNP	16.6	16.9	16.8	16.0	15–17[a]
					21–26[b]
					8.5[c]

[a]Defense Intelligence Agency/Central Intelligence Agency estimates.
[b]Estimate of intelligence analyst W. T. Lee.
[c]Official Soviet estimate.

Source: U.S. Defense Intelligence Agency, *The Economist*, December 15, 1990, p. 20.

valuations fail to indicate the *comparability* of defense efforts. What does it mean to say that the Soviet Union spends 110 billion rubles on its military, while the United States spends 300 billion dollars? How can these two calculations be compared? (See Table 2-4.)

It is for the purpose of comparability that the intelligence community often utilizes dollar costing of foreign defense activities. According to the CIA, dollar costs "provide an appreciation of the size, quality, and trend" of defense activities. American officials are used to seeing costs in terms of dollars, and accordingly the CIA costs out Soviet and other foreign defense activities on a dollar basis. Soviet defense activities, for example, are compared with U.S. activities, and U.S. prices are assigned to labor and defense production. A Soviet soldier is thus given the salary of an American soldier, a Soviet tank the price of an equivalent American tank, and so on for each comparable activity. On this basis, the total Soviet defense effort can be compared with that ongoing in the United States.[40]

Yet a third method of demonstrating the relative size of military effort is simply by comparing the actual numbers of weapons produced and the numbers of soldiers and sailors. For example, between 1978 and 1987, the U.S. intelligence community estimates that the Soviet Union produced 25,300 tanks to America's 7600; 65 attack submarines to 33 for the United States, and 7700 combat and interceptor aircraft to America's 3600. On the basis of these numbers alone (with no accounting for quality differences), the Pentagon concluded in 1988 that Soviet weapons production had "resulted in a wide advantage in their favor in most categories of conventional weapons. . . ."[41]

Many criticisms have been leveled at intelligence community methodologies and estimates.[42] One critique is that the methodology is oblivious to the economic principle of *comparative advantage.* Military forces reflect not only strategic requirements, but the relative abundance of particular factors of production in each country. It seems ludicrous to assign dollar costs to Chinese soldiers on the basis of American wages, since labor is relatively plentiful in China and relatively scarce in the United States. Obviously, if we assign dollar costs to the Chinese army, spending on wages must far exceed the wages given to the American army. But are the wage structures of the Chinese and American armies really comparable?

A further critique of intelligence community estimates is that Soviet defense spending has historically been *exaggerated.* The benign view is that this has been done owing to methodological weaknesses; the malign view, that it has been done for the political reason of supporting domestic (i.e., U.S.) defense spending. Indeed, despite a pervasive academic view that Soviet defense spending had slowed down in the early 1980s, the United States government continued to point to the growing Soviet threat as a fundamental reason for the large peacetime expansion of the armed forces.[43]

The professed desire on the part of Soviet leaders to cut defense spending and convert military industries to civilian production, along with the dissolution of the Warsaw Pact, has had a profound impact on the U.S. defense and intelligence communities. It now seems clear that public officials did a poor job in

Table 2-4 Choosing an Appropriate Measure of Defense Spending

Problem	Methodology
How much does the U.S.S.R. spend on defense?	Current ruble prices
What are the trends in Soviet defense spending?	Constant ruble prices
How do Soviet defense activities compare with U.S. defense activities?	Constant U.S. dollar prices

Source: Adapted from Directorate of Intelligence, *A Guide to Monetary Measures of Soviet Defense Activities*, SOV87-10069, November 1987, p. 17.

reading the economic signals being sent from the Soviet Union, and in recent years the CIA has been criticized for undercounting Soviet military expenditures and overcounting Soviet gross national product.[44]

In recognition of the profound changes in the Soviet bloc, Secretary of Defense Richard Cheney by late 1989 was ordering "deep budget cuts" that would result in employee reductions, changes in force structure, and a dampening of procurement. Some congressional leaders estimated that defense spending would be cut by as much as 150 billion dollars between 1991 and 1993, or 50 percent from 1990 levels. There was widespread talk of a "peace dividend" that could be applied to social spending or deficit reduction.[45]

Will the planned cuts actually be made? Does the defense budget accurately reflect military requirements, based on an objective assessment of the external environment? Or is the budgeting process a giant congressional pork barrel, as critics have charged? In the next section, we will explore the political economy of defense budgeting.

DEFENSE BUDGETING

In theory, national security strategy drives the defense budget. An objective assessment of the external security environment is made by responsible public officials, appropriate force structures and levels are determined, and scarce economic resources are allocated to the defense effort as efficiently as possible. As former Secretary of Defense Caspar Weinberger once wrote, "Our national security strategy and the defense budget are inseparable. National security strategy is the foundation upon which the defense budget is built. . . ."[46]

A very different perspective on defense budgeting has been provided by former Office of Management and Budget director David Stockman. In his account of Reagan economic policymaking, entitled *The Triumph of Politics*, he described the making of the administration's defense budget:

> At seven-thirty Friday evening, January 30 [1981], I gathered in the Secretary of Defense's office at the Pentagon. It was a very unusual Pentagon meeting: no charts, no computer printouts, no color slides, no colonels with six-foot wooden pointers. The only implements we had were my Hewlett Packard pocket calculator and a blank piece of paper. It is somewhat fitting that the

largest peacetime budget in US defense history was about to be tabulated on a $70 pocket calculator manufactured by a major defense contractor. . . . When I finally took a hard look at the numbers (cranked out that evening) several weeks later, I nearly had a heart attack. We'd laid out a plan for a five year defense budget of 1.46 trillion dollars! This was double what candidate Ronald Reagan had promised in his defense budget.[47]

Defense budgeting, like all budgeting, is a political process. It involves resource allocation, and the manner in which scarce resources get allocated is one of the central problems in political theory. The question of defense budgeting is particularly complex, however, given the number of actors involved in the process, the saliency of the issues that are involved, and, perhaps most important, the large amount of discretionary dollars at stake.

Defense budgeting brings us to the classic problem of *guns versus butter*, that is, the trade-off of defense goods against nondefense goods. When private firms think of such trade-offs, they devise a *production possibility frontier*, which suggests different levels of output for the different types of goods they might produce. The challenge is to find the optimal output, the output that maximizes the revenues of the firm. For the public official, the challenge is to optimize a fixed federal budget in such a way as to produce the best mix of defense and nondefense goods. That mix would meet both the national security and social welfare goals set by the central authorities.

The defense budgeting process varies greatly from one country to another. In the United States, the process is intensely pluralistic, meaning that numerous actors are "pulling and hauling" on the budget. Since the defense budget represents the largest pool of discretionary cash in the federal budget, it is not surprising that so many people want to get their hands on it.

In western Europe, in contrast, defense budgeting is much more centralized. Cabinet-level officials take the leading role in shaping defense policy, budgets, and weapons procurement. Parliaments and national assemblies play a smaller role than does the U.S. Congress in shaping defense programs and priorities.[48]

The defense budget is the vital link between military policy on the one hand and the nation's economy on the other. It is the end product of a process that includes (in the U.S. case) the following elements: first, identifying U.S. security interests; second, assessing the threats to those interests; third, formulating a defense policy to respond to those threats and to secure U.S. interests; fourth, determining the most effective mix of forces, weapons, and labor to execute defense policy; finally, proposing a defense budget that meets program requirements.

Traditionally, the most difficult part of the process has been the fourth step: determining an effective force structure. The weapons we buy today will remain in the field into the next century, and the career officers and other personnel we train today will serve just as long. How can a force be built that reflects the range of likely contingencies the United States will face during this time period?

But in the 1990s, it is not just step 4 that has become difficult. For the first time in postwar history, the United States is facing a changing international system in which containment and nuclear deterrence assume less importance. Public officials must once again confront the basic questions concerning U.S. security interests and threats in a post–cold war world. The answers provided will shape the defense budget for many years to come. Thus, a great deal of systemic-level complexity has been added to the defense budget debate.

Incredible as it may seem, it takes more than two years to get a defense budget approved. Every January, the President submits his federal budget proposal to Congress for the fiscal year beginning the following October. During this nine-month period, officials of the Department of Defense make frequent trips to Capitol Hill, explaining their proposals and modifying them at the direction of Congress. To this nine-month period, we must add the eighteen-month budget planning process within the Department of Defense that precedes the submission of the January budget proposal. Adding the twelve months of the fiscal year itself, during which the Pentagon is spending (or obligating itself to spend) the money that has already been appropriated, results in a total cycle of thirty-nine months—over three years—for each annual defense budget.[49]

At any given moment the Department of Defense is actually involved with three or four different budgets in various stages of development. It is spending according to the current budget, testifying in support of the next one, and planning for one or two after that. According to some analysts, the budgeting process itself is the major contributor to inefficiency in defense spending.

Technically, the Pentagon budgets according to a resource allocation mechanism called the planning, programming, and budgeting system (PPBS). The "Whiz Kid" Robert McNamara and his cohorts from the RAND Corporation created PPBS in 1961 in order to achieve centralized control over the operations of the Department of Defense and in order to allocate resources on the basis of cost-benefit criteria (indeed, the economic side of the Pentagon is still largely run by RAND alumni). The PPBS involves a cycle of decision making that includes plans, programs, and budgets. Plans are the specific objectives the Pentagon seeks to achieve. Programs are the basic units around which the major plans and defense budget are built. For example, the Air Force's Minuteman missile and the Navy's Polaris missile are two of the program elements within our nuclear deterrent triad (the third being manned bombers). As part of the PPBS, a considerable effort is made to define the relative "cost effectiveness" of each weapon system (for example, how many bombs could be delivered on a target per unit cost by one weapon versus another). Budgets are the price tags attached to the individual weapons programs.[50]

As has already been mentioned, at any one time Pentagon officials are going through several PPBS cycles. First, they are managing expenditures for the current fiscal year's budget; second, they are defending the budget submission to Congress for the upcoming fiscal year; and third, they are beginning to prepare the budget for the following fiscal year. Thus, during the summer of 1990, for example, the Pentagon was overseeing the expenditures of the fiscal year 1990 budget that ran from October 1, 1989, to September 30, 1990; defending the budget the President presented to Congress in January 1990 for the fiscal year 1991; and finally, beginning preparations for the fiscal year 1992 budget, which would begin on October 1, 1991. The myriad elements of the defense budget, the simultaneous consideration of three different budgets, and the need to coordinate the efforts of thousands of individuals—all make the PPBS exercise a mind-boggling one.

In order to simplify matters, some analysts—like Robert Art of Brandeis—have called on Congress and the Pentagon to adopt a biennial, or two-year, budget. Indeed, since 1986 the Pentagon has prepared a two-year budget for congressional review. To date, however, Congress has appropriated funds only on an annual basis. The Department of Defense is thus ready to launch a two-year budget cycle, but Congress is reticent to do so.[51]

A two-year budget, advocates say, would lead to more effective defense spending by the Pentagon. In theory, effective procedures for allocating resources are those that enable top-level decision makers to do three things well: (1) develop a planning framework for guiding their decisions; (2) make intelligent trade-offs in how resources are allocated among the multiple objectives they have to achieve; (3) evaluate the results of their trade-offs and incorporate those evaluations into the next set of trade-offs they must make. Ideally, then, in making current decisions, managers must have a strategic vision of where they want to go; they must make the necessary trade-offs to get there; they must evaluate the results of their trade-offs; and ultimately they must alter their future decisions to reflect the lessons they have learned and the new information that they receive. In sum, good decision making over defense resources is a feedback process.

Efficient procedures are thus ones that enable managers to perform their important tasks of planning, decision making, and evaluation with a minimum of wasted effort. One contention of defense budget critics, therefore, is that the process wastes enormous human, financial, and capital resources and ultimately leads to poor defense resource allocation decisions.

The problem with annual budgeting is that defense managers spend too much time in minutiae and not enough in planning and evaluating. Indeed, Pentagon officials call their struggle the "annual budget war." With annual budgeting, managers are unable to win the time that might allow them to make the decision-making system more effective, and they have even less time available for evaluating the results of their decision-making process. As one Pentagon official has said, "As it is now, we are always budgeting—we have biweekly budgeting."[52] In the words of another, "The inherent advantage in biennial budgeting is that it frees up time for efficient and effective management of resources. With annual budgeting, we use all the time we have for resource allocation. Where is the exam time around here? If we devote twelve months to allocation, there is not time for exams—review and assessment."[53]

Why then do we have annual budgets, if it is so obvious that a biennial budget would lead to more effective decision making? According to Art, "Annual budgeting is a product of two powerful sets of political forces in the American political system: on the one hand, the rivalry for power among congressional committees and, on the other, the struggle for power between the Congress and the Presidency."[54] Since the early 1960s, annual budgeting has been the mechanism through which all congressional authorizing committees (e.g., the Senate Armed Services Committee) have gained power at the expense of the appropriations committees. In their quest for greater control over defense policy and in their belief that control over money is control over policy, the Senate and House Armed Services Committees have become more like budgeteers and less like policy setters and policy overseers. And since the founding of the republic, the annual appropriation process has been the mechanism by which the Congress has preserved its power vis-à-vis the presidency. The annual defense budget war, Art says, reflects the ongoing committee wars within Congress and the longer-running struggle for power between Congress and the President.[55]

Let's look a little more closely at what happens to a defense budget once the President has presented it to Congress. First, the House and Senate Budget Committees address overall federal budget levels, or "ceilings." This is the absolute amount the federal government is permitted to budget for that fiscal year. Then, the appropriate House and Senate authorization committees (in the case of the defense budget, the Armed Services Committee of each house) hear testimony leading to specific authorizations of each program element. Authorizations are made for everything from weapons systems to labor force to reserve strength. After this, the appropriations committee of each house hears testimony on providing the money for each line item in the budget. In theory, the authorization committees are approving the "functions" for which a budget is required, and the appropriations committees are approving the funds for those

Congress complains about waste, but is it the source of the problem?

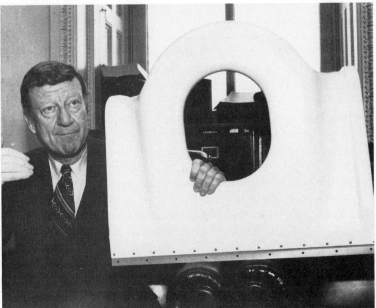

(AP/Wide World Photos)

Table 2.5 Department of Defense Budget Authority (billions of dollars)

	FY88 Request	FY88 Congressional Action	FY88 Budget
Military personnel	78.3	−2.2	76.1
Operations/maintenance	86.6	−5.9	80.7
Procurement	84.0	−3.0	81.0
Research & development	43.7	−7.0	36.0
Construction	6.6	−1.2	5.4
Family housing	3.5	−0.4	3.1
Other	0.6	−0.4	0.2
Total	303.3	−20.1	283.2
	% Share		
Army	26.8		
Navy/Marines	35.4		
Air Force	31.1		
Defense agencies	6.7		

Source: U.S. Department of Defense.

functions; in reality, the hearings are highly redundant. The outcome of the process, however, is usually to reduce the defense budget requested by the President (see Table 2-5).

In addition to the budget, authorization, and appropriations committees, a number of other committees have oversight of specific areas of the defense budget (for example, the banking committees oversee the Defense Production Act). Still more committees have jurisdiction over defense procurement practices, including buying computers and legislating against "waste, fraud, and abuse."

When Congress makes changes to the defense budget, the effects reverberate throughout the PPBS; remember that the Pentagon is also planning for the "out-years" while this year's budget war is ongoing. To understand the magnitude of this effect, it must be realized that a typical weapon system takes from twelve to fifteen years to evolve; thus, reducing a program's budget for the current year results in a reassessment of the "out-year" budget needs (not only to compensate for the lost money, but also to cover cost increases owing to inflation and to the production inefficiencies introduced by stretching out the program). This budgetary change will, in turn, ripple out to affect the amount of money available for other programs in the out-years, and so it permeates all future budgets, affecting many more programs than the single one changed by Congress. Needless to say, the net result is to undermine the coherence of the planning process.

Unfortunately, in recent years, some members of Congress have gone beyond making just a few important changes; aided by their large and growing staffs—some members of which have been doing defense budgeting longer than anyone in the Pentagon—they pore over each new budget proposal line by line, making countless adjustments, redirections, and other "improvements." This detailed micromanagement occurs annually, causing dramatic disruptions of the planning process.[56]

Given efforts to economize each year's annual budget, there is a tendency to stretch out weapons acquisition programs over several years to give the appearance of cost savings. The hope is that the needed dollars will be found for the program in each annual budget. If the anticipated funding is not provided, defense planners are left with the unpleasant choice of either canceling the program or going for a further stretch-out. This leads to inefficient production runs for systems and, consequently, to cost increases. More on this when we talk about procurement.

What can be done to improve the defense budgeting process? We've already talked about one recommendation—biennial budgeting. But to enact this would require that Congress accept binding resolutions on out-year budgets, and this they are unlikely to do. An alternative explanation of congressional action derives from the perspective of corporate finance theory; basically, one could argue that Congress wants the *option* of changing the defense budget each year, and it is willing to pay the price associated with the purchase of that option. It will forgo the option only when the costs of holding it outweigh the potential benefits.

Indeed, leaving aside the constitutional issue of *whether* Congress can authorize multiyear budgets, some representatives have argued that they want to retain the "flexibility" to change the budget each year, to reflect changing external and internal circumstances. But flexibility is the opposite of stability from a budgeting perspective, and there is serious discussion within Congress about coming up with some way to incorporate a longer-term perspective in the planning process.

There have been many other proposals for improving congressional management of the defense budget; one prominent idea worthy of discussion here is called "mission orientation." Basically, this idea requires that Congress think of meeting the "mission needs" of the Pentagon rather than of local politics and the pork barrel. There are many programs that the Defense Department does not support, but they are added on to the defense budget anyway. For example, in 1981 the Carter administration requested no funds for a particular helicopter, but the delegation from Texas put them in the budget. In the same year, the administration refused to provide new funds for a fighter aircraft manufactured by Grumman in New York, but the congressional delegation from that state managed to add several to the budget. During that year one aircraft and one helicopter were produced per month by the respective factories in New York and Texas—a remarkable display of inefficiency. In 1985 it was estimated that more than 5 billion dollars of programs *not* requested by the Pentagon were added on by Congress. To be sure, Congress has a legitimate oversight role when it comes to defense planning and spending; but does it have a legitimate role in the add-on process? It would be interesting to find a case where the Congress was right in providing an add-on—in other words, where Congress had put into place, of its own initiative, a program that the Pentagon had scratched and the Congress's decision was ultimately justified by events (for more on these issues, see Chapter 5, on weapons procurement).

At the Defense Department, perhaps the most important requirement is better planning and strategy—there is a need to integrate our national security strategy with our defense budget. Rather than think of such discrete entities as the various services, the various congressional districts, and the various weapons programs, the Pentagon must think in terms of missions and what is required to perform those missions. Indeed, some have suggested that the Office of the Secretary of Defense formulate specific mission statements and then open a "competition" among the armed services, and perhaps even our allies, to bid on a contract for those particular missions. The current practice of focusing on service requirements allows each service to go its own way, and it creates enormous overlap among the services.

In conclusion, defense budgeting is a highly complex political-economic task. Since it is the largest single item in the federal budget, since it contains so many discretionary funds, and since defense spending is so important to so many constituencies, it is perhaps the most highly politicized budgetary item recommended by the President. This is ironic, in that national security is allegedly a "state" goal that transcends special interests. But the defense budget, like every other item of government business, reflects the American way of conducting political business. Schemes to reform the budgetary process must take this into account.

Selected Bibliography

Art, Robert, "The Pentagon: The Case for Biennial Budgeting," *Political Science Quarterly* *104* (1989): 193–214. This is an excellent introduction to the politics of defense budgeting.

Benoit, Emile, *Defense and Economic Growth in Developing Countries* (Lexington, Mass.: Lexington Books, 1973). This is a pathbreaking book whose findings continue to be debated in the scholarly literature.

Chan, Steve, "The Impact of Defense Spending on Economic Performance: A Survey of Evidence and Problems," *Orbis* (Summer 1985): 403–434. This illuminating and comprehensive review article is written by a leading scholar in the field of defense economics.

Hobkirk, Michael, *The Politics of Defense Budgeting* (Washington, D.C.: National Defense University Press, 1983). This rare, comparative study of defense budgeting examines the United States and Great Britain.

Rowen, Henry, and Charles Wolf, eds., *The Impoverished Superpower* (San Francisco: Institute for Contemporary Studies, 1990). This is a powerful exploration of the Soviet defense economy and its devastating impact on economic growth.

U.S. Department of Defense, *Annual Report to Congress*. This annual report is the best single guide to the defense budget. The Brookings Institution of Washington also publishes an annual analysis of the budget, which provides a useful companion volume.

Notes

1. See Joseph E. Stiglitz, *Economics of the Public Sector* (New York: Norton, 1986), p. 99.
2. Mancur Olson and Richard Zeckhauser, "An Economic Theory of Alliances," *Review of Economics and Statistics 48* (August 1966): 266–279.
3. For an economic textbook treatment of this subject, see Lee Olvey et al., *The Economics of National Security* (Garden City, N.Y.: Avery, 1984).
4. For two recent reviews, see Murray Weidenbaum, *Military Spending and the Myth of Global Overstretch* (Washington, D.C.: Center for Strategic and International Studies, 1989); and Charles Kupchan, "Defence Spending and Economic Performance," *Survival* (Autumn 1989): 447–461.
5. Steve Chan, "The Impact of Defense Spending on Economic Performance: A Survey of Evidence and Problems," *Orbis* (Summer 1985): 403–434.
6. Interviews with ACDA officials, November 1990.
7. See Kurt W. Rothschild, "Military Expenditure, Exports and Growth," *Kyklos 26* (1973); 804–814; and Bruce Russett, *What Price Vigilance? The Burdens of National Defense* (New Haven, Conn.: Yale University Press, 1970).
8. For useful review essays, see Chan, "Impact of Defense Spending," and Gordon Adams and David Gold, *Defense Spending and the Economy: Does the Defense Dollar Make a Difference?* (Washington, D.C.: Defense Budget Project, 1987).
9. Robert DeGrasse, *Military Expansion, Economic Decline* (Armonk, N.Y.: M. E. Sharpe, 1983).
10. See Steve Chan, "Defense Burden and Economic Growth: Unravelling the Taiwan Enigma," *American Political Science Review 82* (1988): 913–920; Bruce Russett, "Defense Expenditures and National Well-Being," *American Political Science Review 76* (1982): 767–777; Karen Rasler and William Thompson, "Defense Burdens, Capital Formation, and Economic Growth," *Journal of Conflict Resolution 32* (1988): 61–86; and Ron Smith, "Military Expenditure and Investment in OECD Countries, 1954–1973," *Journal of Comparative Economics 4* (1980): 19–32.
11. William Domke, Richard Eichenberg, and Catherine Kelleher, "The Illusion of Choice: Defense and Welfare in Advanced Industrial Democracies, 1948–1978," *American Political Science Review 77* (March 1983): 19–35.
12. Steve Chan, "Military Burden, Economic Growth, and Income Inequality: The Taiwan Exception," paper delivered to the 1990 Annual Meeting of the International Studies Association, Washington, D.C., April 10–15.
13. Chung-In Moon and In-Taek Hyun, "Muddling through Security, Growth and Welfare: The Political Economy of Defense Spending in South Korea," paper presented to the International Studies Association, April 10–13, 1990, Washington, D.C.
14. Leonard Silk, "The New Guns-and-Butter Battle," *New York Times,* May 22, 1988, p. 1.
15. See David Calleo, *Beyond American Hegemony: The Future of the Western Alliance* (New York: Basic Books, 1987).
16. Eric Rosengren, "Is the United States for Sale? Foreign Acquisitions of U.S. Companies," *New England Economic Review* (November/December 1988): 47–56.
17. Aaron Friedberg, "The Political Economy of American Strategy," *World Politics 41* (April 1989): 381–406.
18. Ibid.
19. See Adams and Gold, *Defense Spending and the Economy.*
20. *Defense Spending and the Economy* (Washington, D.C.: Congressional Budget Office, February 1983).

21. Ibid.
22. Kupchan, "Defence Spending."
23. *Defense Spending.*
24. Kupchan, "Defence Spending," p. 7.
25. Ethan B. Kapstein, "From Guns to Butter in the USSR," *Challenge* (September/October 1989): 11–15.
26. Richard DuBoff, "What Military Spending Really Costs," *Challenge* (September/October 1989): 4–10.
27. See, for example, Lloyd Dumas, "National Security and Economic Delusion," *Challenge* (March/April 1987): 28–33.
28. See Charles Kupchan, "Defense Spending and Economic Performance," *Survival* (Autumn 1988).
29. *Defense Spending,* p. 37.
30. Ibid.
31. The classic expression of this view is Emile Benoit, *Defense and Economic Growth in Developing Countries* (Lexington, Mass.: Lexington Books, 1973).
32. *Defense Spending,* p. 39.
33. Jacques Gansler, *Affording Defense* (Cambridge, Mass.: MIT Press, 1989), pp. 89 ff.
34. Ibid., p. 81.
35. *The U.S. Aerospace Industry and the Trend toward Internationalization* (Washington, D.C.: Aerospace Industries Association of America, March 1988).
36. "The Tank Trap," *The Economist,* December 15, 1990, p. 19.
37. Ibid.
38. See Judy Shelton, *The Coming Soviet Crash* (New York: Free Press, 1989); and Henry Rowen and Charles Wolf, eds., *The Impoverished Superpower* (San Francisco: Institute for Contemporary Studies, 1990).
39. See Directorate of Intelligence, *A Guide to Monetary Measures of Soviet Defense Activities,* SOV87-10069, November 1987.
40. Directorate of Intelligence, *Dollar Costing of Foreign Defense Activities: A Primer on Methodology and Use of the Data,* July 1988.
41. *Your Defense Budget* (Washington, D.C.: Department of Defense, February 1988).
42. For some of the critiques, see Franklyn Holzman, "Politics and Guesswork: CIA and DIA Estimates of Soviet Defense Spending," *International Security* 14 (Fall 1989): 101–131; Raymond Vernon, "The Politics of Comparative Economic Statistics," in William Alonso and Paul Starr, eds., *The Politics of Numbers* (New York: Russell Sage Foundation, 1987): pp. 77–82.
43. See Richard Kaufman, "Causes of the Slowdown in Soviet Defense," *Soviet Economy 1* (January 1985): 179–192.
44. For a powerful critique, see Rowen and Wolf, *The Impoverished Superpower.*
45. Molly Moore and George Wilson, "Pentagon Drafts Major Cuts in Forces, Weapons," *Washington Post,* November 28, 1989, p. 1.
46. Caspar Weinberger, "Strategy: The Driving Force behind the Defense Budget," *Defense 87* (March/April 1987): 2.
47. David Stockman, *The Triumph of Politics* (New York: Harper & Row, 1986), pp. 277–278.
48. On the British system, see Michael Hobkirk, *The Politics of Defense Budgeting* (Washington, D.C.: National Defense University Press, 1983).
49. My analysis of the defense budget has been greatly influenced by the writings of— and by discussions with—Professor Robert Art of Brandeis University. See, for

example, Art, "The Pentagon: The Case for Biennial Budgeting," *Political Science Quarterly* 104 (1989): 193–214.

50. For a critical analysis of the PPBS, see Robert P. Meehan, *Plans, Programs and the Defense Budget* (Washington, D.C.: National Defense University Press, 1985).

51. See Art, "The Pentagon," and Art, "From Resource Wars to Real Wars: The Pentagon and Biennial Budgeting," mimeograph, January 1989.

52. Cited in Art, "From Resource Wars."

53. Ibid.

54. Ibid.

55. Ibid.

56. For one examination of congressional politics in this area, see David Morrison, "Only the Beginning," *National Journal,* August 18, 1989: 2077–2082.

3

Mobilization, War, and Conversion

"... When the Army marches abroad, the Treasury will be
emptied at home." ——*Sun Tzu,* The Art of War
"I cannot recall any time in our history when the Congress has
attempted to assess the full economic impact of a war."
——*Senator William Proxmire, April 24, 1967*[1]

This chapter examines economic aspects of industrial mobilization and war and
discusses conversion from military to commercial enterprise at the end of the
defense buildup. It might appear at first glance that preparation of an economy
for conventional war would no longer be of major concern to defense planners in
the nuclear age. Indeed, writing in 1960 (in the last major defense economic
textbook published), Charles Hitch and Ronald McKean argued that "preoccu-
pation" with the "mobilization base in the nuclear era is dangerous. It can . . .
only lead to the diversion of resources into activities that have become useless."[2]

As we will see in the following sections, however, one need not contemplate a superpower crisis in order to be concerned with mobilization and the
economics of warfare. Even regional wars like those fought by the United States
in Korea and Vietnam had severe economic impacts, and the U.S. and coalition
response to Iraq's invasion of Kuwait in August 1990—Operation Desert Shield
and Desert Storm—cost over 80 billion dollars. According to U.S. Senator Jim
Sasser of Tennessee, the shooting war cost the U.S. from $1 billion to $2 billion per
day. Sasser has argued that "the economic consequences of war demand attention."[3]

It should also be recalled that the economics of mobilization and war
remains a significant issue for many small states. The Iran-Iraq war and the Arab-
Israeli conflict exemplify how economic preparation for war continues to
preoccupy contemporary societies. As with the other chapters, the objective here

is to provide a framework for analysis as we examine the political economy of war, rather than to provide a description of the problem in the context of a single case study.

Once again we will see that economic preparation for war has both macroeconomic and microeconomic elements. Further, it is an *international* as opposed to a purely national problem. During war, countries continue to rely on trade for needed goods and services. Owing to this vulnerability, countries may engage in or threaten *economic warfare;* they may use economic tools—such as *boycotts, embargoes,* and *preemptive purchases*—to harm adversaries, or they may use military tools to attack targets of economic value within and outside enemy territory.

At the war's end, countries face the problem of reconstruction and industrial conversion from wartime to civilian economic pursuits. Although general economic reconstruction will not be discussed in detail here, it is important to note that this phase may also have a significant international economic and security dimension. Countries often have to rely on external sources for food, raw materials, and money when a war is over. The manner in which the war-torn countries are reconstructed by the victorious powers can influence regional peace and stability. At the end of World War I, on top of the myriad economic problems caused by war, Germany was forced to pay billions in reparations to the Allies, causing severe hardship and political resentment. Ultimately, Germany's economic problems were "solved"; but only after Adolf Hitler had come to power.

Indeed, in part owing to the failure of post-World War I reconstruction policy, the United States led in the creation of new economic development institutions after 1944, including the United Nations Relief and Rehabilitation Agency, the International Bank for Reconstruction and Development (today's World Bank), and the International Monetary Fund. When it became apparent that the resources of these institutions were insufficient to handle the job, the United States launched perhaps the greatest foreign policy initiative in its history, the *Marshall Plan* (named after then Secretary of State George Marshall), which was announced in June 1947 at Harvard University. The Marshall Plan made 13 billion dollars available over the next four years to the war-torn nations of Europe and Asia.[4]

The following sections indicate that war planning, prosecution, and termination present complex economic problems for both market and command economies. Even during periods of "total war," when societies are waged in life and death struggles, basic civilian requirements must still be met. The political economy of war is shaped not only by the state's industrial and raw material capabilities, but also by the willingness of its citizens to sacrifice current consumption for the common cause.[5]

SURGE AND MOBILIZATION

For historian Martin van Creveld, the concept of mobilization implies preparation for total war. According to van Creveld, "Mobilization warfare is a system of war based upon the total mobilization of a country's social and economic resources in addition to its purely military ones."[6] Mobilization implies that society is undergoing a significant shift from civilian to defense consumption.

The first stage in economic mobilization, and one that may be self-contained depending on the nature of the crisis, is when industry is called upon to engage in *surge production.* The U.S. Department of Defense defines surge capability as "the ability of the existing production base to meet accelerated production requirements in the absence of a declared national emergency."[7] Most producers of weapons and war materiel are required by law to maintain surge capability for specific items.

According to John Hiller and Judith Larrabee, "Several possible applications of production surge distinguish it from mobilization demands."[8] An ally, for example, may be called upon to provide materiel support during a conflict in which it is not directly engaged; one example is the support the United States provided to Israel during the 1973 Yom Kippur War, which required American suppliers to boost production of certain items. Alternatively, the threat of a conflict may cause decision makers to order that defense production facilities operate on a three-shift, around-the-clock basis; mobilization, in contrast, would require the conversion of civilian production to military purposes.

Even before surge production can occur, however, defense officials will be forced to draw down stockpiles from existing inventories of weapons and materiel to supply regular and reserve troops and sailors. Indeed, this is why military establishments maintain relatively large inventories of raw materials, intermediate goods, and end-items during peacetime. Peacetime inventories that are large enough to meet emergency requirements are called the *cold-base* level, the level needed to sustain troops in preparation for or during the early days of combat while production lines are still cold. Once the industrial base is primed and production lines are "hot," inventories will be maintained at lower levels, since military requirements will be met primarily from existing production. Wartime inventory levels are thus called the *hot-base* level. Countries could not, of course, sustain combat operations solely on the basis of existing inventories. The ability of a country to produce materiel domestically and engage in foreign procurement where necessary will determine its ability to engage in sustained hostilities.

Industrial mobilization, which signifies the shift from cold-base to hot-base inventory management, may be "defined as the transformation of a nation's industry from a peacetime status to an emergency status. The objective of industrial mobilization is to support the armed forces while providing the minimum essentials for the civilian population and allies."[9] Industrial mobilization includes the following components:

1. Determination of what to produce

2. Determination of which firms produce what items and arrangements therewith for production
3. Arrangements for manufacturing facilities, materials, tools, labor force, and other components of the productive process
4. A system for scheduling and controlling manufacturing production to include items for the civilian population as well as for the security effort[10]

Industrial mobilization normally entails substantial government intervention in economic decision making, although the type and the degree of such intervention remain a subject of controversy; more on this below. This means that governments must have the *authority* to intervene; in this regard, democratic systems of government may be at some disadvantage to command economies, since the granting of extraordinary powers over the economy will inevitably involve political debate. Writing in 1960, James Schlesinger warned that democracies must be prepared to execute at the outset of a war "an overall plan of production." Schlesinger asserted that the efficient use of economic capabilities early in a war could provide the critical margin needed for victory.[11]

Schlesinger's call for peacetime mobilization planning echoed earlier work done by two Princeton University economists, Lester Chandler and Donald Wallace. Analyzing the American experience during World War II, they found that the country's mobilization effort was impeded by President Roosevelt's failure to gain the necessary authority from Congress to direct the economy. For example, the organization established to direct the economic effort, the War Production Board "steadfastly refused" to direct manpower to industries suffering labor bottlenecks; in Britain, in contrast, laborers were drafted to serve in at least one critical industry, the coal mines. Yet another example of the "weakness" of American central government, even during a major war, is provided by Secretary of the Interior Harold Ickes's failed attempt to create a national oil company during World War II. Congress refused to authorize such a "socialistic" idea, despite an oil shortage that threatened the war effort. On the basis of these past experiences, Chandler and Wallace argued that "legislation should be enacted in advance, so that authority for the needed controls will be in existence whenever a full emergency breaks."[12]

The economic controls deemed necessary for mobilization include "production programming; controls over use of manpower, facilities, and materials; stabilization controls; procurement controls; and foreign economic controls."[13] In short, the state must be able to take over the everyday economic life of the country. Mobilization, therefore, will depend on not only the economic *capabilities* of the state, but also its political *capacity* to turn guns into butter. If citizens are unwilling to give up current consumption or a particular life-style to help advance the state's national security objectives, then full-scale mobilization cannot be achieved.[14]

Of interest, the legislative basis for mobilization in the United States does not stem from World War II, but rather from the Korean war. Indeed, the Korean war model is of particular relevance to the contemporary period. The United States possessed a vast nuclear superiority over its adversaries during the Korean war, but chose instead to rely on a sustained conventional war strategy

"I Want YOU": This famous poster has called
millions to arms.

and, concomitantly, on economic mobilization.[15] This mobilization occurred at a
difficult period in postwar history—just as the world was beginning to recover
from the devastations of 1939–1945. A long, conventional war, bringing with it
the threat of high inflation (see Chapter 2, on defense spending), could undo all
the progress made during the Marshall Plan years of postwar reconstruction.

The legislative basis for mobilization is found in the *Defense Production Act*
(DPA), which was enacted into law on September 8, 1950, and amended many
times since then. The act states that "the United States is determined to develop
and maintain . . . military and economic strength. . . . Under present circumstances, this requires diversion of certain materials and facilities from civilian use
to military and related purposes."[16] In executing the act, the President is granted
widespread powers.

Two students of the DPA argue that its legislative support (it passed only
three months after the outbreak of the Korean war) may be attributed to three
different factors in addition to the war itself: first, the World War II experience;
second, the famous "NSC-68" report—a National Security Council document
that compared U.S. and Soviet military and economic capabilities; and finally,

the existence at the time of a *National Security Resources Board* (NSRB), a federal agency with specific responsibilities for mobilization readiness (it has since evolved into the Federal Emergency Management Agency—FEMA, an organization that deals with both mobilization and disaster relief).[17]

The DPA provided nothing less than the legislative foundation for a federal industrial policy. During the Korean war, and in the ensuing years, its provisions were used to increase aluminum, copper, and tungsten production and to create a domestic titanium industry. To cite the Mobilization Concepts Development Center of the National Defense University, "During the 1950s . . . the DPA was a principal mechanism providing Government support for the creation of a healthy national industrial base."[18] In later amendments, the DPA was used during the energy crises of the 1970s as the basis for a national program of synthetic fuels development and for the creation of a strategic petroleum reserve, a stockpile that in 1990 contained some 600 million barrels of oil. The government has also cited the DPA's provisions when purchasing defense-related industrial items like machine tools from domestic suppliers and when creating stocks of finished goods and raw materials in support of a national emergency.

By the 1970s, however, warnings about the industrial readiness of the United States were being sounded by observers within and outside the government. According to historian Paul Kennedy, the Vietnam war was partly to blame for the decline in preparedness. Despite a paper strategy of "flexible response," which advocated that the United States be able to fight along the entire spectrum of conflict, in fact the United States was having difficulty maintaining the needs of its forces in regional trouble spots. Kennedy argues that the military made unproductive use of its resources during the long conflict, permitting the Soviet Union to achieve nuclear parity and superiority in conventional arms and allowing western economic competitors to surpass the United States in the production of various goods and services.[19]

The Department of Defense itself admitted in a 1976 report that the country's mobilization capacity had been greatly weakened since the Korean war. Military exercises revealed a defense industry characterized by declining productivity; reliance on sole-source suppliers for critical components; dependence on foreign sources for electronics, strategic minerals, and energy; outdated plants; critical labor shortages; and an absence of planning. A Defense Science Board (DSB) task force proclaimed that American industry was inadequately prepared to serve "as an effective element in support of the Nation's deterrent posture."[20]

Upon coming to office, the Reagan administration placed renewed attention on the mobilization capacity of American industry. What made the initiatives of the 1980s particularly interesting was the fact that they were embedded in deeper concerns about the international competitiveness of the American economy. The United States, some observers argued, had lost the industrial capacity to produce both the "high" and "low" technologies required by the military. This meant that in times of crisis, the United States would rely heavily on such allies as Japan and the Federal Republic of Germany for defense-related inputs.

The decline of U.S. manufacturing capacity in general, and defense-related production in particular, polarized political discussion of mobilization planning in the 1980s. Some within the Pentagon argued that the United States must think in terms of *coalition mobilization*. Rather than serve as the "arsenal of democracy," as it had done during World War II, the United States must now work closely with its allies to overcome any adversary. Japan, for example, had become an important source of critical defense technology. Mobilization planning should, they argued, incorporate this international dimension at the outset.[21]

Opposing this view were public officials who espoused the doctrine of *Fortress America*. They wanted to restore the defense-industrial base so that the United States could once again be self-sufficient during a war. According to a major proponent of this view, Ohio Congresswoman Mary Rose Oakar (who oversees the congressional subcommittee responsible for the Defense Production Act), the United States should be "able to produce all of the defense items needed to protect ourselves. . . ."[22]

As this review suggests, mobilization planning has become a deeply politicized issue. The polarized nature of the debate has made it difficult for the Pentagon to articulate a clearly defined mobilization strategy. In addition, nuclear deterrence on the one hand and the end of the cold war on the other have rendered mobilization policy a stepchild. As the National Defense University put it, "Many people are unsure of the role that mobilization should play in the nuclear age."[23]

Strategist Paul Bracken of Yale offered strong support for the continued relevance of economic mobilization in an influential article that appeared in the journal *International Security*. Bracken wrote:

> A mobilization option could prove useful in several politico-military situations. A rapid armament build-up induced by provocation, treaty abrogation, or some other stimulus would offer definite advantages not found with the immediate use of a nuclear option. The period of competitive build-up could be described as a *mobilization war*. Little or no large scale fighting would occur, rather there would be a maneuvering for position based upon the respective armament build-ups.[24]

Note that Bracken uses the term "mobilization war" in a different way than that employed by historian Martin van Creveld. For Bracken, mobilization war is, in essence, a phony war that would ultimately deter the enemy. For van Creveld, mobilization war implies the complete engagement of a national economy in war fighting.

At the present time, mobilization planning in the United States is characterized by an absence of clear lines of responsibility and a complex management structure. Emergency preparedness policy is stated in Executive Order 12656 of November 16, 1988, and it gives the National Security Council primary responsibility "for consideration" of such policy. The Director of the Federal Emergency Management Agency—an independent federal agency—serves as the NSC's adviser "on issues of national security emergency preparedness, including mobilization preparedness. . . ."[25] Under the executive order, "all appropriate Cabinet members and agency heads shall be consulted regarding national security emergency preparedness programs and policy issues."[26] The various federal and state agencies and branches are given responsibilities over particular aspects of mobilization planning (the Agriculture Department, for example, oversees stockpiling of food), and as a result, almost every employee of the U.S. federal and state governments must be involved in mobilization planning.

Mobilization planning is tested on a regular basis using simulation exercises and "war games." These activities bring together the key mobilization planners in government and place them in a hypothetical conflict situation. With the use of computers and data banks, these planners respond to military and civilian requirements. The games provide a test of the responsiveness of the American economy to meet crises and wars.

In recent years, the exercises have demonstrated the profound shortcomings associated with the present, decentralized mobilization "system." One postgame report stated that there "was no central data base" and that military planners "paid little attention to the resource and economic implications of military operations." The report concluded that "there was no single agency in charge of managing mobilization. . . ."[27]

As stated at the outset of this chapter, the international dimension of mobilization planning has become of increasing importance to the United States. Whereas the country was viewed as a relatively self-sufficient enclave during World War II and the Korean war, by the 1980s not only had it become dependent on foreign sources for a variety of raw materials, military components, and critical technologies, but it had become a net debtor as well. War games suggested that by the second week of a major conflict, the United States would have to "exert pressure on other nations to loan money and even to donate resources to help pay for the war."[28] Indeed, American financial weakness became apparent early in the Persian Gulf crisis of 1990, when Secretary of State James Baker and Secretary of the Treasury Nicholas Brady were forced to go on a world tour, dubbed "Operation Tin Cup," in search of funds. Further, according to the war games, the United States would be faced with having to source materiel and weapons systems from abroad—a difficult prospect at a time of intense conflict.

In sum, mobilization planning is now being conceived of under important political and economic constraints, both foreign and domestic. With the outbreak of peace, and the decline of the Soviet threat, it appears that concern with emergency preparedness will recede into the shadows of defense planning. Mobilization has always been of secondary concern in the (peacetime) military world, and there is no reason to believe that its visibility will improve in the 1990s.

And yet with demobilization of active forces and reduction in the defense-industrial base, it would be logical to conclude that mobilization has taken on fresh strategic importance. Part of the U.S. buildup in the Persian Gulf in 1990, for example, was drawn from reserve forces. If troops are not already in the field and if production lines are not hot, the ability to mobilize will be crucial in any future conflict that is larger than a brushfire operation. As former defense official Thomas Etzold has argued, "Mobilization issues are going to continue to increase in importance because of new strategies, contracting and changing military forces and relationships . . . and new technologies. . . ."[29]

To the extent that there is a political debate over mobilization, however, it will increasingly be tied to industrial policy. In 1990, for example, the Department of Defense even was asked by Congress to issue a "Critical Technologies Plan" stating how it planned to promote on national soil twenty technologies deemed critical to national security.[30] As economic competitiveness becomes an increasingly important political issue, pressure will be placed on the Pentagon to support particular industries and perhaps even specific firms. But decisions regarding the industrial and technological base must be taken within the context of overall defense policy and strategy. To be sure, industrial and military issues are inextricably linked; the ability of executive branch planners to coordinate policies in these areas, however, remains in doubt. The United States has a decentralized system of government, and nowhere is that more evident than in a discussion of mobilization planning.

THE POLITICAL ECONOMY OF WAR

The political economy of war is concerned with the sustainable equipping of a country's armed forces engaged in combat. As noted above, sustainability is a question not only of capital, land, and labor availability, but also of a multitude of political and psychological factors. Klaus Knorr described the "war potential" of nations on the basis of "three broad categories: economic capacity, administrative competence, and motivation for war."[31]

The utility of a perspective that goes beyond resource capabilities becomes obvious in any number of historical examples, including in recent times the Vietnam war and the Arab-Israeli conflict. By any measure of "power resources," the United States certainly dominated North Vietnam by a substantial margin. Over the long haul, however, it lacked the "motivation for war" that is critical to ultimate victory. Similarly, according to most measures of natural resources and human capital, the Arab states as a collectivity far outweigh tiny Israel, a country the size of Massachusetts. Yet the Israelis enjoy technical superiority over their adversaries, and the will to fight for their homeland.

The political economy of war is different from that of mobilization for several reasons, and that is why they are treated separately in this chapter. Of greatest importance, "when a nation stands on the brink of . . . a war which calls for the utmost degree of mobilization, it may choose not to fight at all. . . ."[32] War requires the dedication of resources to combat; mobilization may be nothing more than a bluff. Indeed, in the nuclear age, mobilization capabilities may be retained largely for their deterrent value.

The political economy of war is largely about the ability of societies to endure extreme deprivation as they engage in maximum sustainable production. The Iran-Iraq war provides only the most recent example of two economies almost completely devoted to war fighting. Thus, as in previous chapters, we seek here to develop a broad framework rather than one that is narrowly defined in terms of specific cases.

In building this framework, it will be useful to recall our traditional economic categories of microeconomics, macroeconomics, and international economics. The major microeconomic problems during a war concern research and development, labor and resource availability, and sustainable production; the macroeconomic problems associated with war are control of inflation and investment; and the international economic questions concern maximization of necessary imports (or exports to allies), while denying adversaries critical economic inputs. All of these activities occur within a complex system of government controls, and it is problems of administration which must first be examined.

Wartime Administration

During wartime, government controls over economic activity normally expand and, in the event of total war, become almost complete. Why is this so? Why are free markets unable to allocate goods during wartime? Why must government control prices, wages, and resource allocation?

Before the Second World War, it must be pointed out, such pervasive exercise of economic control did not exist. As military historian Martin van Creveld tells us, during World War I "the extension of control . . . was carried out in fits and starts. . . ."[33] Governments engaged in a "gradual extension of controls" over war materiel, and laborers were denied the right to strike, but wage restraints were "frequently ineffective." The First World War represented an experiment with economic control rather than its realization.[34]

Among academic economists, there was widespread skepticism concerning the efficacy of government controls, even during wartime. As John Kenneth Galbraith stated in his seminal work, *A Theory of Price Control*, which was based on his experience in the Office of Price Administration during World War II, many economists believed that economic controls were "unwise and . . . impossible." Government efforts to control prices and wages and to allocate resources could make the productive situation in a country less rather than more efficient, defeating the very objectives that controls were expected to serve.[35]

It must also be stated at the outset that the development of a *command economy* in almost every country during World War II—an economy in which the allocation and price of all goods and services were directed and determined by government—did not settle the issue. Drawing on the World War II example, President Truman was quick to institute broad controls at the outbreak of the Korean war. This approach was criticized by many economists, who urged that free-market principles carry the day. Indeed, the Korean war saw an extensive political debate in the United States over the power of the executive branch in conflicts short of total war.[36]

Government administration of the Vietnam conflict was completely different from that in previous American engagements. According to one Vietnam veteran who worked for the Joint Chiefs of Staff, the Pentagon treated the conflict as "business as usual," except for the fact that a real war was going on.[37] To be sure, the government drafted thousands of young men, placed additional procurement orders with industry, and developed an infrastructure in southeast Asia to support the war. But President Johnson did not institute wage and price controls or take any exceptional measures to control the economy. Indeed, despite the fact that expenditures for the conflict quickly outshot official estimates, the President failed to request any new taxes during the period of rapid buildup, 1966–1968; only with the Tax Reform Act of 1969 was a tax surcharge added to increase government revenues.[38]

The Costs of War

The prosecution of international conflict brings significant costs to an economy. The impact of wartime defense expenditures is different from those that occur in peacetime, largely because spending requirements are volatile. War, it has been said, is fought in a "fog," and economic forecasting during conflicts is similarly clouded. In fact, the tremendous uncertainty associated with the prosecution of a war is one of the most important factors relating to its economic impact.

Industrial mobilization during World War II relied heavily on American women.

(National Archives)

The Vietnam conflict provides an interesting case in point, both because spending requirements increased more rapidly than had been foreseen by public officials and because, in mobilizing the economy, the Pentagon consciously sought to learn the lessons—or avoid the mistakes—brought home by earlier conflicts, notably the Korean war. Vietnam was budgeted for in an entirely new way, and given that future conflicts are more likely to resemble localized, Vietnam-type wars rather than world wars, an analysis of how it was financed is particularly revealing for our purposes.

At the outset of the Korean war, the Pentagon had provided Congress with an estimate of the size and duration of the conflict and requested funds on the basis of these estimates. It was assumed that the war would be quite short and that economic mobilization would be unnecessary; thus it was budgeted for accordingly. Of course, the war turned out differently, and as a result the Pentagon was forced to make several supplemental requests during each fiscal year the war was waged. In practice, these supplemental requests turned out to be much larger than the amounts actually expended, so that by the end of the conflict the military had a large unexpended balance. Indeed, "during the 4 fiscal years 1955–58 no additional funds had to be appropriated for Army procurement; the Army lived off excess funds appropriated during the war."[39]

The Pentagon approached the Vietnam conflict in a different way. Rather than provide an estimate of the scope and duration of the war—and thus a "ballpark" figure for total war costs—the government avoided giving Congress such figures. In fact, throughout the war Congress and the Pentagon would have an ongoing debate about the quality of information "the people" were being provided, and thus of the integrity of the budget requests themselves.

During the early years of the American engagement, the Department of Defense refused to supply separate figures for the costs associated with the war. As reported by *Fortune*, "The official position of the Defense Department is that it does not know what the costs of the war are, and that it does not even try to compute them."[40] The magazine cited a Pentagon official as saying, "We have no intention of cost-accounting the war in Vietnam. Our business is to support the conflict there. . . . We have no estimate of costs."[41]

This approach soon became unacceptable to the U.S. Congress. By 1966, the sudden increases in defense spending were having an adverse effect on the management of monetary and fiscal policy, and interest rates and inflation levels were spiking to postwar highs. Led by such senators as John Stennis and William Proxmire, Congress demanded more economic data from the Pentagon. In 1967, the Department of Defense began to comply.

After 1967, the Vietnam war was viewed by the President and Congress in light of its "incremental cost," that is, "the costs over and above the normal costs of the defense establishment."[42] These incremental costs were estimated at some 23 billion dollars for fiscal year 1968—the peak year—before declining to 21.5 billion dollars in fiscal year 1969 and to 17.6 billion dollars in fiscal year 1970 (see Table 3-1). These incremental expenditures totaled less than 3 percent of gross national product. In contrast, during the Korean war, Department of Defense

Table 3-1 Vietnam War Costs

Fiscal Year	Number of Troops	Incremental Costs
1968	534,700	$23.0 billion
1969	538,700	21.5 billion
1970	414,900	17.6 billion
1971	250,000	12.6 billion

Source: Charles Schultze et al., *Setting National Priorities* (Washington, D.C.: Brookings Institution, 1971), p. 107.

spending increased from almost 7 percent of GNP in fiscal year 1951 to over 12 percent in fiscal year 1952.

But Vietnam entailed economic costs beyond those suggested by its small fraction of GNP. According to economist Murray Weidenbaum, "1966 witnessed the most rapid inflation since Korea."[43] The Johnson administration had woefully underestimated the costs of the defense buildup, but nonetheless it continued to pursue numerous "Great Society" social programs. As Weidenbaum argued before Congress, "The increases in government, civilian and military demand . . . exceeded the capablity of the American economy to supply goods and services at then current prices."[44] The largest item in the changing budget, however, was defense; national defense expenditures increased from 7.5 percent of GNP to 8.6 percent of GNP between 1964 and 1966.

Beyond the domestic monetary and fiscal ramifications of Vietnam, the war also had an adverse impact on the U.S. balance of payments. During fiscal year 1968, the war led to a direct deterioration of the country's balance-of-payments position by somewhere between 1 billion and 1.5 billion dollars. This helped fuel an existing fire in the balance of payments, which would ultimately lead America to stop exchanging dollars for gold at fixed exchange rates in 1971. Indeed, during the war angry Europeans—led by General Charles de Gaulle—decried the United States for exporting the inflationary costs of Vietnam to the continent, since Washington was shipping over dollars that were becoming less and less valuable in terms of the goods and services they could purchase.[45]

It is important to note that the President refused to acknowledge the exceptional costs associated with the war. The President's annual *Economic Report,* prepared by his Council of Economic Advisers, made only passing references to the war in its editions of 1966, 1967, and 1968. In fact, the stress was placed not on the current monetary, fiscal, and balance-of-payments problems associated with the war, but rather on the problem of economic conversion at the war's end.

But real economic costs *were* associated with the war, and beyond those that can be calculated are an array of charges that even today cannot be readily quantified. The war tore at the political and social fabric of the United States and weakened its international economic and political leadership. The war resulted in the deaths of 68,000 American soldiers, and it crippled hundreds of thousands more. Estimates of lost wages can be approximated, but the human tragedy associated with death and suffering is incalculable.

In short, it may be concluded that Vietnam was much more costly to the United States than can be suggested by such macroeconomic numbers as "2.5 percent of GNP." Ironically, despite its relatively small dollar price tag, it was a war that President Johnson refused to make the American people pay for directly at the time, indicating the delicacy of public support even in the early years. Instead, it was paid for through deficit financing, the legacy of which remains with the United States to this day. Wars are political acts, and the ways in which they are financed represent political as much as economic decisions.

ECONOMIC WARFARE

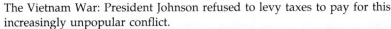

Wars are fought not only with bullets and guns, but with economic instruments as well. Economic warfare is part and parcel of any international conflict, as efforts are made to deny the enemy access to needed goods and services, and military operations are conducted against the enemy's defense-related industries. While the value associated with such operations remains the topic of substantial debate, it is likely that economic warfare will endure as part of every state's political-military strategy for victory over adversaries, as exemplified by the United Nations embargo against Saddam Hussein in 1990.

To cite another recent example, the United States made economic warfare against the Sandinista regime of Nicaragua a central element in its overall

The Vietnam War: President Johnson refused to levy taxes to pay for this increasingly unpopular conflict.

(UPI/Bettmann)

strategy. It reduced trade with that country and ordered the Inter-American Development Bank to cut back on the credits available for internal investment. The United States claims that these tools, in addition to the Contra war, laid the groundwork for democratic elections, which resulted in victory for the opposition UNO party in February 1990. (For more on economic warfare, see Chapter 7.)

Economic warfare has many dimensions, but the major categories can be listed as follows:

1. Export embargo, or a prohibition on exports to the enemy and its allies
2. Boycott, or a prohibition against buying goods from the enemy and its allies
3. Blacklist of domestic or third-country firms that trade with the enemy
4. Strategic purchasing, or the buying of defense-related commodities on world markets
5. Dumping, or the sale of stockpiled commodities to lower their price and thus lower the earnings of countries selling those commodities
6. Impounding, confiscating, or nationalizing enemy-owned assets
7. Strategic bombing, sabotage, or other military operations against enemy economic targets
8. Propaganda, or the deliberate use of economic misinformation to create panic, hoarding, and confusion in enemy territory[46]

The United States has been actively involved in economic warfare since the country's birth. During the War of 1812, the Madison administration engaged in an embargo of the European market and a boycott of British goods. During the Civil War, Secretary of State Seward threatened Britain with an economic boycott should it enter the war on behalf of the South. And, of course, in more recent times the United States has pursued economic warfare in any number of actions, from blocking the sale of oil and steel to Japan after the invasion of Manchuria in 1937 (which some historians claim precipitated the Japanese attack on Pearl Harbor), to strategic bombing of German industry during World War II, to complete embargoes on trade with Communist China, North Korea, Cuba, and North Vietnam, at various times after World War II, to the freezing of Iranian and Libyan assets in the 1980s.[47]

In peacetime, the U.S. government's major tools of economic warfare are the Export Administration Act (EAA), which gives the President the ability to control international trade for reasons of domestic shortage, foreign policy, and national security, and the Office of Foreign Assets Control (OFAC) in the Treasury Department. The EAA, with the sweeping authority it gives the President to intervene in the international economy, stands in sharp contrast to America's free-trade ideals. For its part, OFAC "prepares, monitors and enforces economic sanctions of various kinds," including the freezing of assets, embargoes on trade, and seizures of property. The office was particularly active during the Reagan administration, when at one time or another the President brought sanctions against Nicaragua, South Africa, the Soviet Union, and Libya.[48]

In wartime, the Defense Department plays a larger role in planning economic warfare. This will include the establishment of blockades and the strategic bombing of industrial targets. Since World War II, strategic bombing of industry has played a large role in U.S. war fighting. In fact, some of the important public officials engaged in target selection during World War II, such as Walter Rostow, returned to the government during the Vietnam conflict, and they attempted to apply the lessons learned from their earlier experience to southeast Asia.

During wars, efforts will be made to establish an economic quarantine of the enemy. During the Korean war, for example, the United States engaged in a widespread denial campaign against North Korea and Communist China. By invoking the Trading with the Enemy Act of 1917, the President prohibited American citizens from *all* dealings with these countries, and in the United Nations the United States called for other countries to do the same. The United States also conditioned its economic and military aid to foreign countries based on their participation in the embargo campaign.[49] Although the United States invoked the Trading with the Enemy Act against North Vietnam, it had little success winning alliance cooperation in this conflict, given differing views among the allies regarding the wisdom of the war effort.

It is interesting to ponder what will become of economic warfare as the world economy becomes more integrated and interdependent. The tools of economic denial only work when one side possesses something that another wants or needs. In the emerging global economy, however, there are fewer and fewer capabilities that are concentrated within a single geographical region.

Indeed, the embargo of Iraq during the Persian Gulf crisis may provide important lessons for economic warfare in the future. To the extent that the embargo and blockade succeeded in undermining Saddam Hussein's war economy, it was due to the near unanimous support of the United Nations. In a "unipolar" world where the United States had become the only great power capable of exercising military force throughout the world, more and more countries appeared willing to join with it in seeking collective goals. To be sure, there was "cheating" on the blockade as goods continued to flow to Iraq through Jordan, Iran, and other countries. But the largest part of Iraq's foreign trade had been cut off. At least one lesson seems clear-cut: in a global economy, economic warfare requires global support to succeed.

FROM GUNS TO BUTTER

At the war's end, or during a period when defense spending is in steep decline (as of this writing, for example), industrial societies will face the task of converting the military economy to civilian ends. In the United States, military industries have faced the prospects of conversion four times since 1944: after World War II, the Korean war, the Vietnam conflict, and the Reagan buildup. In the contemporary Soviet Union, which is still in the process of shifting from a wartime to a peacetime economy, conversion from military to civilian production has been held out as an important policy measure for the restoration of overall economic health.[50]

Conversion is not merely a microeconomic task at the plant level, but it also has important macroeconomic and regional economic dimensions. Further, depending on the postwar political and economic climate, it may have an important international aspect, as foreigners invest in the country or provide economic assistance.

In the wake of sharp declines in defense spending, as occur after wars or rapid military buildups, public policy is faced with two major problems: first, the loss of demand for military goods and services; second, the matching of resources once employed by the military with new civilian requirements. The macroeconomic task will thus be to stimulate demand, while policies may also be created to facilitate the transfer of resources among industrial sectors. Governments must be fully involved in this conversion process if unemployment is to be contained and if a postwar recession is to be prevented.

Government policy to maintain economic growth and investment has five general instruments at its disposal: (1) tax policy, especially tax cuts; (2) monetary policy, specifically lower interest rates; (3) increased government purchases of nondefense items; (4) increased transfer payments and adjustment assistance to displaced workers and industries; and (5) export promotion policies.[51] The success of economic conversion at the plant and regional levels will largely be a function of these aggregate offset policies. The higher the general demand in the economy, the faster market forces will operate, facilitating the shift of resources from defense to commercial sectors.

These policies are not, however, sufficient to ensure a successful conversion. We must also consider regional economic balances, as well as the particulars of each industrial plant involved in the process. Even at these levels, central governments can play an important role in adjustment from a military to a peacetime economy

Conversion is best viewed as a step-by-step process; and when viewed as such, the complications entailed in the process are fully illuminated. Each step involves discrete analytical tasks, which must be incorporated into a larger plan of action. As an actual—as opposed to theoretical—economic problem, transforming guns into butter is quite sophisticated. Indeed, the technical economic literature on "guns into butter," which focuses on the problem of equalizing the marginal rate of transformation (i.e., the *ability* to turn guns into butter) and the marginal rate of substitution (i.e., the *willingness* of consumers to substitute butter for guns), gives us little sense of the enormous difficulties involved.

In practice, the conversion process requires that decisions must be taken regarding which plants to convert, when they should be converted, and to what they should be converted. The economic and technical analyses at every stage are complex, given the number of variables involved. They are also dynamic, since changes occur over a relatively long period of time; if experience is any guide, the conversion process can take anywhere from one to ten years to complete.[52]

To take an example, consider postwar French efforts to convert their shipbuilding to other activities. The French took the decision to convert a substantial portion of their shipyards to civilian production in the early 1960s, after the Algerian war; they planned to convert five of twelve active yards. The first decision that had to be taken was which yards to convert and which to maintain. In making their choices, the French were concerned not only with efficiency questions, but with regional economic balances as well. In many cases, shifts from military to civilian production involved layoffs, which were especially problematic as veterans returned from overseas; labor politics was thus an additional factor in the equation.

These problems became especially acute on the Atlantic coast of Brittany; a region then suffering high unemployment. Some of the shipyards were not difficult to convert, but thousands might be left without jobs as a result. French officials had no choice but to consider the regional implications of each conversion decision.[53]

The decision to convert having been taken—and the French converted shipyards into such tasks as smelting, forging, metal working, and scrapping— they found that in each case the conversion of enterprise required substantial fresh capital injections. The state was required to make investments far higher than those initially projected, since the ease and degree of convertibility had been underestimated. This is a lesson that should not be lost on American and Soviet public officials as they contemplate conversion, since both countries are running large budget deficits.

Further, in many cases the French found that their decision to convert conflicted with their hope of making the new operations self-financing. (Again, this seems relevant to the Soviet case, given Mikhail Gorbachev's insistence that factories operate on a self-financing basis.) Although the output of the converted yard was in demand by the civilian sector, it proved that it would have been cheaper to expand the production of existing civilian plants rather than convert shipyards from military to commercial work. The profits were low in the converted operations, and they required continued state support.

Unfortunately, even these financial problems paled next to the human resource ones. Ironically, human resources proved the least transferable of all. Depending on the age and educational level of the work force, retraining efforts were much longer than expected, and the ensuing productivity of the converted work force was low. Furthermore, the French found that the labor mix required for the new civilian operations was different from that used by a military shipyard. The converted plant needed marketing people, salespeople, distribution experts, quality control specialists, and so forth. These scarce resources were difficult to employ, given existing demands for their skills. Bidding for these skilled workers created inflationary pressures, and indeed, inflation often accompanies the conversion process owing to the scarcity of factors of production.

Finally, the French also came up against a host of infrastructure problems that involved substantial amounts of time and money to resolve. Phone lines, roads, and postal services had to be expanded and improved in the process of conversion. Distribution networks had to be established. All these changes stretched out the process way beyond projected time horizons.

In short, as the French looked back at their conversion experience a decade later, they were disappointed. As one student of French economic policy has concluded, "Overall, there is no conversion policy in France; that is to say, no liaison between the decision to convert and the search for an appropriate solution, including the programming of the date of closure, the date of opening the replacement, and the retraining and organization of the labor force."[54]

The American experience after World War II provides additional insights into the conversion process; incidentally, conversion has become a major political and economic issue after each major downturn in defense spending. The United States began to plan for wartime demobilization as early as 1943. The issue of economic conversion soon became one of considerable political importance in the country; indeed, by the late 1940s it was rated in public opinion polls as one of the most topical issues of the day.

In the United States the debate revolved around the social and economic ends to which conversion should contribute. Should it be a tool to maintain employment, or should it be used to maximize consumer goods production? Should industrialists be given free rein to run the process, or should the converted firms be run as a government-contractor partnership (as a GO-CO plant, to use the contemporary acronym). For his part, Interior Secretary Harold Ickes suggested that the government should establish a giant holding company—an American version of the Italian IRI—which would sell shares to World War II veterans.

One fact to be recalled is the substantial ownership of plants held by the U.S. government at the war's end. The government held title to 90 percent of the synthetic rubber, aircraft, and magnesium industries and to over 50 percent of the aluminum and machine tool plants. In short, conversion was a process of some consequence for the American political economy. As one historian of the process has commented, "The ways these plants were transferred from wartime to peacetime service held the potential for economic and social change."[55]

The conversion process was also difficult at the plant level. It turned out that much of the wartime plant and equipment was not readily transferable to civilian production. Machine tools that had been engineered for the military were inappropriate for civilian production. Plant layout had to be altered for civilian output, and a new work force mix was needed; of course, the United States had a huge influx of veterans to train. The government ended up hiring hundreds of engineers who conducted detailed industrial surveys of each plant under its ownership, and these surveys provided recommendations for alternative uses.

The United States was still engaged in postwar conversion in 1950 when the Korean war erupted. Thus, six years after the process was launched, it was still ongoing. There are important lessons to be drawn from the American experience. First, even given macroeconomic policies that encouraged postwar growth, the conversion process proved difficult to execute. Second, plant location was a critical factor in the success of the process. In some cases it was better to dismantle a factory and sell the tools and equipment to an enterprise in a growing region than to convert the plant to civilian production. Third, the labor mix required for commercial enterprise was quite different. Finally, conversion turned out to be a lengthy and costly process. The U.S. government devoted thousands of labor-hours and millions of dollars to postwar economic conversion.

Perhaps of more contemporary relevance to American defense manufacturers is the Vietnam experience. After the Vietnam conflict drew to its close, defense firms had a difficult time converting from guns to butter. On the macroeconomic level, the American economy was performing badly in the 1970s, suffering from a mix of stagnation and inflation—stagflation—that followed from poor economic policymaking in the wake of the Arab oil embargo of 1973 and the war's end in 1975. Scrambling for new niches in this dismal environment, defense companies experimented with various civilian pursuits outside their expertise, from building buses (Grumman) to bathtubs (Boeing). For its part, General Dynamics lost millions on commercial shipbuilding and asbestos mining.[56]

Based on a study of current defense industry strategies for coping with decline, the *Economist* magazine divides the prime contractors into three categories: "the hawks, who plan to remain as dependent as ever on defense, the doves, who intend to reduce their reliance on Pentagon business, and the turkeys, who haven't a clue."[57] The hawks include General Dynamics, Raytheon, and Martin Marietta; the doves are General Motors, Boeing, United Technologies, and General Electric; and the turkeys are the weak airframe manufacturers McDonnell Douglas, Grumman, and Lockheed; one could probably add Northrop, which is dependent for its livelihood on the controversial B-2 Stealth bomber program, to this list.

In sum, a comparative perspective illustrates some of the macroeconomic, regional, and microeconomic issues that countries are likely to face as they proceed with the shift from guns to butter. Success requires the right policy mix at all levels. Governments must enact aggregate offset policies that maintain demand in the wake of decreased defense spending, while assisting the regions and firms that are most seriously affected by the postwar adjustment problems.

CONCLUSION

During periods of mobilization and war, governments will seek to command a large share of societal resources for military operations. As James Schlesinger wrote thirty years ago, the efficiency with which scarce resources are used may provide states with the margin of victory in times of war and crisis. Even relatively small wars, like the Vietnam conflict, consume enormous resources in the modern age.

But the ability of governments to extract resources will depend in large measure on relations between the state and its society. There are limits to coercion even in authoritarian societies, and if citizens do not make common cause with their government, it will prove difficult to sustain hostilities. In this context, it is useful to recall Adam Smith's view that wars should be paid for out of direct taxation rather than debt financing, since the willingness of citizens to be taxed provides a test of their belief in the war cause. During the Vietnam conflict, the American government attempted to finesse the people, paying for the war through deficit financing rather than increased taxes, thus shielding them from its direct costs. This strategy may have helped prolong the war, but ultimately it could not substitute for public support of U.S. soldiers in the field and the mission they were conducting.

When wars are over and defense spending declines, societies face the difficult task of turning guns into butter. Factors of production do not shift effortlessly from one task to another, and again governments will play an important role in facilitating the transfer and in maintaining aggregate demand. This is a critical point to emphasize, especially as a free-market-oriented administration (the Bush administration) must now direct a major downsizing of defense spending, with all the industrial and regional adjustments this entails.

This is not to say that liberalism does not speak to the war economy. To be sure, even in war, states must retain incentives for entrepreneurs and firms to create new technology, maximize output, and ensure quality control. And in the aftermath of war, market forces may well be the most effective method for allocating scarce resources. But the tools of neoclassical economics are unlikely to solve all the dilemmas posed by the political economy of mobilization, war, and reconstruction.

Selected Bibliography

Backman, Jules, et al., *War and Defense Economics* (New York: Rinehart, 1952). Although dated, this text still provides a good introduction to issues of wartime economics.
Bolton, Roger, ed., *Defense and Disarmament* (Englewood Cliffs, N.J.: Prentice-Hall, 1966). This book contains excellent essays on the economics of defense and conversion.
Knorr, Klaus, *The War Potential of Nations* (Princeton, N.J.: Princeton University Press, 1956). This is a classic statement of defense economics.
Lynch, John, ed., *Economic Adjustment and Conversion of Defense Industries* (Boulder, Colo.: Westview Press, 1987). The book includes essays that describe base and plant closings and conversion of military enterprise.
Merritt, Hardy, and Luther Carter, eds., *Mobilization and the National Defense* (Washington, D.C.: National Defense University Press, 1985). This is a useful introduction to mobilization issues.

Notes

1. U.S. Congress, Joint Economic Committee, *Economic Effects of Vietnam Spending* (Washington, D.C.: Government Printing Office, 1967), vol. 1, p. 1.

2. Charles Hitch and Ronald McKean, *The Economics of Defense in the Nuclear Age* (Cambridge, Mass.: Harvard University Press, 1960), p. 313.

3. Jim Sasser, "Is Uncle Sam Getting Stiffed?" *New York Times*, December 19, 1990, p. A25.

4. See Michael Hogan, *The Marshall Plan* (New York: Cambridge University Press, 1988); Alan S. Milward, *The Reconstruction of Western Europe, 1945–1951* (London: Methuen, 1984); and John Maynard Keynes, *The Economic Consequences of the Peace* (New York: Harcourt, Brace and Howe, 1920).

5. For a nuanced account of state-society relations and war preparation, see Michael Barnett, "High Politics Is Low Politics: The Domestic and Systemic Sources of Israeli Security Policy, 1967–1977," *World Politics 42* (July 1990): 529–562.

6. Martin van Creveld, "The Origins and Development of Mobilization Warfare," in Gordon McCormick and Richard Bissell, eds., *Strategic Dimensions of Economic Behavior* (New York: Praeger, 1984), p. 26.

7. John Hiller and Judith Larrabee, *Production for Defense* (Washington, D.C.: National Defense University Press, 1980), p. 124.

8. Ibid.

9. George Lincoln, *Economics of National Security* (Englewood Cliffs, N.J.: Prentice-Hall, 1954), p. 329.

10. Ibid., p. 331.

11. James Schlesinger, *The Political Economy of National Security* (New York: Praeger, 1960), p. 76.

12. Lester Chandler and Donald Wallace, *Economic Mobilization and Stabilization* (New York: Henry Holt, 1951), p. 18.

13. Ibid.

14. For a brilliant study that emphasizes state-society bargains in wartime, see A. S. Milward, *War, Economy and Society: 1939–1945* (Berkeley: University of California Press, 1979).

15. Paul Bracken, "Mobilization in the Nuclear Age," *International Security 3* (Winter 1978/1979): 80–105.

16. The text of the act may be found in Jules Backman et al., *War and Defense Economics* (New York: Rinehart, 1952), pp. 403–449.

17. Leon Karadbil and Roderick Vawter, "The Defense Production Act," in Hardy Merritt and Luther Carter, eds., *Mobilization and the National Defense* (Washington, D.C.: National Defense University Press, 1985), pp. 37–59.

18. Ibid.

19. Paul Kennedy, *The Rise and Fall of the Great Powers* (New York: Random House, 1987), p. 406.

20. Ethan B. Kapstein, "Economics and Military Power," *Naval War College Review* (Summer 1989): 102; the task force report is quoted in Defense Science Board, *1980 Summer Study Panel on Industrial Responsiveness*, Department of Defense, January 1981.

21. On the debate, see Ethan B. Kapstein, "Losing Control—National Security and the Global Economy," *The National Interest* (Winter 1989/1990): 85–90.

22. Quoted in ibid.

23. Ralph Sanders and Joseph Muckerman, "A Strategic Rationale for Mobilization," in Merritt and Carter, *Mobilization*, p. 8.

24. Bracken, "Mobilization," p. 81.

25. "Assignment of Emergency Preparedness Responsibilities," Executive Order 12656, November 18, 1988, *Federal Register 53* (November 23, 1988): 47491–47512.

26. Ibid.

27. NMIG Special Working Group, "Evaluation of War Mobilization Board Play in Global War Game 88," August 1988, mimeograph.
28. Ibid.
29. Thomas H. Etzold, "National Strategy and Mobilization: Emerging Issues for the 1990s," *Naval War College Review* (Winter 1990): 28.
30. *Critical Technologies Plan* (Washington, D.C.: Department of Defense, 1990).
31. Klaus Knorr, *The War Potential of Nations* (Princeton, N.J.: Princeton University Press, 1956), p. 41.
32. Ibid., p. 45.
33. van Creveld, "Origins and Development," p. 31.
34. Ibid.
35. John Kenneth Galbraith, *A Theory of Price Control* (Cambridge, Mass.: Harvard University Press, 1951).
36. See the essays in Chandler and Wallace, *Economic Mobilization.*
37. Telephone interview, Joint Chiefs of Staff, the Pentagon, May 15, 1990.
38. See U.S. Congress, *Economic Effects of Vietnam Spending;* and Charles Schultze, *Setting National Priorities: The 1971 Budget* (Washington, D.C.: Brookings Institution, 1970).
39. Robert Anthony, in U.S. Congress, *Economic Effects,* p. 5.
40. William Bowen, "The Vietnam War: A Cost Accounting," *Fortune,* April 1966; of interest, one consultant on this *Fortune* article was Alan Greenspan.
41. Ibid.
42. Anthony, in U.S. Congress, *Economic Effects,* p. 50.
43. Murray Weidenbaum, in U.S. Congress, *Economic Effects,* p. 176.
44. Ibid.
45. Ibid.; also see Kennedy, *Rise and Fall of the Great Powers,* pp. 434–435.
46. Adapted from Thomas Schelling, *International Economics* (Boston: Allyn and Bacon, 1958), p. 488.
47. For an overview, see David Baldwin, *Economic Statecraft* (Princeton, N.J.: Princeton University Press, 1985).
48. Peter Kilborn, "They Who Dig the Trenches for Economic Warfare," *New York Times,* January 15, 1986.
49. Schelling, *International Economics,* p. 491.
50. See Ethan B. Kapstein, "From Guns to Butter in the USSR," *Challenge* (September/October 1989).
51. See Roger Bolton, "Defense Spending: Burden or Prop?" in Roger Bolton, ed., *Defense and Disarmament* (Englewood Cliffs, N.J.: Prentice-Hall, 1966), pp. 1–54.
52. See the cases cited in John E. Lynch, ed., *Economic Adjustment and Conversion of Defense Industries* (Boulder, Colo.: Westview Press, 1987).
53. On the French case, see Jean Chardonnet, *L'Economie Française* (Paris: Dalloz, 1970).
54. Ibid.
55. Gerald White, *Billions for Defense* (University, Ala.: University of Alabama Press, 1980).
56. "The Pentagon's Menagerie," *The Economist,* June 16, 1990, p. 69.
57. Ibid.

PART TWO

Micro Issues

4

Defense Industries in the World Economy

". . . not only the wealth but the independence and security of a country appear to be materially connected with the prosperity of manufacturers." ——Alexander Hamilton, Report on Manufactures, 1791

"In the councils of Government, we must guard against the acquisition of unwarranted influence, whether sought or unsought, by the military-industrial complex. The potential for the disastrous rise of misplaced power exists and will persist." ——President Dwight David Eisenhower, Farewell Address, January 17, 1961

Public officials are often torn between the requirement for national security and the requirement for economic efficiency. For most public officials, national security means having access to sufficient military capability to advance foreign policy objectives, to deter potential aggressors, and, when deterrence fails, to beat enemies on the battlefield. In short, national security means autonomy and superiority. This requirement, in turn, has argued for at least some domestic capacity in the area of armaments production.

Liberal models of economic efficiency, in contrast, emphasize free markets and comparative advantage. Economic principles dictate that states abandon inefficient industries in order to move factors of production to their most productive uses. The implication is that some countries may simply find it "uneconomic" to be engaged in defense-related production.

This chapter explores the "defense-industrial base." In the first section we will focus on the American defense industry; in subsequent sections, the chapter examines defense industries in Europe, the Soviet Union, and Japan, and the emerging defense industries of the third world, emphasizing the case of Brazil. In gaining a comparative perspective, it will be seen that the structure and operations of national defense industries reflect the particular political-economic systems in which they are embedded and the particular strategic goals (both military and economic) of the countries they serve.

At the same time, however, the defense industry is becoming increasingly "globalized." Defense firms are sourcing components from firms located outside national boundaries, and many military end-items, including missiles and aircraft, are being produced by international collaborative ventures. In short, liberal economic trends are being pitted against national security interests, posing policy dilemmas for public officials.

DEFINING THE DEFENSE-INDUSTRIAL BASE

What is meant by the "defense-industrial base"? Writing from an economic perspective, one authoritative report states that the "defense industrial base is defined as the aggregate ability to provide the manufacturing, production, technology, research, development, and resources necessary to produce the materiel for the common defense. . . ."[1] Obviously, the defense-industrial base encompasses myriad industrial activities, from shipbuilding to semiconductor manufacture. At the extreme, the defense-industrial base is inseparable from the national-industrial base. In 1987, over 38,000 firms provided goods and services to the U.S. Department of Defense.[2]

From a more politicized perspective, the defense-industrial base is really a euphemism for the "military-industrial complex" (MIC). The theory of the MIC "suggests that military decision makers, corporations which produce primarily for the defense sector, and political representatives of regions in which defense spending is concentrated exert pressure for levels of defense expenditure in excess of legitimate national needs."[3] The complex, it is argued, comprises an "iron triangle" that has become bigger and more influential than even President Eisenhower could have imagined. Of interest, the military-industrial complex has come under attack not just in the United States, but in recent years in the Soviet Union as well.

From the perspective of public policy, a more restricted conceptualization of the defense-industrial base has taken hold since the 1980s. There has been less concern with access to such traditional resources as energy and steel (and we should recall that coal, petroleum, and steel were *the* critical defense resources until the end of World War II), and more with high technology. Indeed, the U.S. Office of Technology Assessment (OTA) has focused attention on the "defense technology base." According to the OTA, "The defense technology base is that combination of people, institutions, information, and skills that provide the technology used to develop and manufacture weapons and defense systems."[4]

Defining the defense-industrial base is not a trivial exercise. If appropriate public policies are to be articulated, we must know what the objectives of such policies are and what groups are being targeted. Do we wish to use the defense budget as a tool for promoting domestic industries in general or specific industries in particular?

(Library of Congress)

A World War II Defense Plant: How should we define the defense-industrial base today?

Given scarce budgetary resources, and a general recognition that it is impossible to protect *all* domestic industries, states are now focusing their attention on what have been called *strategic industries.* According to one defense analyst, "Strategic industries are those which best foster technological development."[5] This conceptualization has found favor because it provides a mechanism for state support of industry which even liberal economists can support.

In economic terminology, technology generates "positive externalities." Once a technology is created, it diffuses widely among industries and even between countries. In short, the social benefits created by new technology outweigh the private benefits. As a result, firms will invest less than socially optimal amounts in the research and development that generates technology since they cannot capture all the rents that accrue from this activity. The tendency of private-sector firms to underinvest in R&D provides a justification for government sponsorship that even neoclassical economists generally accept.

A further economic problem is that the costs of basic R&D are growing as a percentage of the cost of military production, making the "up-front" investment of risk capital difficult for even the world's largest defense firms. This means not only that firms will underinvest, but that they will tend to do less "parallel investment" than they did in the past; they will fund fewer competing lines of research. A second argument for government intervention, then, is that it helps to maintain technological options by promoting multiple R&D paths.

It is important to point out that the liberal defense for government support of the defense technology base does not come out of a neo-mercantilist desire to "pick winners" or promote "national champion" firms. Instead, the objective is to *perfect the market*—to make it work better than it would otherwise. This suggests that government should not support just a few technologies or a few firms, but a broad array of possible innovations "along the technological frontier."[6]

In sum, issues associated with the defense-industrial base are embedded in larger economic and technological trends. Policy officials are hard-pressed to adopt appropriate responses that meet their security objectives on the one hand and social welfare objectives on the other. We may expect that public policies toward the defense-industrial base will remain hotly contested issues around the world for the foreseeable future.

THE U.S. DEFENSE INDUSTRY

An appropriate place to begin the examination of any industry is in terms of its particular political-economic structure. These structural issues are important for several reasons: first, they indicate the degree of competition within the industry and between the industry and its purchasers; second, they point to whether the industry is seasonal, cyclical, or steady; third, they position the industry in terms of its relative maturity—is it growing, mature, or in decline? A final point we wish to consider is business-government relations in the industry, including the degree of government intervention and the extent of regulation. Is the industry a regulated utility? Or does management exercise a wide latitude of discretionary decision-making power?

If we examine the *prime contractors* in the U.S. defense industry—the major firms that conduct the bulk of research, development, and production of weapons systems—the following characteristics emerge:

- Concentration: According to defense analyst Jacques Gansler, "The defense industry is relatively concentrated; the top 100 firms do about 75 percent of the business." While Gansler points out that "this is no more concentrated than most segments of the commercial sector,"[7] it must be recognized that in particular segments the defense industry is highly concentrated. Only one firm, for example, produces aircraft carriers (Newport News); only two firms produce submarines (General Dynamics and Newport News); and only two firms produce jet aircraft engines (General Electric and Pratt-Whitney). Indeed, it is safe to assert that the industry is quite concentrated when it comes to particular military *platforms* (ships, aircraft, vehicles), and *systems* (avionics, computers, fire control systems).

- Cyclical business: As Gansler notes, throughout American history defense budgets have been subject to sharp cyclical increases and declines. This complicates the industrial planning process since commercial firms generally plan on the basis of relatively constant growth or predicted seasonality.[8]
- Monopsony: The defense market is characterized by one buyer, the Department of Defense. To be sure, a percentage of defense production is exported, but for most firms the number is small, below 10 percent. Further, the determination of military specifications (milspecs) for all hardware is established by the Department of Defense. From the perspective of economic theory, this would lead us to predict that the buyer exercises considerable leverage in the marketplace; in practice, we will see that the reality is far more complex.
- Annual budget process: Firms make investment decisions using a long planning horizon—often ten years or more. It takes a long period of time to bring a capital-intensive project on line, whether the project be an oil well or a fighter aircraft. Firms that are gambling on these projects must make assumptions about the cost of capital and other inputs, and the prices they can expect to receive for the final output. The U.S. government, however, provides funds for defense procurement on the basis of an annual budget process. At any point in time, funds for a given program can be increased, decreased, or cut. This uncertainty lends further complications to defense-industrial planning.
- R&D-intensive: In the opening of the chapter we noted that public officials are becoming increasingly concerned with the state of their national defense technology base. Pressure is being placed on firms to produce "high technology," but at the same time the costs of advanced R&D are rapidly rising. Firms must be prepared to invest a substantial portion of risk capital "up front" if they hope to win defense contracts. The corollary to the R&D-intensive nature of the business is that it is highly risky; firms may gamble huge sums on a new generation of weapons system without any assurance of winning a procurement contract (see Chapter 5 for more on this issue).
- Political: The defense industry is intensely political. Firms are heavily monitored not only by their program managers at the Department of Defense, but by various congressional bodies as well, including congressional committees, the General Accounting Office, and the Congressional Budget Office. Since defense contracts are a high-stakes business, members of Congress are active in ensuring that a piece of the pie goes to their local constituents. This means that economically optimal decisions are often set aside for politically expedient ones.[9]

However, political scientist James Kurth suggests that the risks associated with defense production are substantially mitigated by what he has labeled *the follow-on imperative*. Kurth argues that defense officials perceive the defense industries (or at least the major prime contractors) as a "national resource." In Kurth's words, "The Defense Department would find it risky and even reckless to allow a large production line to wither and die for lack of a large production contract."[10]

Given that defense officials find it difficult if not impossible to allow prime contractors to fail, they must constantly feed firms with contracts. This is the "follow-on imperative," and as Kurth has observed, "About the time a production line phases out of one major defense contract, it phases in production of a new one, usually within a year."[11] It is this imperative that gives the defense industry a surprising continuity despite cyclical changes in the defense budget.

The characteristics listed above suggest that the U.S. defense industry is different from what we would call competitive industries in a free-market sense. There is no free market in defense, and the industrial structure reflects that fact. It is within this structural context, however, that policy decisions regarding the industry must be made by public officials and investment decisions must be made by corporate executives and pension fund managers.

In examining the defense-industrial base, it is also appropriate to think about the national security strategies that the industry is expected to serve. In the United States, for example, the industry is expected to provide a nuclear strategic triad (land, air, and seaborne nuclear forces) in addition to a substantial conventional deterrent force. The industry must produce equipment that can meet a range of contingencies in a variety of environmental conditions. The Brazilian defense industry, in contrast, does not have as complex a strategic mission to equip. Thus, the defense industry will reflect threat analysis on the one hand and economic capabilities on the other.

The structure of the American defense industry reflects a long and winding historical development, as opposed to the articulation of a rational master plan. Much of the contemporary defense-industrial base was constructed by the government during the crisis conditions of the Second World War and the Korean war, and even today a large percentage of defense plants are owned by the government and then leased to private firms. In times of crisis, the defense industries were not built with considerations of economic efficiency, high-technology competence, and integrated efforts to "spin off" developments into the civilian economy.

While it may seem surprising, defense industry operations are often outmoded when compared to their commercial counterparts. Numerous studies have found that defense contractors invest in new manufacturing equipment and technologies at only about half the rate of comparable commercial firms. The instability associated with weapons programs, and the uncertain economic payback, acts to discourage fresh investment.[12]

Consider, for example, the case of the B-2 Stealth bomber. The B-2 had been a high priority for the Bush administration, and the administration had planned to build 75 airplanes at a cost of over 65 billion dollars during the 1990s. In deliberations over the fiscal year 1991 defense bill, however, the House voted to bar construction of additional planes, leaving the Air Force with only 4.1 billion dollars for fifteen B-2s. After the House voted, the executive vice president of Boeing (a major B-2 subcontractor; the prime is Northrop), C. G. King, said that "I've never seen a period of greater uncertainty than we have now. . . . It's awfully difficult to plan."[13] In such an environment, firms are loath to invest in new plant and equipment and in worker training. More on this in Chapter 5.

Additional problems that face the defense industry are labor and money. In terms of labor, the industry is moribund, as younger workers have sought more stable opportunities in other sectors. The defense business is not characterized by job security, and, in fact, with the growth in the civilian economy during the 1980s, it proved difficult for defense contractors to hire all the scientists and engineers they wanted.

Indeed, the aerospace industry has labeled the shortage of technical staff as "America's next crisis." Citing a Department of Defense study, the report warns that the decline in technical staff "will affect both civilian and military recruitment. . . . The Department [of Defense], because of a lack of an adequate supply of qualified and competent engineers and scientists, could suffer a degradation of its ability to respond to technical change, and its vital mission of national defense."[14]

For defense industry analysts, the employment trends in critical sectors are discouraging. Employment fell among domestic precision optics firms by 50 percent between 1981 and 1986, and it fell by a similar percentage in steel. Between 1987 and 1989, aerospace companies—which had been relatively buoyant owing to commercial aircraft orders—shed 41,000 workers. The U.S. machine tool industry has shrunk by over 25 percent since 1983, and retrenchment is now upon the defense electronics firms. Further, workers in these industries tend to be older than their counterparts elsewhere. The net result is that the United States risks losing its most precious national resource—skilled labor.[15]

Financial capital has also become a big problem for the industry. If one examines the stock prices of the major contractors, it can be seen that they are depressed by historical standards, reflecting the low price-earnings multiples that characterize these firms (see Table 4-1). As we have already mentioned, defense is a risky business, and investors must be compensated for that risk by receiving a higher return. Defense industries, however, are not profitable relative to other sectors of the economy. According to one study, "The Standard & Poor's Aerospace price/earnings index trailed the Standard & Poor's 400 index [a broad-based index based on New York Stock Exchange issues] by a substantial margin between 1962 and 1987."[16] Table 4-2 compares aerospace earnings with those of other industries.

Table 4-1 Top Ten U.S. Defense Contractors

| Firm | Stock Price (52-week) (Oct. 1989–Oct. 1990) | | Stock Price (10/3/90) | DoD Sales 1989 ($BN) |
	High	Low		
McDonDoug	$71\frac{7}{8}$	34	$47\frac{7}{8}$	10.0
Gen.Dyn.	59	$22\frac{1}{8}$	$22\frac{1}{4}$	9.6
Lockheed	$49\frac{7}{8}$	$24\frac{3}{4}$	26	9.5
Raytheon	85	$57\frac{3}{4}$	$66\frac{7}{8}$	6.2
Boeing	$61\frac{7}{8}$	$35\frac{1}{2}$	$43\frac{1}{4}$	5.7
Mart.Ma.	$53\frac{1}{2}$	$34\frac{1}{4}$	$37\frac{3}{4}$	5.6
Northrop	$23\frac{1}{4}$	$13\frac{3}{4}$	$16\frac{5}{8}$	5.5
Un.Tech.	$62\frac{1}{2}$	$40\frac{1}{8}$	$43\frac{7}{8}$	5.5
Rockwell	$28\frac{3}{4}$	$19\frac{3}{4}$	25	5.0
Grumman	$20\frac{3}{4}$	$12\frac{5}{8}$	15	3.4

Sources: New York Times, October 3, 1990; Wall Street Journal, November 21, 1989.

**Table 4-2 Profit Comparisons by
Industry, 1986**

Industry	Return on Equity
Aerospace	9.6%
Automotive	14.2
Drugs	21.2
Food processing	19.0
Computers	11.5
Information/broadcasting	18.5
Textiles and apparel	12.9

Source: Aerospace Education Foundation, *Lifeline in Danger.*

Old plant, old labor, a shortage of capital, declining competitiveness—these are big problems that face a critical industry. What has been its response? First, there has been a trend toward merger and acquisition at home. Second, there have been efforts to "team up" or form joint ventures with domestic and foreign firms on defense programs. Third, the industry has gone global, purchasing an increasing percentage of components abroad (and reflecting similar trends in civilian industry) in order to cut costs. Fourth, the industry has sought new opportunities for export markets. Finally, the industry has made a pitch to codevelop civilian and military products and to have fewer restrictions in commercializing technology developed for the military sector. Let us examine a few of these points further.

As already noted, owing to lower prices and better performance, many weapons components are now purchased abroad from foreign suppliers; indeed, in some cases foreign parts are the only ones available, as American firms have exited the business. The U.S. defense industry now relies on foreign sources for computer memory chips, silicon for electronic switching, gallium arsenide–based semiconductors for data processing, precision glass for reconnaissance satellites, and ball bearings. In some cases, the cause of the shift is that American firms have moved their facilities abroad in order to reduce their labor costs and gain access to foreign markets; in other cases, it is simply that American suppliers have chosen to leave the defense market for the far larger and more lucrative commercial market; in still others, it is that foreign suppliers have had an easier time promoting the "dual-use" characteristic of their technologies, since they are unbridled by American security laws and the like. Regardless of the cause, it is a fact that most U.S. weapons systems and subsystems today are dependent on offshore producers for numerous critical components. The trend is likely to continue. Further, various laws and policies intended to encourage greater weapons cooperation with military allies have virtually promoted the growth of foreign subcontractors.

Foreign dependence is a prominent issue as we face the 1990s, and there is a real danger that Washington could overreact to the problem. Rather than examine cases where foreign dependence poses a security problem and then have the Pentagon or an interagency committee develop an appropriate response—such as stockpiling where necessary—there is a danger that Congress, responding to local political pressures of subcontractors threatened by foreign competition, will enact protectionist solutions. This will only raise costs to the defense industry and exacerbate underlying problems.[17]

Going global also has another side, of course—exports; the arms trade is treated in more detail in Chapter 6. The defense industry, and the aerospace sector in particular, is one of America's largest industrial export businesses; aerospace exports totaled some 35 billion dollars in 1987, nearly half of which came from military aircraft. Exports are important to the industry for several reasons: first, in a cyclical domestic business, exports can help firms ride through the troughs. Second, exports of equipment lead to contracts for maintenance and spare parts, which can ultimately be more profitable than the sale of the original equipment. Third, once an export market has been established for one product, then future products might find the same market. Incidentally, the Department of Defense also profits from exports, since it receives a 2 percent fee on every export deal done; on sales of 15 billion dollars this comes to 300 million dollars.

Yet exports are unlikely to bail out the defense industry as military spending declines. As will be detailed in the following sections, important defense industries have emerged in recent years in western Europe, Japan, and the third world. Further, the Soviet Union is now attempting to become a commercial player in the arms export market. The excellent performance of American weapons during Operation Desert Storm, however, has given exports a major boost.

As stated above, many of the problems inherent in the defense industry have arisen from the fact that it has been separated from the civilian economy; accordingly, some analysts say that the industry must be reintegrated into the commercial world.[18] This would require a loosening of security regulations, in order to allow defense manufacturers to exploit technology developed in a classified setting. Some American officials view it is as a national embarrassment that the world's leading satellite imaging corporation is French, and yet this is a technology the United States virtually monopolized for a generation. Security requirements have prevented the United States from exploiting satellite imaging technology for commercial purposes.

In sum, the U.S. defense industry faces a difficult future. It is characterized by excess capacity, obsolescent capital equipment, a short-term focus, a cutback in R&D spending, growing quality problems, and a concern with mergers and acquisitions as opposed to strengthening of core businesses. In many respects, the problems of the defense industry mirror those of other manufacturing firms, and the question of industrial competitiveness that is plaguing America's traditional industries is now of concern in the defense sector. Indeed, there has been substantial pressure placed on the Pentagon to generate an "industrial policy" for the United States to meet the challenge of declining competitiveness in defense-related industries.[19] Whether it *can* do so and whether it *should* do so are likely to be important political issues over the coming decade.

DEFENSE INDUSTRIES IN OTHER COUNTRIES

Western Europe

The modern defense industries of western Europe have arisen from the ashes of
World War II. Recalling the industrial base in 1945, former NATO Secretary
General Lord Ismay wrote:

> The armament industries of most countries of Western Europe had almost
> ceased to exist; the plants and factories had been destroyed, damaged, or
> switched to civilian production. The economic situation of these countries
> made it impossible for them to devote a large proportion of their resources to
> defense production.[20]

The United States led in the rehabilitation of these defense industries, and
in postwar European rearmament more generally. The United States provided
direct financial assistance to firms, provided European governments with
financial aid to procure American weapons, and even purchased weapons *from*
European manufacturers. Examining the case of France, Edward Kolodziej
concluded that American assistance "provided the additional margin of support
needed to develop France's arms industry as a self-sustaining system."[21]

But over the long term, the Europeans sought to use American assistance to
advance their own end, namely, the restoration of an internationally competitive
industry. Through *collaborative* ventures with American firms and on an intra-
European basis, the technological capacity of the industry grew throughout the
postwar period. By the 1970s, it represented a serious challenge to American
firms in third markets, especially in the developing world.

One fundamental difference distinguishes European firms from their
American counterparts: They cannot generally survive only on domestic
weapons procurement. Whereas the major U.S. defense contractors rely more or
less on Department of Defense contracts, European companies would be hard-
pressed to survive on contracts generated solely from national ministries. This
has forced the firms to adopt an international perspective that may give them
certain advantages in the increasingly competitive environment that character-
izes the weapons marketplace.[22]

Indicative of this trend is the willingness of the largest European defense
contractors (see Table 4-3), such as *Thomson-CSF* of France (1989 sales of 4.5
billion dollars) and British Aerospace (1989 sales of 5.4 billion dollars), to engage
in collaborative ventures and the merging of duplicative activities. Perhaps the
most prominent merger and acquisition deal of recent years was the acquisition
of the British defense electronics firm Plessy by the *German* electronics giant
Siemens and Britain's General Electric Corporation (GEC—no relation to the
American firm). These transnational arrangements are progressing rapidly in
western Europe; American firms—and the U.S. government—remain laggard in
this respect.[23]

European firms are thus reacting to a different set of incentives and
constraints than those shaping their American counterparts. In the U.S. case, we

argued that firms were influenced mightily by the Department of Defense, by the cyclical nature of defense spending, by the increasing R&D costs and concomitant financial risk, and so forth. In the European case, analysts provide a very different list of factors influencing the industry, including the following:

1. Emphasis on cost as a design requirement. The Europeans are much more constrained economically than the Americans when it comes to weapons development. Accordingly, a greater emphasis is placed on cost, whereas in the United States the emphasis is placed on weapons performance. Since many European weapons are simultaneously designed for domestic and export markets, cost even looms larger as a factor in design and production.
2. "Explicit consideration of the industrial base in acquisition decisions and budget planning."[24] European governments regard healthy defense industries as being critical to the health of both the military *and* the civilian economy. Defense industries are regarded as technology drivers, and thus European states work closely with the firms in ensuring that they are able to maintain this distinctive role. At the same time, given international competition in high-technology industries, European officials have permitted integration to pervade the defense industry, making the firms larger and more able to compete.[25]

French defense executive Philippe Cothier focuses on yet additional factors that are shaping the European firms. These are:

1. Relatively small defense budgets
2. The revolution in electronics
3. New military strategies for fighting land battles, which focus on mobility and surprise
4. The high costs of new weaponry
5. The increasing importance of "dual-use" technology—technology that is used by both the civilian and military sectors
6. The emergence of a single European market

Table 4-3 Western Europe's Top Ten Defense Contractors, 1989

Rank	Firm	Sales ($USMM)[a]	Net Income ($USMM)
1	British Aerospace (UK)	5376	576
2	Thomson-CSF (France)	4592	275
3	GEC (UK)	3419	334
4	Aerospatiale (France)	2760	112
5	Daimler-Benz (FRG)[b]	2304	78
6	MBB (FRG)	1712	NA
7	Avions M. Dassault (France)	1480	43
8	Ferranti (UK)	1280	152
9	Philips (Netherlands)[c]	1222	13
10	Matra (France)	992	7.2

[a]*Defense* sales and income only.
[b]Daimler-Benz and MBB merged in 1989.
[c]Philips sold off its defense electronics business in 1989 (to Sweden's Bofors and to France's Thomson-CSF).

Source: Author's estimates, derived from David Greenwood, "The European Defense Industry Stakes," *International Defense Review* (November 1989), p.1573.

7. Increasing competition in export markets, particularly from third world suppliers

8. The potential emergence of Japan as a major producer of weapons and aerospace

The implications of these trends for industry, Cothier says, are clear. These include *consolidation,* with both vertical and horizontal integration becoming prominent in the defense industry; *privatization,* with European states divesting themselves of defense firms; and increasing *financial linkage,* where European (and American) nondefense firms will take an equity share in defense-related industries (one recent example is the decision of General Motors to invest in the Swedish firm Saab-Scania and to collaborate in defense-related activities.)[26]

These ongoing changes in the European defense industry reflect what one observer has called a "crisis."[27] European states are faced with exponentially rising costs of new-generation weapons systems, and an industrial base that is both undercapitalized and stuck with overcapacity.[28] At the same time, export markets are shrinking as new entrants crowd the markets and an increasing number of countries manufacture their own weapons. During the 1970s the French aircraft manufacturer Dassault (producer of the famed Mirage line of aircraft) exported 60–70 percent of its production. In 1982, Dassault had exports worth 17.6 billion francs; in 1987, exports had fallen to 5.6 billion.[29]

European firms and governments have responded to this crisis, sometimes in tandem, sometimes at cross-purposes. The industrial response was noted above. The governmental response, in contrast, has been to promote a paradoxical mix of competition and collaboration. The British government of Margaret Thatcher took the lead, not surprisingly, in promoting more competition among defense industries and in adopting a "value for money" policy in weapons procurement. Bidders from other countries have been permitted to engage in bidding on new systems, and indeed some controversial decisions have been made by the government which resulted in procurement contracts with foreign firms. Prominent among these was the British decision to purchase the Boeing AWACS radar aircraft rather than the domestically designed Nimrod.

Britain has also shown its willingness to allow foreign firms to buy into British companies, as with the United Technologies and Agusta (an Italian defense firm) purchase of Westland Helicopters—a controversial decision, incidentally, that led to the resignation of two cabinet ministers! Thatcher and her defense procurement boss Sir Peter Levene showed themselves willing to shrink Britain's defense industrial base and to focus on the production of those weapons for which the country had a comparative advantage.

The collaborative approach to procurement has been pushed by western European governments as a response to the rising costs of weapons and shrinking domestic markets. Indeed, as early as 1976 the European members of NATO (including France) had joined to create the Independent European Programme Group (IEPG). The objectives of this group were to strengthen European armaments industries, increase American purchases of European equipment, and promote standardization of weapons among the IEPG states. The creation of the IEPG demonstrated a European commitment to the maintenance of a continental defense industry in the face of American competition.[30]

During its first decade, the IEPG was relatively moribund, as European governments pursued "business as usual." But given growing integration under the banner of the European Community's 1992 project, rising weapons costs, industrial consolidation, and vigorous leadership on the part of Britain's Sir Peter Levene, the IEPG became more prominent in the promotion of collaboration during the late 1980s. In November 1988, the IEPG approved an "action plan" that called for the creation of a "common European arms market."

Armaments collaboration in western Europe has occurred on the basis of a principle known as *juste retour*, or "to each according to his contribution." As Harvard's Andrew Moravcsik describes it:

> According to this principle, the share of work each participating nation receives, as well as the burden of financing it bears, is proportional to the percentage of the production it procures. Once this basic rule is established, the precise tasks allotted to each country are carefully negotiated, generally with efforts made to distribute the technologically challenging portions equitably. *Juste retour* has been the basis for nearly all successful European collaborative projects, both civilian and military.[31]

As we can see, the principle of *juste retour* is at odds with the alternative European approach that favors more competition among industrial interests. *Juste retour* basically cartelizes a weapons system, since allocational decisions are not made on efficiency grounds but rather on the grounds of how much one partner is ultimately purchasing. Because of the economic inefficiencies it introduces and because of the high degree of government involvement in the process, *juste retour* has been widely criticized by economists.[32]

Nonetheless, the Europeans have collaborated on many weapons systems, as suggested by Table 4-4. Indeed, collaboration began in the early postwar years when British firms entered into licensing agreements with their French counterparts for the production of weapons systems. The armaments market, it can never be forgotten, is political by its very nature; free-market critiques, while important, are thus ultimately unsatisfying.

In conclusion, the western European defense industry reflects a particular blend of competition and collaboration. The success of this model, however, remains in doubt, but if it fails European firms will find themselves incapable of competing technologically or financially with their American and—perhaps—Japanese counterparts (for more on Japan, see below). On the other hand, the European approach may provide a model for the future, as the world moves away from "free trade" in goods and services and toward a new order of "managed trade" under the guidance of regional blocs. European industries have certainly been preparing for the future through consolidation, privatization, and growing financial linkages. These moves would appear to give them the flexibility to pursue either the competitive or collaborative approach to weapons development. But should European governments open up their weapons markets to more foreign competition, the defense industries may find,

Table 4-4 Selected European Collaborative Arms Projects

Project	System	Start Date	Participating Countries
Jaguar	Aircraft	1965	Great Britain, France
Lynx	Helicopter	1967	Great Britain, France
Tornado	Aircraft	1968	Great Britain, Federal Republic of Germany, Italy
Alpha Jet	Aircraft	1969	France, Federal Republic of Germany
Otomat	Missile	1969	France, Italy
RITA	Radio	1973	France, Belgium

Source: Ethan B. Kapstein, "Corporate Alliances and Military Alliances: The Political Economy of NATO Arms Collaboration," John M. Olin Institute for Strategic Studies Working Paper WP-89-002, Harvard University, Cambridge, Mass., November 1989.

as many of their civilian counterparts have already done, that they are unable to match their counterparts in the United States and, perhaps in the future, Japan.

Japan

Had this book been written even five years ago, it is probable that the Japanese defense industry would have been overlooked. Indeed, the phrase appears to be a contradiction in terms. Japanese firms, we know, have become dominant players across the industrial and financial spectrum. But it would be hard to think of a Japanese firm that is active in defense.

Today, Japan is taking a fresh look at the weapons marketplace. As Eduardo Lachica quipped in the *Wall Street Journal* in 1987, "Japan's defense industry has come out of the closet. . . ."[33] Unfortunately, this development has produced a fresh set of tensions in Japan's relations with its major allies, especially the United States. The controversy in the United States over the codevelopment of the FSX jet fighter aircraft exemplified American qualms about seeing Japan emerge as a major defense-industrial power.

While military expenditures are difficult to compare across countries—as we have already discussed in Chapter 2—by 1987 it appeared that Japan had the third or fourth largest defense expenditure in the world, when measured in absolute (not per capita) dollar terms. The Japanese defense budget that year was over 3.5 trillion yen, and it was projected to rise to over 4 trillion yen in 1990; at an exchange rate of 120 yen to the dollar, this would be equivalent to expenditures of over 34 billion dollars, or about 12 percent the level of spending found in the United States.[34]

Although Japanese defense production is, in the words of the Stockholm International Peace Research Institute, "insignificant" as a portion of total manufacturing output, it still is sufficient to supply the bulk of Japanese Defense Forces (JDF) requirements. Indeed, domestic suppliers provided the JDF with over 80 percent of their needs in the early 1980s. Nonetheless, until recently Japan's Defense Agency (JDA) has been careful to weigh domestic procurement considerations against economic efficiency on the one hand and trade tensions on the other. By using foreign sources, Japan has been able to get advanced technology at a cheaper price than domestic production would allow, while reducing strains in alliance relationships.[35]

Japanese policy now appears to be on the verge of significant changes. The largest defense contractor, Mitsubishi Heavy Industries, derives 17 percent of its sales from the military, while the second largest contractor, Kawasaki Heavy Industries, is reported to have military sales equal to 21 percent of turnover (see Table 4-5).[36] Since bankers commonly view exposure to any one client of over 10 percent as significant, it appears that Japanese industries do more defense contracting than was once commonly believed.

Although Japan's defense industry is only now emerging, it has been in the planning stages for quite some time. In 1970, the director general of the JDA, Yasuhiro Nakasone (who would go on to become prime minister), published a blueprint of a defense-industrial policy entitled "Basic Policy for Development and Production of Defense Equipment." In this document, Nakasone outlined five objectives for the defense industry:

> to maintain Japan's industrial base as a key factor in national security, to acquire equipment from Japan's domestic R&D and production efforts, to use civilian industries, to have a long-term plan for R&D and production, and to introduce the "principle of competition" into defense production.[37]

Of interest, in the same year—1970—the Ministry of International Trade and Industry designated "aerospace as one of three key technologies for the twenty-first century."[38]

Japan did not adopt, however, an autarkic approach to military aerospace development. Indeed, the country had already attempted in the late 1950s to produce an indigenous commercial aircraft, the YS-11. The aircraft was deemed a technological success but an economic failure; by the early 1970s this effort was abandoned. Likewise, the domestically designed and built F-1 jet fighter was regarded as technologically obsolescent when compared with American aircraft available on the marketplace.

Table 4-5 Japan's Top Ten Defense Companies, 1989

Firm	Defense Sales ($USMM)	As % Total Sales
Mitsubishi Heavy Industries	2909	17.4
Kawasaki Heavy Industries	1394	21.5
Mitsubishi Electric	894	4.7
NEC	568	2.6
Toshiba	546	2.2
Ishikawajima Harima Industries	502	9.9
Nihon Seikosho	249	26.4
Hitachi Shipbuilding	219	8.5
Komatsu	189	3.8
Fujitsu	173	3.8

Source: Japan Defense Agency and corporate annual reports.

Thus, the Japanese have sought to develop their aerospace industry in recent years through collaborative projects with western allies. Mitsubishi Heavy Industries undertook the construction of two fighter aircraft, the F-4J and F-15J, designed by McDonnell Douglas. Japanese firms also built antisubmarine aircraft under license. Then, in the early 1980s, the JDA decided to replace its old fighter fleet with a new airplane, the FSX (fighter-support/experimental), which generated substantial controversy in the United States over the costs and benefits of technology sharing with Japan.[39]

More than in any other industrial country, Japanese defense-industrial planning reflects a desire on the part of public officials to advance both economic and security objectives. On the strategic front, in the 1980s Japanese officials became increasingly preoccupied with the Soviet military buildup in the far east (Japan and the Soviet Union never signed a peace treaty after World War II, and outstanding territorial issues continue to stymie an agreement). The Soviets maintain a large troop presence along the Sino-Soviet border, and the Soviet Pacific fleet remains a substantial force that includes nuclear-powered submarines and surface vessels. Yet a further source of regional tension arises from North Korea, which is reputed to be building a nuclear device. While the United States maintains an important naval presence in the Pacific, with major bases in the Philippines, Hawaii, and Japan, American officials have called upon the Japanese to "do more" in light of the domestic "burden-sharing" debate (see Chapter 7, on alliance economic relations, for more on this topic).[40] The Soviet threat on the one hand and the American burden-sharing demand on the other have framed strategic planning in Japan in recent years.[41]

Yet the Japanese are unwilling to develop a defense industry that lacks direct and profitable ties to civilian sectors of the economy. In the words of MIT's Richard Samuels and Benjamin Whipple, "Japan's military aerospace industry arms the nation, serves as the bellwether for commercial aerospace, and provides an important new market for the application of civilian high technology."[42] Jacques Gansler corroborates this view, stating that in the formulation of defense-industrial planning, "The Japanese will select some technologies that have both military uses and significant commercial applications. . . ."[43] These include computers, process technology in manufacturing, robotics, and electronics.[44] What makes the Japanese approach to defense industrialization unique is the conscious effort to maintain—and indeed strengthen—linkages between civilian and military technology.

Ironically, some American officials now appear to view Japan as a future "arsenal of democracy," recalling America's economic role in the First and Second World Wars. Today, Japanese high-technology firms supply allied military equipment with much of its electronic components. As former U.S. Navy Admiral James Lyons stated in 1987:

> All the critical components of our modern weapons systems . . . come from East Asian industries. I don't see change in that, during the foreseeable future. . . . Certainly, the East Asian industries have really become an extension of our own military-industrial complex.[45]

Lyons spoke from direct experience. The U.S. Navy has had significant exposure to Japanese technology, borrowing, for example, specialized modular technology to rehabilitate the aging aircraft carrier *Kitty Hawk*. Contacts between the Pentagon and the Japanese Defense Agency are increasing at a fast pace, as U.S. officials see Japanese firms as being ahead of their American counterparts in certain areas of science and technology.[46]

Yet an important question is whether the Japanese view themselves as an extension of America's military-industrial complex or whether they have a separate agenda. Already, tensions have been produced in alliance relations as the United States has accused Japan of breaching western security. In the most publicized case, the Reagan administration announced in April 1987 that Toshiba Corporation had sold advanced submarine technology to the Soviet Union. As one student of the affair has written, "The sale confirmed a spreading perception that Japan would willingly sacrifice the military strength of its protector and most important ally in order to increase its commercial sales revenues."[47]

The Japanese defense industry, it appears, is attempting to link the state's strategic objectives with private commercial interests in a unique fashion. Through the use of dual-use technology, a focus on the application of specific technologies and techniques, the commercialization of spin-offs that result from research and development, and the capture of needed western technology through coproduction arrangements, the Japanese are clearly developing their military-industrial capabilities. Whether this newfound capability contributes to alliance "burden sharing" or detracts from western security remains an open question. Indeed, as the anti-Soviet strategic consensus erodes in the west, tensions between the United States and Japan over defense-industrial issues are likely to increase.

The Soviet Union

Despite its enormous economic problems, the Soviet Union has managed to create the world's largest military-industrial complex. According to western analysts, the quality of Soviet weaponry saw great improvement during the 1980s, thanks in part to covert and legal access to western technology and manufacturing equipment. While Soviet intentions certainly appear more pacific than at any other time in the postwar era, Moscow's military capabilities remain intact.

The Soviet military-industrial complex (VPK) is composed of several industrial ministries whose output is aimed mainly for the defense sector. These include the ministries of machine building, aerospace, defense industry, shipbuilding, electronics, and communications. While these industries are playing a growing role in civilian production, as efforts are made to convert guns into butter, they remain dedicated to the military effort (see Chapter 3 for more on economic conversion).[48]

In addition to the defense-related industrial ministries, the Soviet Union devotes a substantial portion of its research and development effort to the military. There is no single R&D establishment, but instead these activities are found in the design bureaus of the specialized industries, the military research institutes, and the Academy of Sciences of the U.S.S.R. (Further, the Soviets have devoted an increasing percentage of their foreign covert and legal scientific and industrial activities to the acquisition of western technology.)[49]

> According to the U.S. intelligence community, the VPK is a small but powerful group, responsible for centrally overseeing the research, development and production of all Soviet weapon systems. It coordinates developments between its chief customer, the Ministry of Defense, and the key suppliers, the defense-industrial ministries. As the expediter of weapons-development projects, *it is the principal Soviet military instrument for eliminating or circumventing the inefficiencies characteristic of the Soviet economic system.*[50]

In addition to its domestic responsibilities, the VPK "also has a foreign trade sector."[51] Exports of military equipment have served several functions: (1) they strengthened alliance relationships, although apparently not enough to maintain their alliances intact; (2) they supported revolutionary movements; (3) they earned hard currency; (4) they enabled defense industries to lengthen production runs, which contributes to economic efficiency; and (5) they have contributed to Soviet propaganda and prestige, as exemplified by the publicity associated with recent Soviet demonstrations at western air shows.[52]

According to the Stockholm International Peace Research Institute, the Soviet Union has been the world's largest weapons exporter since 1978, when it overtook the United States. In 1988, exports totaled some 9 billion dollars, and efforts to promote commercial sales of weaponry have increased as the Soviets seek hard cash to bolster their ailing economy (see Chapter 6, on arms trade, for more on export policy).[53]

Although western analysts may have overstated the power of the defense industries in the Soviet economy, there is no question that they have received priority in the allocation of scarce resources. Further, the high status associated with the military in Soviet society has enabled the VPK to attract the country's leading scientific and managerial talent. In program planning, the VPK has also been free of anything resembling congressional oversight, though this may change should political reform proceed in the Soviet Union.

The Soviet economy—including the military sector—is run on the basis of five-year plans. These five-year plans give the VPK a degree of stability in planning that is unheard of in the west. According to Jacques Gansler, such stability

> influences the weapons-acquisition program—even down to the R&D level. Stable budgets and constant manpower levels for the research institutions and design bureaus result in a regular progression of designs and prototypes, and also allow the Soviet research and design bureaus to maintain and develop a corps of experts (in contrast with the shifting of manpower with the cycles in the U.S. defense industry).[54]

Gansler notes that the high quality of Soviet weapons suggests a relatively advanced defense industry. Unlike most western countries, the U.S.S.R. has opted to separate weapons research, development, and production. Development centers conduct basic research and create prototypes, and this work is then tested independently by "research establishments." These research establishments then present their results to senior military officials, who decide which of the competing systems should be placed into production.[55]

Indeed, one irony of the Soviet defense industry is that it is probably relatively competitive in an economy characterized by state monopolies. Development centers compete with one another in the early stages of weapons research, and the research establishments test a variety of designs before proceeding with production. The Soviet defense industry also experiences what economists might call "effective competition" from the west, since military officials are sensitive to the state of their weapons technology vis-à-vis the United States and wish to create similar levels of capability.

According to the Pentagon, "The Soviets . . . made substantial improvements in their defense industrial facilities through a comprehensive modernization program begun in the early 1970s and accelerated in the latter part of the decade."[56] This investment enabled the Soviets to produce their current generation of weapons which incorporated advanced electronics and fire control systems. It also enabled the Soviets to produce greater quantities of selected weapons systems, particularly strategic and naval platforms. During this period, the Soviets reached strategic parity with the United States, began construction of modern aircraft carriers, and outfitted a new generation of fighter aircraft.[57]

Despite its sophistication and dominant position in the Soviet political economy, the defense-industrial base does face considerable challenges. At the macroeconomic level, Mikhail Gorbachev has pledged to reduce defense spending, and while the lion's share of any reductions will undoubtedly come from the work force, it may be expected that defense production will also be reduced. On the microeconomic level, Gorbachev has launched an effort to convert military industries to civilian production; as was discussed in Chapter 3, this effort is not without considerable hurdles. Further, although the defense economy is given preferential treatment in the Soviet Union, it is still embedded within a grossly inefficient and corrupt socialist system.

On the international level, there are yet further problems for the defense economy. During the era of coerced membership in the Warsaw Pact, the Soviets could enjoy long production runs and even weapons coproduction with their Soviet bloc allies. Politically, in the cold war era, they were ready and willing to export weaponry to their friends in Africa and the middle east. Today, the political climate has changed completely, and this may constrain the internationalization of Soviet defense industries. To be sure, defense firms are attempting to commercialize their products, but in the "free" defense market they will face considerable competition.

In sum, the Soviet defense industry has a unique set of strengths and weaknesses. Traditionally, it has been characterized by programmatic stability, appropriate levels of competition in the research and development phases, long production runs, and a supportive political-economic environment. The current political and economic upheaval in the former Soviet bloc, along with the end of the cold war, must inevitably influence defense-industrial planning and output. In any event, it is likely that the VPK and its associated industries will play a considerable role in future Soviet research, development, and production, whether those activities be earmarked for the civilian or the military sector of the economy.

The Developing World

Few changes in the international security environment have been more profound in recent years than the globalization of sophisticated defense industries. Whereas the ability to manufacture advanced weapons systems used to reside solely in the "first" world, armaments are now produced around the globe, from Brazil to Singapore. This development suggests that, in the future, regional conflicts may become more deadly and that the superpowers may find their ability and willingness to prevent and contain such conflicts greatly reduced.

Why have countries throughout the developing world devoted scarce resources to armaments production? Surely these countries could find more productive uses for their labor and capital. While there is no single answer to that question, we will try to formulate a provisional response in this section, focusing on the case of Brazil.[58] Since there is a substantial literature on third world militarization, students will be able to apply the concepts developed in the following paragraphs to other countries.[59]

Although the realization of a sophisticated arms industry is of recent origin in Brazil, it has long been a cherished goal of the armed forces. The military has played a prominent role in economic development since World War I, and from the 1920s onward national security considerations were explicitly incorporated into the state's industrial policy. The lesson that the Brazilian military drew from the two world wars and the great depression—a period when Brazil's trade with the outside world was substantially curtailed—was that the state ought to build an industrial base that could provide civilian and military needs in the event of war or blockade.

Nonetheless, until the 1960s Brazil imported the bulk of its weaponry from the United States. The country lacked the industrial infrastructure that would permit private- or public-sector actors to build technologically advanced end-items, be they military or civilian. Indeed, Brazil had only begun to produce steel at the end of World War II, and in the early postwar years its economy still revolved around the coffee complex.

In the late 1960s, Brazil began to diversify its suppliers of armaments, purchasing an increasing amount from western Europe. Unlike bilateral military relations with the United States—in which America simply exported defense equipment "off the shelf," usually on a grant or credit basis—arms cooperation between Brazil and western Europe "included the gradual transfer of production technology, from direct supply of the first units to local assembly and ultimately indigenous manufacture."[60] Such firms as the British military electronics contractor Ferranti established subsidiaries in Brazil or negotiated licensing agreements with local manufacturers. These contacts between European and Brazilian firms were—and continue to be—instrumental to the arms industries' progress.

The early evolution of the Brazilian arms industry is mirrored in many other countries of the developing world. Small states begin their development dependent on advanced countries for weaponry, and advanced technology more generally. But as development plans proceed—development plans with an explicit national security objective—states seek to build end-items domestically. They do so first by licensing technology and then by entering coproduction agreements. As technology is diffused to the developing country, the state is able to build weapons indigenously. We may call this evolution, borrowing from Raymond Vernon's felicitous description of the "product life cycle" in consumer goods, the *defense industry life cycle* (the product life cycle described the evolution of consumer goods, particularly consumer electronics, from domestic production in advanced countries to exports to foreign direct investment and ultimately to a stage where the initial producer becomes an importer).[61] This evolution, it must be stressed, is the result of purposeful activities on the part of state officials and industrial elites. In the words of former Brazilian Air Force Minister Joelmir Campos Macedo, "It is a condition of security that each nation manufacture its own armaments."[62]

By the 1970s, Brazil had in place what had been labeled a "potential arms production base." It had built steel mills, military academies, research institutes, and a technological infrastructure of sufficient sophistication to build simple weapons, including armored cars, light aircraft, artillery, and the like. As market opportunities expanded for defense producers late in the decade and into the 1980s, Brazil would be able to capitalize on its newfound prowess and compete successfully for sales overseas.

During the 1980s, Brazil exported weapons to some forty countries. Sales were concentrated in the middle east, suggesting that the firms profited nicely from the Iran-Iraq war and other regional conflicts. For several years, Iraq was the single largest purchaser of equipment, with imports of over 1 billion dollars from 1980 to 1987, or two-thirds of total Brazilian weapons exports. During the Iran-Iraq war, Iraq purchased 200 or more armored cars from Engesa, and it was the first customer for the Astros 2 multiple-launch rocket system, built by Avibras.

Notable in recent years has been Brazil's decision to move from being a producer of relatively "low-tech" weapons to a generator of high-technology end-items, including main battle tanks, jet aircraft, missiles, and naval vessels. This transition poses substantial risks for Brazil, and for other developing world producers bent on a similar strategy. Simply stated, these countries lack the capital, domestic market size, and export possibilities to justify the high costs associated with product development. Indeed, two of the major Brazilian defense firms, Engesa and Avibras, entered bankruptcy in early 1990, partly owing to unpaid Iraqi war debts from the 1980s and partly owing to the cash squeeze created by these high-technology programs.

Developing countries that have entered the arms business thus face important constraints in the 1990s, just as earlier decades provided them with opportunities for technological advancement. To the extent that new entrants to weapons production attempt to build sophisticated technology, they will face greater demands on scarce factors of production, including human and financial capital. In debt-ridden countries like Brazil that are unable to borrow money from the international financial markets, the dedication of resources to defense industries means that critical "guns versus butter" trade-offs must be made. Further, these countries cannot finance sales of big-ticket items like tanks, as do firms and states in the "first world."

In sum, the efforts of developing countries to build domestic armaments industries represent a bold attempt to achieve independence and increase their freedom of maneuver in an international system that many of them view as oppressive. While this effort is understandable, it is questionable whether it can succeed in light of the economics associated with weapons research, development, and production. Clearly, many developing countries have built advanced armaments industries. These industries pose a potential threat to international security in that they can contribute considerably to the lethality of regional conflicts. But their continued advance must take place at immense cost to citizens who already suffer from a lack of basic goods and services.

CONCLUSION

National defense industries are deeply embedded in the particular political and economic cultures of the countries where they are situated. Everywhere, however, these industries are expected to serve scientific, technological, and strategic objectives. Defense-related industries are viewed as creators of "high value-added" products and of spin-offs that can bolster the civilian economy. They employ and train technical personnel. In sum, these industries are generally viewed as generators of "externalities"; that is, the social benefits they generate are greater than the private benefits.

And yet these industries are currently being impacted by significant global economic and security trends. Public officials are torn between their desire to promote national security on the one hand and social welfare on the other. This means that subsidization of inefficient industries must come at the expense of the state's internationally competitive firms. The economic and security trade-offs in defense-industrial planning are becoming more and more difficult to make.

The defense industries thus face an uncertain future. Between the outbreak of peace and the globalization of the economy, the case for protection of domestic defense firms becomes less compelling. Thus, while states may be expected to preserve some indigenous defense capability, we can predict that considerable shrinkage will occur in this sector during the 1990s.

Selected Bibliography

Brzoska, Michael, and Thomas Ohlson, eds., *Arms Production in the Third World* (Philadelphia: Taylor & Francis, 1986). This book contains good essays on many of the developing countries.

Davis, Christopher, "Economic and Political Aspects of the Military-Industrial Complex in the USSR," in Hans Hohmann, ed., *Economics and Politics in the USSR* (Boulder, Colo.: Westview Press, 1986). This provides a good introduction to the Soviet defense industry.

Gansler, Jacques, *The Defense Industry* (Cambridge, Mass.: MIT Press, 1980), and Gansler, *Affording Defense* (Cambridge, Mass.: MIT Press, 1989). These are the old and new testaments of defense industry studies.

Notes

1. Center for Strategic and International Studies, *Deterrence in Decay: The Future of the U.S. Defense Industrial Base* (Washington, D.C.: Center for Strategic and International Studies, 1989), p. 11.
2. Ibid., p. 31.
3. Lee Olvey et al., *The Economics of National Security* (Garden City, N.Y.: Avery, 1984), p. 102.
4. *The Defense Technology Base* (Washington, D.C.: Office of Technology Assessment, March 1988), p. 7.
5. Martin Libicki, "What Makes Industries Strategic," mimeograph, Strategic Capabilities Assessment Center, National Defense University, Washington, D.C., June 13, 1989.
6. For a cogent argument, see Theodore Moran, "The Globalization of America's Defense Industries," mimeograph, Georgetown University, Washington, D.C., September 1989.
7. Jacques Gansler, *Affording Defense* (Cambridge, Mass.: MIT Press, 1989), p. 245.
8. Ibid., p. 241.
9. See Kenneth Mayer, "The Politics and Economics of Defense Contracting," Ph.D. dissertation, Yale University, Hartford, Conn., 1988.
10. James Kurth, "The Military-Industrial Complex Revisited," in Joseph Kurzel, ed., *American Defense Annual: 1989–1990* (Lexington, Mass.: Lexington Books, 1989), p. 200.
11. Ibid.
12. See Cynthia Mitchell and Tim Carrington, "Many Defense Firms Make High-Tech Gear in Low-Tech Factories," *Wall Street Journal*, October 8, 1987, p. 1.
13. Andy Pasztor and Rick Wartzman, "Air Force Agrees to Freeze Stealth Bomber Production," *Wall Street Journal*, December 31, 1990, p. 3.
14. *America's Next Crisis* (Arlington, Va.: Aerospace Education Foundation, September 1989), p. 20.

15. Ethan B. Kapstein, "Losing Control—National Security and the Global Economy," *The National Interest* (Winter 1989/1990): 85–90.

16. *Lifeline in Danger* (Arlington, Va.: Aerospace Education Foundation, September 1988), p. 41.

17. See Richard Stevenson, "Foreign Role Rises in Military Goods," *New York Times*, October 23, 1989, p. 1; David C. Morrison, "Halting the Erosion," *National Journal*, July 30, 1988: 1968–1971.

18. See Jacques Gansler, "Integrating Civilian and Military Industry," *Issues in Science and Technology, V*, 1988: 68–73; Philip Gold, "A Call for the Defense Sector to Reinforce Civilian Economy," *Insight*, November 28, 1988: 22–23; Judith Reppy and Philip Gummett, eds., *The Relations between Defense and Civil Technologies* (Boston: Kluwer, 1988).

19. See Department of Defense, *Bolstering Defense Industrial Competitiveness*, Washington, D.C., July 1988.

20. Lord Ismay, *NATO: The First Five Years, 1949–1954* (Utrecht: Bosch, 1954), p. 125.

21. Edward Kolodziej, *Making and Marketing Arms* (Princeton, N.J.: Princeton University Press, 1987), p. 42.

22. On this point see, for example, Artemis March, "The Future of the U.S. Aircraft Industry," *Technology Review* (January 1990): 26–36.

23. On European armaments collaboration, see Andrew Moravcsik, "The Future of the European Armaments Industry," *Survival* (Spring 1990).

24. Gansler, *Affording Defense.*

25. Ibid., pp. 308–310.

26. Philippe Cothier, "European Defense Industries," paper presented at the workshop on International Arms Collaboration, Harvard University, Cambridge, Mass., November 8, 1989.

27. Moravcsik, "Future of European Armaments Industry."

28. On overcapacity, see "Europe's Defence Companies Join the Modern World," *The Economist*, December 10, 1986: 67–68.

29. Jean-François Jacquier, "Dassault: Le Plan Serge," *Le Nouvel Economiste*, July 15, 1988: 28–34.

30. On the IEPG, see Paul Hammond et al., *The Reluctant Supplier* (Cambridge, Mass.: Oelgeschlager, Gunn & Hain, 1983).

31. Moravcsik, "Future of European Armaments Industry."

32. A prominent critic is Britain's Keith Hartley, of the University of York. See Hartley, *NATO Armaments Collaboration* (London: George Allen & Unwin, 1983).

33. Eduardo Lachica, "Japan's Arms Builders Openly Vie for Orders," *Wall Street Journal*, August 19, 1987, p. 1.

34. On Japanese defense expenditures, see SIPRI, *SIPRI Yearbook: 1989* (Oxford: Oxford University Press, 1989), pp. 159–162; Walter Galenson and David Galenson, "Japan and South Korea," in David Denoon, ed., *Constraints on Strategy* (McLean, Va.: Pergamon-Brassey, 1986), pp. 152–194.

35. Ibid.

36. SIPRI, *SIPRI Yearbook*, p. 161.

37. Cited in Gansler, *Affording Defense*, p. 312.

38. Richard Samuels and Benjamin Whipple, "Defense Production and Industrial Development," in Chalmers Johnson et al., *Politics and Productivity* (Cambridge, Mass.: Ballinger, 1989), p. 275.

39. Ibid.

40. See Galenson and Galenson, "Japan and South Korea."

41. For a variety of perspectives on Pacific security, see Andrew Mack and Paul Keal, eds., *Security and Arms Control in the North Pacific* (Boston: Allen & Unwin, 1988).
42. Samuels and Whipple, "Defense Production," p. 277.
43. Gansler, *Affording Defense*, p. 313.
44. Samuels and Whipple, "Defense Production," p. 276.
45. Cited in James Kurth, "The US and the North Pacific," in Mack and Keal, *Security and Arms Control*, p. 35.
46. Lachica, "Japan's Arms Builders."
47. Dan Granirer, "Multinational Corporate Power in Inter-State Conflict: The Toshiba Case," senior honors thesis, Harvard College, Cambridge, Mass., March 1989, p. 1.
48. On the Soviet defense industry, see Department of Defense, *Soviet Military Power: 1989* (Washington, D.C.: Government Printing Office, 1989); Christopher Davis, "Economic and Political Aspects of the Military-Industrial Complex in the USSR," in Hans Hohmann, ed., *Economics and Politics in the USSR* (Boulder, Colo.: Westview Press, 1986); Gansler, *Affording Defense*, pp. 314–318; SIPRI, *SIPRI Yearbook*, pp. 150–155.
49. See the U.S. intelligence community report, *Soviet Acquisition of Militarily Significant Western Technology: An Update* (Washington, D.C., September 1985).
50. Ibid.
51. Davis, "Economic and Political Aspects," p. 97.
52. Ibid.
53. SIPRI, *SIPRI Yearbook*, p. 229.
54. Gansler, *Affording Defense*, p. 315.
55. Ibid.
56. Department of Defense, *Soviet Military Power*, p. 35.
57. Ibid.
58. Except where noted, the material for this section comes from Ethan B. Kapstein, "The Brazilian Defense Industry and the International System," *Political Science Quarterly* 105 (Winter 1990–1991): 579–596.
59. See, for example, Michael Brzoska and Thomas Ohlson, eds., *Arms Production in the Third World* (Philadelphia: Taylor & Francis, 1986); Edward Azar and Chung-In Moon, eds., *National Security in the Third World* (London: Elgar, 1988); Edward Kolodziej and Robert Harkavy, eds., *Security Policies of Developing Countries* (Lexington, Mass.: Lexington Books, 1982); Uri Ra'anan et al., *Arms Transfers in the Third World* (Boulder, Colo.: Westview Press, 1978); James Everett Katz, ed., *Arms Production in Developing Countries* (Lexington, Mass.: Lexington Books, 1984); James Everett Katz, ed., *The Implications of Third World Military Industrialization* (Lexington, Mass.: Lexington Books, 1986); and Arthur Manfredi et al., *Ballistic Missile Proliferation Potential of Non-Major Military Powers* (Washington, D.C.: Congressional Research Service, 1987).
60. P. Lock, "Brazil: Arms for Export," in Brzoska and Ohlson, eds., *Arms Production*, p. 81.
61. Raymond Vernon, *Sovereignty at Bay* (New York: Basic Books, 1971).
62. Ibid.

5

Weapons Procurement

"Nobody likes the weapons acquisition process." ——*Thomas McNaugher*[1]

The weapons acquisition process is often associated in the public's mind with scandal and crime. We think about the *iron triangle* of military officers, members of Congress, and defense contractors, who are plotting the development of costly new weapons. We think about the inside deals, the payoffs, the white-collar crime. In creating this image, we tend to overlook the fact that weapons procurement is an enormously complex problem, and one that is driven not just by a rational process based on cost-benefit analysis but by politics as well.

Further, in building weapons, defense officials in every country are pursuing multiple economic and security objectives. These include support of domestic (and even alliance) industries and firms, employment of scientists and engineers, funding for research and development, and, of course, the fielding of equipment that meets perceived national security requirements. Weapons procurement is really about how these various objectives get reconciled.

This chapter examines the *process* by which weapons are acquired in the United States, the Soviet Union, and western Europe.[2] The purpose of this comparative analysis is to highlight the point that defense procurement cannot be understood apart from the domestic politics of each country.[3] This does not mean that one state's defense bureaucracy cannot learn from another's, but it does force us to consider the political environment in which procurement occurs. Efforts to reform weapons acquisition, with their focus on making the system more "rational," have largely overlooked the political system in which the process is embedded.

THE UNITED STATES

Appropriations for defense represent the largest *discretionary* item in the federal budget. Unlike payments for medicare, social security, or other social welfare programs, most of which are more or less etched in stone, the defense budget can be continuously tampered with by Congress. For students of American politics who associate themselves with the *pluralist* paradigm—the view that political outcomes reflect the pulling and hauling of a multitude of interest groups—the discretionary nature of defense spending means that particular groups will lobby heavily for their special programs. The congressional decision-making process will be exemplified by *logrolling,* or the trading of favors.

In such a political-economic environment, the procurement of costly weapons is likely to be a messy process.[4] After all, of the discretionary dollars in the defense budget, none are so important to regional economies as those in the procurement account (see Table 5-1). Each year the Pentagon spends about one-third of its budget, or some 100 billion dollars, on procurement. The manner in which this money is spent can make a vital difference to communities in which defense facilities are located, and elected officials are naturally concerned to make certain that their area gets its fair share.

It is important to recognize that two major categories of items are purchased by the Department of Defense each year: major weapons systems (high-technology, performance-driven, and purchased in small quantities at high unit costs) and commercial-type "standard" items (items bought in large quantities at low unit costs). An overwhelming majority of the contract actions involve standard items, but the largest share of the defense dollars goes for a few major weapons systems. In 1985, for example, the Air Force spent 78 percent of its dollars on just 3 percent of its contracts.[5] This chapter focuses on the procurement of major weapons systems, rather than on how the Pentagon "conducts" its daily, routine purchases.

Before addressing the question of *how* weapons are bought, we must first emphasize *who* does the buying. In the United States, weapons are not purchased by the secretary of defense for all the armed forces, but by the individual armed services (Army, Navy, Air Force, Marines, Coast Guard) themselves. The services manage "*all* phases of the procurement process." Indeed, the secretary of defense is not authorized to buy weapons; his role (all secretaries of defense have been male as of this writing) is limited to supervision and review.[6]

While we will return to the issue of *who* buys weapons and procurement reform later in the chapter, it should be stated that many criticisms of the acquisition process begin right here. The system, these critics argue, is inherently bloated and flawed because it leads to duplication of effort, needless interservice rivalry, multiple bureaucracies, and an absence of rational planning. Were the process centralized in the Office of the Secretary of Defense, it is argued, the United States would be able to get a "bigger bang for the buck."[7]

Political scientist Kenneth Mayer has suggested that "every major weapon that one of the armed services buys passes through four stages as it moves from conception to deployment: concept definition, concept validation, full-scale

Table 5-1 Department of Defense Procurement Forecasts for Leading Industries, 1989–1994 ($USMM constant 1988)

Industry	1989	1990	1991	1992	1993	1994
Communications equipment	40,195	38,702	38,634	39,127	40,060	40,840
Aircraft	17,356	16,285	16,032	16,407	17,406	18,274
Missiles	15,691	15,414	15,381	15,400	15,436	15,583
Shipbuilding	8,943	8,132	7,842	7,535	7,421	7,432
Airplane engines	7,094	6,905	6,816	6,776	6,926	7,058
Electronics and computers	5,542	5,185	5,161	5,181	5,256	5,350
Ammunition	4,922	4,657	4,566	4,568	4,650	4,754
Tanks	4,505	3,846	3,377	3,223	3,390	3,427
Steel	4,490	4,015	3,898	3,833	3,760	3,707

Source: U.S. Department of Defense.

development, and production."[8] (See Figure 5-1.) Each of these stages, in turn, is made up of several subsets, or hurdles that weapons must overcome if they are to proceed to full production and fielding.

The first stage, *concept definition,* may arise from any one (or a combination) of three different sources: threat assessment, military doctrine, and technological change. Threat assessment and military doctrine—which Jacques Gansler has called the *user pull* side of the equation—are based on the services' perceptions of deficiencies in their current weapons systems or of likely future threats from the Soviet Union and other potential enemies.[9] In simple economic terms, the services have a "demand" for a new weapon to meet a perceived need.

In formulating a threat assessment, the intelligence community (comprising the Central Intelligence Agency, the Defense Intelligence Agency, the National Security Agency, and the intelligence branches of the armed services) may, for example, identify the development of new capabilities (e.g., Stealth technology) in an adversary's aerospace program and then communicate these findings to the Pentagon. The armed service most affected by the capability would then seek an appropriate response (e.g., new radars).

Figure 5-1 The Weapons Procurement Process

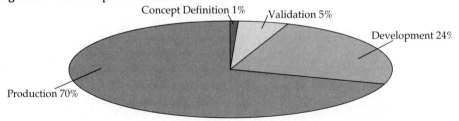

Concept Definition 1% Validation 5%

Development 24%

Production 70%

Sources: Adapted from Jacques Gansler, *Affording Defense* (Cambridge, Mass.: MIT Press, 1989), p. 157; and Kenneth Mayer, "The Politics and Economics of Defense Contracting," Ph.D. dissertation, Yale University, New Haven, Conn., 1988.

Alternatively, the armed services themselves may undergo a doctrinal change owing to new threats, the development of new technology, or a change of military leadership. During the 1980s, for instance, the Army placed its war-fighting emphasis on mobility. The execution of this doctrine required weapons with unique capabilities (e.g., new helicopters), and this also catalyzed the procurement process.

Finally, new weapons can also result from "technology push," or the recognition that a new technology may offer a significant military advantage. According to Jacques Gansler, "Radar, jet engines, and atomic weapons are all examples of how 'technology push' has changed force structure and war-fighting capabilities dramatically."[10] The downside of technology push, as Gansler points out, is *gold-plating*—the addition of costly features to a weapons system that only provide marginal benefits in terms of performance (in other words, the costs outweigh the benefits).

Once a military requirement is defined, concept definition can move forward into the laboratory. A military service will take the lead in this effort, with significant help from potential industrial sources. Research teams in government laboratories (for example, the Lawrence Livermore Laboratory in California, Sandia Labs in New Mexico, and the Argonne National Laboratory in Illinois) and industry (generally the prime contractors) will produce "paper designs" of a system. At this stage, preliminary cost estimates will also be forwarded to the armed service for consideration, along with other program requirements (labor, research and development needs, and so forth).

Theoretically, these research teams are operating in a highly competitive environment where many systems are vying for scarce budget dollars. That is, the design of the weapon has not yet been established, so there is ample room to propose new ideas, so long as they meet the general criteria that have been established. When President Reagan, for example, decided that the United States needed a "shield in space" against nuclear weapons, or a strategic defense initiative (SDI—popularly known as "Star Wars"), he did not have a particular design for such a system in mind. Instead, the principal defense laboratories explored alternative ideas that would carry out the mission of striking ballistic missiles in space.

This competition is in principle healthy, at least from the Darwinian perspective of neoclassical economics. However, it does not encourage realistic estimates of costs and schedules since each laboratory will seek to win the development contract. Invariably, when a program finally receives budget approval, it embodies highly overstated requirements and generally under-stated costs. As a General Accounting Office official has said, "The planning estimates sent through the DoD are not honest. . . . They are highly optimistic for a specific purpose, and that is to get the program started."[11]

Getting a program started requires that a decision coordinating paper be drafted by one of the armed services, stating the rationale for and feasibility of a new weapons program. This paper is forwarded to the Defense Acquisition Board (DAB) in the Office of the Secretary of Defense. The Defense Acquisition Board, headed by the undersecretary of defense for acquisition, was created in

1987 at the instigation of the *Packard Commission* (named after its chairman, David Packard), a blue-ribbon panel established by President Ronald Reagan for the purpose of evaluating the acquisition procedures of the Department of Defense (the Packard Commission is the most recent in a long line of such presidential commissions which have studied this problem).[12] Under the Packard Commission procedures, weapons programs are reviewed by DAB at critical project "milestones," at which time decisions can be made to continue or to stop development. Again, as we will see, this is the function of DAB *in principle;* in reality, numerous actors—including Congress—are involved at each step of the process, and they have a loud voice in determining program execution.[13]

Once development funding has been approved by the DAB, funds must be allocated to the program in the defense budget. The program will be listed as a new line item (unless it remains hidden in the budget as a classified "black" program), and congressional approval for the weapon will be required as it considers the annual defense budget request.

While the budget is being prepared for the new program, the weapons system must be specified in detail. We now move into the *concept validation stage.* A program office is established by the appropriate armed service, and a program manager is given overall responsibility for the execution of the ensuing developmental and testing stages. Specifications for the desired weapon, which run to thousands of pages, are written. Potential bidders from industry are, of necessity, involved in the specification process (since industry will ultimately build the weapon), and they try to influence the design characteristics. This is an important step in the process, because it will affect all future elements in the program, from contracting to final production.

The next step in the validation stage is the competition among firms for the responsibility to develop and produce the weapon. In the early postwar years, it was normal practice for the Pentagon to contract with several firms for the development of prototypes of the weapons system; these prototypes could then be tested and evaluated before final contracts were let. However, given the high up-front costs associated with weapons development—that is, the costs associated with basic research and initial development—multiple sourcing of prototypes is generally no longer possible. In today's environment, the most significant competition takes place earlier in the acquisition process, often when preliminary research is still ongoing.

The basis for industrial competition in the validation stage is the *specification document.* In order to win a contract, a firm must demonstrate that it will meet the project specifications (specs) at the lowest possible cost. Asking that the specs be changed puts a firm in a bad position in the competition; it may even be ruled ineligible for the contract. It should be noted that firms spend millions of dollars simply in responding to the *request for proposal* (RFP) issued by the Pentagon to address the specification document. As of December 1989, for example, Lockheed and Northrop (jointly with their respective industrial partners) had each invested over 600 million dollars in the preliminary design of the advanced tactical fighter, the "next-generation" attack aircraft that will replace the F-15.[14]

After the selection of a contractor, "the burden then shifts back to the program manager, who has the impossible task of managing an overspecified and underfunded program."[15] His task becomes increasingly difficult as more and more actors become involved both within and outside the Pentagon. The various laws and regulations that govern the development process may require the manager to use small or minority businesses, to produce at least some equipment in specific locations, to purchase from American firms, etc. Incidentally, the officials who write the procurement regulations generally are not concerned with the schedule, cost, or even the performance of the weapons program.

The next phase of weapons acquisition is called *full-scale development*. This is the penultimate stage during which the weapon is built as an operational system, ready for a complete array of military tests. During these tests, systems can be adapted to meet changes in adversarial capabilities, to accommodate new requirements, or to overcome design shortcomings. In sum, this is when the weapon is completed and prepared for "mass production" (such as it is in military hardware; given the costs associated with modern weaponry, rarely are more than a thousand copies of an aircraft ever produced, and even the numbers of tanks and artillery weapons are far smaller than in previous eras).

In most cases, only one contractor is involved in full-scale development. The B-2 Stealth bomber, for example, was developed by Northrop, and the Ohio class nuclear submarine (equipped with Trident nuclear strategic weapons) was built by the Electric Boat Division of General Dynamics. Contractors are desperate to win the full-scale development contract since this means they are almost certain to be awarded the production contract. Further, by this stage firms may have invested hundreds of millions of dollars in the system; the failure to win the contract could be catastrophic from the perspective of the firm.[16]

Finally, a weapon is ready for *production and deployment*. A contractor is selected to build a weapon, and Congress authorizes and appropriates a certain amount of funds for the program. In recent years, the Pentagon has often awarded contracts using *second-sourcing* techniques. Thus, even though one firm may have led in the research and full-scale development of a weapon, it is denied a monopoly at the final stage by the establishment of a second production line at another firm. This technique was widely used by Secretary of Defense Caspar Weinberger (and in particular by Secretary of the Navy John Lehman) during the Reagan administration, as a way of curbing the rapidly rising costs associated with new weaponry, and as a way of overcoming the criticisms being lodged at the "iron triangle." According to Weinberger, "The most powerful force for efficiency in production is competition."[17]

As noted above, Navy Secretary John Lehman made extensive use of second-sourcing techniques. By using second sourcing, he lowered the costs associated with several naval platforms. The price of the Aegis cruiser, for example, dropped from 1.2 billion dollars to 900 million dollars per copy, while the F/A-18 fighter's cost fell from 22.5 million dollars to 18.7 million. All things being equal, the Navy could purchase eight Aegis cruisers for the price of six, thus expanding the size of the fleet toward Lehman's 600-ship goal. With the exception of aircraft carriers, the Navy has more than one producer for each of its platforms.[18]

Yet another approach to cost-effectiveness in weapons procurement has been to purchase more from abroad. Among the foreign weapons acquired by the Pentagon in recent years are the British Harrier VTOL (vertical takeoff and landing) jet fighter, the RITA communications system from France, and a minesweeper from Italy. In addition, after an intense competition, the Coast Guard purchased a new series of helicopters from the French firm Aerospatiale. As former Deputy Secretary of Defense William Taft quipped in 1987, "We're trying to get as much bang from the German mark as well as from our own bucks."[19] Nonetheless, foreign procurement remains a small fraction of the overall procurement budget.

Further, protectionism has even influenced the *way* in which the Pentagon buys foreign weapons. Rather than purchase the Harrier "off the shelf" from British Aerospace, for example, the Pentagon was pressured by Congress to coproduce the weapon with McDonnell Douglas in St. Louis. This raises overall system costs to the taxpayer, since it would be cheaper simply to import the weapon from the original producer.

The length of the weapons acquisition process, from initial research to fielding of a new system, is upward of ten to fifteen years.[20] During this period, any number of external and internal factors can influence the developmental process. In economic terminology, weapons acquisition is a "stochastic process," with many of the associated variables changing over time and thus altering the function to be described. Threats can change, new technology may emerge, program managers come and go, funding levels rise and fall, and new Presidents will be elected and secretaries of defense appointed. Any of these factors will work to alter some aspect of the weapon—its specifications, fielding, production run, and so forth. Indeed, as stated at the outset, it is hardly surprising that the process is criticized by so many different people and from so many different angles!

Congress is intimately involved in every step of the acquisition process.[21] In the yearly budget, the program manager must sell the program to the relevant committees and subcommittees in the House and Senate. This helps to explain why there is an effort by the Pentagon to spread the subcontracts through as many congressional districts as possible. For their part, the defense industries engage their political action committees and lobbyists in support of each new program.[22] Nonetheless, when budget cuts occur, weapons programs are often *stretched out* (if not canceled, which rarely occurs); when a program is stretched out, fewer dollars are allocated in a single fiscal year, but the prolonged cycle of development and production leads ultimately to higher costs, to constant tinkering, and, as with the B-1 bomber, to the ultimate fielding of obsolete technology.[23]

(U.S. Air Force)

The B-1 Bomber: Obsolete before its time?

REFORMING PROCUREMENT

The Reagan administration was responsible for the largest peacetime buildup of the U.S. armed forces since the end of World War II. As the building of hundreds of new ships, aircraft, and tanks was under way, a series of newspaper stories began to appear about Pentagon fraud, waste, and abuse. The Defense Department, it was reported, had paid 436 dollars apiece for hammers, 600 dollars apiece for toilet seats, and 7600 dollars apiece for coffee makers. These scandals caused such public uproar as to force President Reagan to appoint a blue-ribbon commission, the Packard Commission, to study the problem, and caused Congress to write hundreds of new regulations.[24]

Indeed, there have been consistent calls to reform the weapons procurement process throughout the postwar era.[25] A major thrust of these studies has been to centralize oversight for acquisition in the Office of the Secretary of Defense and to lessen the power of the armed services. Analysts perceived that the services were rife with the "revolving door" syndrome, in which retired military officers, after doing favors for defense industries during their careers, would then go and work for those very same firms in an effort to lobby their former colleagues! The abuses associated with the revolving door were well known: leakage of specification and other classified documents, favoritism directed toward particular contractors, and a failure to penalize firms for poor performance. Many of these abuses were brought to light in 1989 and 1990 as a result of *Operation Ill Wind,* a probe by the Justice Department of illegal contracting procedures on the part of such major defense firms as Boeing and General Dynamics.

As a result of the Packard report, Congress created a new position, the undersecretary of defense for acquisition, who would serve as a procurement "czar." The czar was expected "to provide centralized direction for the 150,000 acquisition officers who carry out 15 million separate contracting actions a year."[26] The first czar was a former president of Bechtel, Richard Godwin, who was expected to make the Pentagon operate more like a private-sector enterprise.

After a year, however, Godwin resigned in frustration. He said in his final remarks that "I did not think it was doable" to change the standard operating procedures of the Department of Defense. The armed services appeared to retain their overwhelming power in the acquisition process, despite the many changes legislated by Congress. As Godwin said, "I had the authority to write a letter." A Herblock cartoon that followed Godwin's resignation (and that is reproduced here, see Figure 5.2) captured the official's despair.[27]

During the summer of 1989, Defense Secretary Richard Cheney announced a major overhaul of the acquisition system. Cheney proposed that a senior-level executive committee should be formed that would establish policy and oversee weapons procurement. The committee would include the secretary, his deputy, the undersecretaries for acquisition and policy, the chairman of the Joint Chiefs of Staff, and the three service secretaries. Cheney's objective was to stop the turf battles and the duplication among the services and to professionalize the acquisition function.

In this regard, Cheney has also sought to improve the pay and the career and educational benefits for civilian acquisition employees and establish a career path for uniformed acquisition personnel. The plan also called for the elimination of several layers of procurement management. It consolidated all Pentagon contract administration services into a new Defense Contract Management Agency. Further, Cheney asked that Congress review and streamline its procedures concerning weapons procurement.[28] It must be emphasized that a very significant share of the procurement legislation emanates from Congress and is used not to better the weapon or make it cheaper, but to pursue some unrelated social or political objective. Thus, there are congressional mandates that Department of Defense funds be used to support small and minority business and that funds be placed in areas of high unemployment; the result is often some scam, like the scandal involving the New York City–based Wedtech Company, an alleged "minority" defense contractor from the Bronx that was, in reality, a shell corporation established to obtain lucrative defense contracts.

Many proposals for reform of defense procurement have indeed focused on congressional *micromanagement*, that is, the attempt by Congress not only to oversee, but to direct, major weapons programs. With the growth in professional congressional staff members, the costs associated with defense acquisition, and increased media (and public) interest in procurement, it has proved tempting for Congress to become intimately involved with every programmatic detail. Fur-

Figure 5-2

© 1987 by Herblock in *The Washington Post*.

ther, given the "pork" associated with weapons programs, it has been almost impossible for members of Congress to resist efforts to get some piece of a contract for local constituents.

As a response, some recent studies have called on Congress voluntarily to limit its role in defense procurement to actual oversight. Greater onus should be placed on program managers and on the Office of the Secretary of Defense (notice how Congress legislated the creation of an undersecretary for defense acquisition without in any way limiting its own role). In short, weapons acquisition should become a true, managerial task.[29]

But it would be simplistic to place all the problems of weapons procurement on the shoulders of Congress. In December 1990, the Bush administration's acquisition czar, John Betti, was forced to resign over the growing scandals associated with the Navy's new A-12 attack aircraft program.[30] While senior Pentagon officials attempted to allocate the blame to Congress and the defense contractors for the cost overruns, delays, and possible criminal wrongdoing, there has been a clear absence of leadership on procurement issues in the Defense Department, one that some would say goes as far back as Robert McNamara's tenure as defense secretary in the Kennedy administration. In part this is because acquisition authority remains divided between the Office of the Secretary of Defense and the various services, which jealously guard their acquisition activities; ironically, the Department of Defense was created in 1947 largely to overcome the bureaucratic battles between the services.

Despite the many calls for change in the process, why has weapons acquisition proved so difficult to reform? Political scientist Fen Hampson has stated the problem succinctly: "The way America buys its weapons," he writes, "is a supremely political process and one plagued by inefficiency, waste, and political mismanagement."[31] In other words, weapons acquisition is embedded in the American political system. The process is decentralized, and efforts to concentrate it have been successfully resisted, as have all efforts to concentrate political or economic power in the United States. The process involves hundreds if not thousands of defense officials, members of Congress, and industry executives. Each group is pursuing its narrow interests, with little regard for the overall quality and cost of the ultimate weapons system; the costs can be widely diffused to the American taxpayer.

This is not to suggest that the system cannot be improved. But significant improvements cannot occur until there is widespread agreement about what the problem *is*. In reforming acquisition, what are we trying to accomplish? Are we trying to make weapons cheaper? To make the process more transparent and honest? Are we trying to give individuals more responsibility in decision making? Are we trying to involve Congress more in the process or less? At present, few analysts share the same priorities when it comes to reform.

Nonetheless, a study of procurement reform during the 1980s does reveal certain common themes. As lawyers William Burnett and William Kovacic have said, "The most striking feature of defense . . . reform . . . has been its emphasis, previously unequalled, on competition oriented strategies for buying major weapons systems."[32] Echoing the ideological preferences of the Reagan and Bush administrations, efforts have been made to introduce the magic of the marketplace into the procurement process. Defense firms are being required to team up to bid on major systems contracts, and they have been forced to do much more research and development up front. The current competition for the advanced tactical fighter (ATF), which pitted two industrial teams against each other, exemplifies the new approach that has taken hold in the Pentagon.

But despite this emphasis, there are limits to competitive rivalry in defense contracting. First, the number of players is relatively small, making it plausible that firms are still able to collude even while appearing to compete.[33] Second, since defense firms literally must bet the capital of the company on each new project, in that new projects only come along once or twice a generation, competition may produce even greater efforts to secure secret information from the Pentagon or engage in other illegal activities. This is one of the important lessons brought home by the Justice Department's Operation Ill Wind. Finally, competition can only succeed when the Pentagon makes clear that it is willing to see major contractors go out of business. With the current downturn in defense spending, it will be interesting to see whether the Pentagon or Congress is willing to stand on the sidelines should large production lines be forced to shut down, or whether the "follow-on imperative," which keeps firms alive, will endure.

In sum, defense procurement defies quick-fix approaches to reform. The process is embedded in the American political-economic system. While competition, less congressional micromanagement, and more centralization in the Office of the Secretary of Defense are sensible proposals, we should not hold out unreasonable expectations for what they can accomplish. Modern weapons, with their incredible price tags, will continue to mobilize public opinion against fraud, waste, and abuse.

For all the complaints we hear about weapons acquisition, however, most analysts continue to agree that the United States fields weapons that are superior to those produced in any other country. They are better technologically and are more reliable, as amply demonstrated during Operation Desert Storm. How do we account for this apparent success? How do we measure the effectiveness of Department of Defense weapons procurement?

Two general approaches have been taken. The first is to look at the long-term trends from generation to generation of weapons systems and to determine whether performance has improved and costs have gone down—in civilian goods this would be a clear indication of improved production techniques. Color televisions, for example, are far cheaper today than they were in the 1960s, yet the quality is superior. The second is to look at an individual weapons system and to determine whether the cost and performance objectives set for the program at the outset were achieved.[34]

One important observation that emerges from the first approach to effectiveness is that the Department of Defense has emphasized the performance of weapons in the postwar era, without regard to cost. Thus, a tremendous technical improvement in weaponry has been achieved, but at an extremely high price. For example, whereas in the 1950s the United States bought 2000 fighter aircraft per year, by the 1970s the number was down to 300. As defense executive Norman Augustine has said, if current trends continue, by the year 2054 the

United States will only be able to buy one fighter plane per year![35] Indeed, this trend toward decreasing quantities and increasing costs is one of the greatest concerns of contemporary defense analysts.

If we look at the second measure of effectiveness, comparing results with objectives, the performance is somewhat better. In comparison with many other organizations, the Department of Defense does a relatively good job controlling cost overruns. However, cost overruns have nonetheless been significant—running in the range of 40–100 percent for entire programs, from initiation to completion.

In an effort to control program costs, the Department of Defense has increasingly attempted to introduce competition into the weapons procurement process. The introduction of even one additional firm in the construction of a weapon can lead to significantly lower costs, as borne out by the case of the Aegis cruiser program, in which costs per unit fell from 1.2 billion dollars to 900 million dollars after the introduction of a second supplier.

A second important development has been the trend toward more sourcing of commercial products. As of this writing, the Department of Defense has user specifications for every product it buys, and so the Pentagon has been encouraged to do more "off-the-shelf" purchasing of standard items. Even here, however, Congress has intervened in the process. To take a now famous example, after Congress found out that the Pentagon was going to buy twelve tons of fruitcake for Christmas from a commercial supplier, a law was passed prohibiting it from awarding the contract to a "brand-name" producer. The lawmakers wanted small bakers to bid on the contract! Congress was not necessarily wrong to do this, but it suggests the extent to which Pentagon managers' hands are tied when it comes to procurement.[36]

Examined in historical perspective, the weapons acquisition trend in the Department of Defense is toward fewer new programs, which will be more expensive, take longer to complete, and result in fewer weapons per dollar than their predecessors. Some analysts view these trends as most dangerous, both for the economy and for the national security.

Yet there is no escaping the conclusion that the procurement process is a political one. As a result, the Department of Defense is subject to intense regulation and scrutiny, and it is often directed to act in a way that is at odds with good commercial sense. To be sure, the Pentagon has had scandals, some of which have been mentioned in the preceding pages. But the biggest waste in the system is created by the system itself.

PROCUREMENT IN OTHER COUNTRIES

It has been argued in this chapter that weapons acquisition in the United States is, above all, a political process. Defense officials are pursuing multiple economic and security objectives in the construction of defense hardware, from support of particular firms and industries, to research and development of advanced technology, to the actual design of weapons that meet a perceived threat. These various objectives are being balanced in a political arena characterized by intense "pulling and hauling."

Is such the case in other countries? Or does procurement reflect the more "rational" objective of meeting national security requirements? In this section, we will briefly examine weapons procurement in the Soviet Union and western Europe.[37]

The Soviet Union

According to a leading student of Soviet military power, Chris Donnelly, "The Soviet procurement system can produce most items of military hardware of a combat effectiveness equivalent to that of Western equipment but in half the time and at half the cost."[38] During the 1970s, the Soviets initiated a substantial program aimed at improving the output of the defense-industrial base, and the best domestic machine tools—and a significant amount of legally and clandestinely obtained western technology—were devoted to the weapons sector. As a result of this investment program, the Soviets enjoyed increased production of many types of conventional weapons, particularly aircraft and naval vessels.[39] There are some indications, however, that strategic programs were cut at the hands of these conventional improvements; in other words, conventional weapons were allocated an increasing share of the procurement pie from 1970 to 1980.[40]

As in the United States, weapons procurement is a big business in the Soviet Union. In 1982 (a year for which relatively good unclassified data are available), the Soviets allocated almost 50 billion rubles to procurement, an amount that represented over 40 percent of the defense budget; since Soviet defense spending constituted some 15 percent of GNP that year, weapons procurement alone accounted for approximately 6 percent of GNP. In the United States, the corresponding figure would be about 2 percent of GNP spent on weapons procurement.[41]

Defense analyst Stan Woods has determined that defense procurement in the Soviet Union goes through three stages: *exploratory work, development work,* and the *production phase*.[42] Exploratory work on new weapons systems is undertaken by a research institute, under the supervision of a scientific-technical commission. Woods argues that this commission—which is composed of both defense officials and industrialists—"is the linchpin of the R&D cycle. It provides the detailed specifications of the projected weapon."[43] A document is generated during the exploratory phase which provides the raison d'être for the new weapon, along with its projected operational and cost specification.[44]

Next comes development work. On the basis of the technical document generated by the research institutes and the commissions that provide oversight, the military will decide whether or not to go ahead with the next phases of weapons development. These include the selection of one or more *design bureaus* that will initially produce paper studies of the weapon, and then if the military goes forward, the prototype. Oftentimes, several prototypes will be built and will be placed in competition with one another. Should the decision be taken to produce a weapon on the basis of these tests, a "technical conditions" document is prepared.

Not only does the technical conditions document outline in detail the specifications of the weapons system, but it gives a prominent role to the "chief designer" and his overseers on the scientific-technical commission who report directly to the ministry of defense. The chief designer and the commission are independent of the research institutes, design bureaus, and the industrial plants where the weapon is actually built. The objective of this aspect of the procurement process is to ensure that the defense ministry's quality standards are upheld.

Weapons acquisition in the Soviet Union is animated by three guiding principles: simplicity, standardization, and evolutionary change.[45] These three, it must be stressed, are not at all shared by the United States, and are only shared to a slight degree by the other western allies. Soviet designs are "primitive," lacking the fine design features that characterize American weaponry. They are standardized, meaning that common components (propulsion and fire control systems, for example) are found across a range of platforms. This allows for longer production runs, interchangeability of parts, and the efficiencies that arise from economies of scale and learning effects; that is, the more of a particular item a worker builds, the more efficient he or she tends to become in the production process.

Finally, Soviet systems exemplify evolutionary as opposed to revolutionary change. This may reflect problems associated with basic research and development in the Soviet Union and the difficulties related to incorporating western technology in the design process, as much as any articulated preference of defense planners. Indeed, during the 1980s, it appeared that Soviet planners were beginning to sacrifice simplicity and standardization (and the long production runs associated with these preferences) for more technically advanced conventional weaponry.[46]

The severe economic problems that face the Soviet Union of the 1990s place both constraints on—and opportunities for—weapons procurement. On the one hand, the shortages and bottlenecks that encumber the civilian economy have, according to the CIA, also caused a slowdown in weapons procurement. Further, the CIA believes that weapons procurement has slowed owing to the failure of the Soviets to incorporate all the technology they have obtained from the west into their new designs and prototypes.[47]

On the other, *perestroika* and economic modernization offer "the prospect of long-term benefits for the defense industrial sector."[48] Gorbachev has targeted specific sectors for priority investment, including computers, electronics, machine tools, and robotics—the very sectors that make up the defense-industrial base. Should *perestroika* succeed, an ironic spin-off may be greater productivity in the defense sector.[49]

In both the Soviet Union and the United States, of course, weapons procurement decisions in the future will also reflect the state of arms control agreements and treaties. As of January 1990, analysts were focusing particular attention on the conventional forces in Europe (CFE) talks, which held out the promise of greatly reduced U.S. and Soviet conventional forces in the Central Front. Should the leadership in Washington and Moscow agree that the threat of conventional war between the superpowers has receded, it will be much more difficult for either side to legitimize long production runs of tanks, armored cars, artillery, and other such types of war materiel. Thus, on both economic and strategic grounds, weapons procurement is at a crossroads in the superpowers as we enter the 1990s.

Western Europe

Unlike the United States and the Soviet Union, western European countries enjoy comparatively small domestic procurement markets. This means that the high costs associated with weapons development and production must be amortized either by exporting armaments or by establishing collaborative programs in which two or more countries join together in building a common weapons system. Both these alternatives increase the complexity of the procurement process, and indeed western Europe is now in the midst of a wide-ranging political-economic debate with regard to defense acquisition.[50]

In recent years western European governments have procured weapons in the following ways: first, importing defense goods from abroad (principally from the United States); second, producing weapons under a licensing agreement from a foreign (usually American) company, or *coproduction;* third, designing and producing weapons on a collaborative basis with other countries, or *codevelopment;* finally, designing and producing weapons systems domestically.

In fact, despite the high costs associated with domestic procurement, the major European states continue to purchase the bulk of their weaponry at home. Britain and France, for example, purchase 70–80 percent of their weapons from domestic industry, while they import, coproduce, and codevelop the remainder. The increasing costs associated with domestic procurement, however, have caused European governments to reconsider their procurement policies.[51]

Traditionally, weapons acquisition decisions in western Europe have been largely removed from the pulling and hauling of domestic politics. Procurement decisions were undertaken by a relatively small "iron triangle," which included the civil service, military, and industrial elite.[52] National assemblies, unlike the U.S. Congress, have played an insignificant role in oversight and regulation. It is only in recent years, with increasing public debate about defense budgets in general and the role of domestic armaments industries in particular (this latter caused in part by scandals concerning shady arms export deals and sales to such countries as Iraq), that public representatives have begun to examine weapons programs in detail.[53]

Any analysis of European weapons acquisition must therefore recognize its international dimension at the outset. Even though the bulk of weapons continue to be produced domestically, they are frequently designed with export markets in mind. And, increasingly, collaborative ventures are being developed by defense industries across territorial boundaries. Indeed, in the Federal Republic of Germany, the armed service staffs in charge of defense procurement are expected to explore "possibilities for international cooperation" at the outset of planning new weapons programs.[54]

The acquisition of modern weapons in western Europe is, as elsewhere, a multistage process. In Germany, six distinct stages have been identified: the *preconcept phase;* the *concept phase;* the *definition phase;* the *development phase;* the *procurement phase;* and finally, the *utilization phase.*[55] The armed services direct the process completely, giving them an authority over procurement that is even greater than that enjoyed by their American counterparts. While the Ministry of Defense is ultimately responsible for decision making concerning the advancement of a program from one stage to the next, the technical knowledge needed to make informed decisions appears to rest largely with the service staffs. In collaborative programs involving alliance partners, however, the ministry's control over management increases. These programs are often viewed as political as much as technical and economic; thus the ministry reserves for itself wide scope for independent action.

Although the Germans have made paper efforts to increase competition for weapons procurement contracts, in practice the degree of competition is small, and in fact is likely to decrease in the 1990s with the formation of the armaments giant *MBB,* a subsidiary of Daimler-Benz that was created with the merger of the two most important defense-aerospace firms. Despite its support for competition, prime contractors are selected early in the acquisition process. Whereas in the United States the prime is often selected only at the production stage, in Germany it is common to select a prime in the initial concept and definition phases. This prime, in turn, is then "responsible for selecting sub-contractors and integrating individual components."[55] Again, unlike the process in the United States, in Germany micromanagement of procurement does not appear widespread.[56]

The British government under Margaret Thatcher, in contrast, made vigorous efforts to introduce meaningful competition into defense procurement. According to two analysts of the British defense industry, "Reforming defence procurement . . . became an important element in Mrs. Thatcher's efforts to apply the principles of the market economy and reduce the protection industry derived from the state."[57] This reform effort was driven by a host of political and economic pressures, but Thatcher's essential problem was to increase defense procurement without dramatically enlarging the defense budget. The guiding principle instituted by the government in procurement matters was "value for money," and it was exemplified by the decision to purchase the Boeing AWACS radar aircraft over the domestically produced Nimrod, despite intensive lobbying on the part of industry and labor for the latter.

The procurement reforms (known as the Levene reforms, after Minister for Defense Procurement Sir Peter Levene) "rest on three main principles: that suppliers should compete for development and production contracts; that suppliers, and not the customer, should bear the risks of failure . . . and that budgetary control should be strengthened. . . ."[58] At the same time, the government *privatized* its shareholdings in major defense firms, including British Aerospace, Rolls-Royce, and Royal Ordnance. This placed the economic burden

of weapons research and development on industrial managers and their shareholders.

Despite the government reforms and professional supervision of defense
procurement in western Europe, defense ministers are still faced with the
unpleasant specter of rising costs, decreasing quantities, and increasing competition for export markets. This has drawn the European industries closer together,
and the intergovernmental response has been to form the *Independent European
Programme Group.* The IEPG, which consists of the European members of NATO,
has the following objectives:

1. *Opening markets to competition.* The IEPG is working to reduce protectionism in
   procurement policies (this is also an objective, incidentally, of the European
   Community's 1992 project).
2. *Juste retour.* The concept of *juste retour* (fair return) is critical to European
   collaborative programs. It argues that "the share of work each participating
   nation receives, as well as the burden of financing it bears, is proportional to the
   percentage of the production it procures."[59] Under *juste retour*, collaborative
   programs are cartelized on a national basis; states divide work among themselves not on the basis of efficiency or comparative advantage, but simply on the
   basis of what percentage of the end-item (be it a jet aircraft or a missile)
   production the country buys.
3. *Technology transfer.* IEPG is working to remove barriers to trade in intellectual
   property and technological know-how. The organization is also exploring the
   potential for developing a common program for basic research and development.[60]

Western Europe, therefore, may be on the verge of establishing a united
armaments industry, characterized by cross-border mergers and acquisitions
and multinational collaborative programs. At the same time, however, defense
procurement still remains shielded behind a wall of protectionism. Defense
acquisition in western Europe, therefore, is caught between the conflicting
pressures of competition and protection. It is the political tension created by this
conflict that has brought procurement into the broader public eye for the first
time in modern history.

CONCLUSION

The process of weapons acquisition, it has been argued, is embedded in domestic
politics. Procurement in the United States is a decentralized process, characterized by pulling and hauling and intense political pressure. In the Soviet Union
and western Europe, the process tends to be centralized; in France, for example,
all procurement decisions are taken within a single government ministry, the
General Directorate for Armaments. Micromanagement by national assemblies
in these countries is almost unheard of.

All countries, however, have found weapons acquisition in recent years to
be economically burdensome. As a result, reforms have been introduced,
notably by the Packard Commission report in the United States and the Levene

reforms in Great Britain. The common objective of these reform packages has been to curtail the inflationary spiral of costs associated with modern weapons production.

As we enter the 1990s, the task of weapons procurement will grow more complex. There is less agreement now than in the Cold War past about the nature of the military threat faced by the great powers, and less public agreement about what if anything governments should do to counter such threats as third world arms proliferation, drugs, and terrorism. Further, given declining defense budgets in almost every country, the task of justifying costly programs will become more difficult to make.

The debate over weapons procurement is thus likely to become more rather than less politicized in the future. While such debate may be politically healthy from the perspective of liberal political theory, it is doubtful that the end product will be cheaper and more plentiful conventional weapons. Indeed, as programs are dragged out, it is probable that overall costs will rise. Paradoxically, the weapons that are produced by such an intensely political process may not even be truly reflective of national security requirements.

Selected Bibliography

Art, Robert J., *The TFX Decision: McNamara and the Military* (Boston: Little, Brown, 1968). This remains a classic account of the weapons acquisition process.

Edmonds, M., *International Arms Procurement* (New York: Praeger, 1986). This introduction to procurement is set in an international context.

Hampson, Fen, *Unguided Missiles* (New York: Norton, 1989). This useful book would have been stronger had it attempted to explain some procurement successes, rather than just the "failures."

Kotz, Nick, *Wild Blue Yonder* (New York: Pantheon, 1988). This book is a highly readable account of the B-1 bomber program.

McNaugher, Thomas, *New Weapons, Old Politics: America's Military Procurement Muddle* (Washington, D.C.: Brookings Institution, 1989). This book would be even more valuable had some procurement success stories been analyzed.

Notes

1. Thomas McNaugher, *New Weapons, Old Politics: America's Military Procurement Muddle* (Washington, D.C.: Brookings Institution, 1989).
2. There is a rich literature of case studies in weapons procurement. For some of the classics, see Robert J. Art, *The TFX Decision: McNamara and the Military* (Boston: Little, Brown, 1968); Harvey Sapolsky, *The Polaris System Development* (Cambridge, Mass.: Harvard University Press, 1972); Robert F. Coulam, *Illusions of Choice: The F-111 and the*

Problem of Weapons Acquisition Reform (Princeton, N.J.: Princeton Universtiy Press, 1977); and Ronald Fox, *The Defense Management Challenge* (Boston: Harvard Business School Press, 1988).

3. There is a serious shortage of works analyzing weapons acquisition in other countries, one that scholars would do well to address.

4. For two critical studies of the congressional role, see William Gregory, *The Defense Procurement Mess* (Lexington, Mass.: Lexington Books, 1989); and Gordon Adams, *The Iron Triangle: The Politics of Defense Contracting* (New York: Council on Economic Priorities, 1981).

5. Jacques Gansler, *Affording Defense* (Cambridge, Mass.: MIT Press, 1989), p. 144.

6. Kenneth Mayer, "The Politics and Economics of Defense Contracting," Ph.D. dissertation, Yale University, Hartford, Conn., 1988, pp. 59–60.

7. See, for example, the President's Blue Ribbon Commission on Defense Management (Packard Commission), "A Formula for Action: A Report to the President on Defense Acquisition," Washington, D.C., April 1986; see also the Pentagon response, Secretary of Defense Richard Cheney, "Defense Management: Report to the President," June 12, 1989.

8. Mayer, "Politics and Economics," pp. 59–60.

9. Gansler, *Affording Defense*, p. 144.

10. Ibid., p. 145.

11. Ibid., p. 146.

12. President's Blue Ribbon Commission on Defense Management, "A Formula for Action."

13. See Fen Hampson, *Unguided Missiles* (New York: Norton, 1989); and Secretary of Defense Richard Cheney, "Defense Management."

14. Richard Stevenson, "New Jet Fighter: Risks Are High," *New York Times*, December 27, 1989, p. D1.

15. Gansler, *Affording Defense*, p. 147.

16. Hampson, *Unguided Missiles*, p. 12.

17. Secretary of Defense, *Annual Report to the Congress: Fiscal Year 1987* (Washington, D.C.: Government Printing Office, 1988), p. 23.

18. Ethan B. Kapstein, "Economics and Military Power," *Naval War College Review* (Summer 1989): 105.

19. Eduardo Lachica, "Pentagon Turns More to European Arms," *Wall Street Journal*, February 10, 1987, p. 42.

20. See Mayer, "Politics and Economics," p. 73; Hampson, *Unguided Missiles*, p. 14; President's Blue Ribbon Commission on Defense Management, "A Formula for Action," p. 47; and Gansler, *Affording Defense*, p. 148.

21. For an acquisition study that emphasizes the role of Congress, see Hampson, *Unguided Missiles*.

22. See Mayer, "Politics and Economics," for a sophisticated study of Department of Defense efforts in this regard.

23. See Nick Kotz, *Wild Blue Yonder* (New York: Pantheon, 1988), for an account of the B-1's history.

24. George Melloan, "Even Generals Get the Arms-Procurement Blues," *Wall Street Journal*, June 23, 1987, p. 31.

25. For an earlier review, see Robert J. Art, "Why We Overspend and Underaccomplish: Weapons Procurement and the Military-Industrial Complex," in Steven Rosen, ed., *Testing the Theory of the Military-Industrial Complex* (Lexington, Mass.: Lexington Books, 1973), pp. 247–266.

26. "Pentagon Procurement Has Armor That Repels Reform," *New York Times*, September 27, 1989, p. E4.

27. Ibid.

28. Secretary of Defense Richard Cheney, "Defense Management."

29. For the most recent recommendation of this kind, see Gregory, *Defense Procurement Mess.*

30. Molly Moore, "Pentagon's Chief Weapons Builder, under Fire and over Cost, Quits Post," *Washington Post*, December 13, 1990, p. 21.

31. Hampson, *Unguided Missiles*, p. 298.

32. William Burnett and William Kovacic, "Reform of United States Weapons Acquisition Policy," *Yale Journal of Regulation 6* (Summer 1989): 252.

33. See Barbara J. Alexander, "Prime Contract Competition Regimes and Subcontracting among Military Aircraft Manufacturers," Ph.D. dissertation, Harvard University, Cambridge, Mass., 1990.

34. Adapted from Gansler, *Affording Defense*, pp. 169–179.

35. Norman Augustine, *Augustine's Laws* (New York: Penguin, 1986).

36. See Gansler, *Affording Defense.*

37. There is a paucity of research on arms procurement in countries other than the United States; for one review see M. Edmonds, *International Arms Procurement* (New York: Praeger, 1986).

38. C. N. Donnelly, "Future Soviet Military Policy," *International Defense Review* (January 1989): 21.

39. Department of Defense, *Soviet Military Power: 1989* (Washington, D.C.: Government Printing Office), p. 35.

40. See Richard Kaufman, "Causes of the Slowdown in Soviet Defense," *Soviet Economy 1* (January–March 1985): 179–192.

41. David Epstein, "The Economic Cost of Soviet Security and Empire," *Working Papers in International Studies* (Hoover Institution, Stanford University, Palo Alto, Calif., December 1988).

42. Stan Woods, "Weapons Acquisition in the Soviet Union," *Aberdeen Studies in Defence Economics 24* (Summer 1982).

43. Ibid.

44. Ibid.; see also Matthew Evangelista, *Innovation and the Arms Race: How the United States and the Soviet Union Develop New Military Technologies* (Ithaca, N.Y.: Cornell University Press, 1988).

45. Ibid.

46. Department of Defense, *Soviet Military Power.*

47. Kaufman, "Causes of the Slowdown."

48. Department of Defense, *Soviet Military Power.*

49. Ibid., pp. 35–36.

50. For an overview, see Andrew Moravcsik, "1992 and the Future of the European Armaments Market," *Survival* (January 1990): 65–85.

51. Ibid.

52. See William Walker and Philip Gummett, "Britain and the European Armaments Market," *International Affairs 65* (Summer 1989): 418–442.

53. On the Federal Republic of Germany, see Regina Cowen, *Defense Procurement in the Federal Republic of Germany* (Boulder, Colo.: Westview Press, 1986); on France see Edward Kolodziej, *Making and Marketing Arms* (Princeton, N.J.: Princeton University Press, 1987); and on Britain, Keith Hayward, *The UK Defence Industrial Base: Development and Future Policy Options* (London: Brassey's, 1989).

54. Cowen, *Defense Procurement*, p. 114.
55. Ibid.
56. Ibid.
57. Walker and Gummett, "Britain."
58. Ibid.
59. Moravcsik, "1992," p. 19.
60. Adapted from Walker and Gummett, "Britain."

PART THREE

International Issues

6

The Arms Trade

"For Graham a gun was a series of mathematical expressions
resolved in such a way as to enable one man, by touching a
button, to project an armour-piercing shell so that it hit a target
several miles away plumb in the middle. It was a piece of
machinery no more or less significant than a vacuum cleaner or a
bacon slicer. It had no nationality and no loyalties. It was neither
awe-inspiring nor symbolic of anything except the owner's ability
to pay for it. His interest in the men who had to fire the products
of his skill as in the men who had to suffer their fire—and,
thanks to his employer's tireless internationalism, the same sets
of men often had to do both—had always been detached."
——*Eric Ambler,* Journey into Fear, *1937*[1]

With the invasion of Kuwait by Iraq in August 1990, the arms trade has once
again become the topic of widespread public and official scrutiny. Journalists,
public officials, and other informed observers have claimed that had the world
not sold advanced weaponry to Iraq during the 1980s, the invasion would never
have occurred. During the crisis, President George Bush articulated his commitment to seek new controls on the proliferation of biological, chemical, and
nuclear weapons and ballistic missiles. In August 1991, members of the United
Nations Security Council met in Paris to discuss curbing arms sales. Editorialists
called upon the President to launch an international effort at the end of the crisis
not only to halt the trade in those technologies, but to win new controls on the
entire array of advanced weapons systems.[2]

Trade in armaments has assumed critical political and economic importance for states and firms in the postwar era. States have come to view arms sales
as the "currency of foreign policy," while firms use sales to achieve economies of
scale in production and to diversify away from dependence on the home market.
At the same time, public debate over arms sales has increased, as the benefits of
such sales from the perspective of international security and regional stability

(Reuters/Bettmann)

Saddam Hussein: He spent billions on weapons in
his quest for regional hegemony.

become more questionable. Further, arms sales have become tainted by scandals
involving bribes to foreign officials.

Of course, concern with arms transfers is hardly new. During the 1920s, as
the world reflected upon the bloodletting of World War I, the League of Nations
formed a commission to study the role of arms merchants in military policymaking. Among its many findings, the commission concluded that:

1. Armament firms have been active in fomenting war scares and in persuading
   their own countries to adopt warlike policies and to increase their armaments;
2. Armament firms have attempted to bribe government officials both at home and
   abroad;
3. Armament firms have disseminated false reports concerning the military and
   naval programs of various countries in order to stimulate armament expenditure;
4. Armament firms have sought to influence public opinion through the control of
   newspapers in their own and foreign countries;
5. Armament firms have organized international armament rings, through which
   the armaments race has been accentuated by playing off one country against
   another;

6. Armament firms have organized international armament monopolies that have increased the price of armaments sold to governments.[3]

As a result of the popular revulsion against such "merchants of death" as Basil Zaharoff, who sold weapons to all the major protagonists during the war, the arms trade after 1918 came under increasing official scrutiny, if still lax public control; the writing of spy novelist Eric Ambler, quoted at the opening of the chapter, is suggestive of public opinion at the time. Indeed, the gradual extension of state control over the arms trade is one of the most important developments in this issue area since the interwar period.

But debate has not ended about the appropriate role of the state in fostering or curtailing the arms trade. In recent years the sale of arms has become increasingly politicized, and the issues surrounding this trade have grown in complexity as new entrants have made the sector no less competitive than many commercial domains.[4] In fact, the competition has grown so intense that some commentators see an end to state control, and a "de facto de-regulation of the arms trade."[5]

This chapter provides an introduction to the arms trade and to the arms transfer policies of the United States, the Soviet Union, and several other major exporters. The chapter suggests that neither unilateral control regimes on the one hand nor free trade regimes on the other are likely to be politically acceptable methods of dealing with the problems associated with arms transfers. Unilateral controls will be viewed as ineffective so long as other major producing countries continue to sell weapons, while free trade in arms was halted by states before World War II, owing to both national security concerns and public revulsion. Although a multilateral regime to control arms sales still appears a long way off, this may offer states the best hope for achieving their multiple economic and security objectives in the issue area.

INTRODUCTION TO THE ARMS TRADE

During the 1980s, the arms trade was dominated by the superpowers (see Table 6-1). The United States and the Soviet Union supplied the world with well over half the armaments sold, and the arms that they offered became increasingly sophisticated. Further, there has been a significant shift in the *way* weapons are sold. In the past, the major powers sold mostly completed systems "off the shelf." Today, the friends and allies of the superpowers, and many developing countries, have increasingly demanded coproduction and codevelopment of armaments, in which weapons are produced jointly and arms technology is transferred (for more on armaments collaboration, see Chapter 7). As the developing-country manufacturers have increased their capabilities, they have found niches in the arms market, allowing them to become new entrants in an already crowded field.

According to the U.S. Arms Control and Disarmament Agency, arms sales have averaged around 50 billion dollars per annum during the 1980s; of this amount, the Stockholm International Peace Research Institute (SIPRI) argues that around 35 billion dollars is in the form of major weapons systems.[6] In terms of total world trade the number is insignificant. Total world exports averaged around 2 trillion dollars per annum during the 1980s, and of that amount some 1.4 trillion dollars was manufactured goods.[7] Even for countries like France, which are widely regarded as dependent on arms sales for export revenues, the numbers suggest the relative unimportance of this trade. In 1986, France had export sales of 125 billion dollars, and arms sales made up only 4 billion dollars of the total.

A detailed econometric model produced at the University of Michigan lends support to the thesis that, in the developed world, the economic effect of arms exports on the macroeconomy is relatively small. The researchers modeled a multilateral arms embargo by all the major industrial countries and found that "the adjustment problems would not be of major proportions in most cases." [8] For the industrial world, exports would be reduced by under 1 percent, while the labor force reduction would total some 423,000 workers.

Of course, arms sales are more important when viewed from the perspective of particular industries and particular regions in arms-exporting countries. For aerospace and defense manufacturers, arms sales are often viewed as critical to industrial health, especially when domestic spending for the outputs of these firms is experiencing a cyclical downturn. Further, in particular regions—like those surrounding Toulouse, France; Los Angeles, California; or Boston, Massachusetts—defense-related sales are important to overall employment and manufacturing levels.

Nonetheless, if arms sales are trivial from a macroeconomic perspective, they assume major importance in terms of foreign policy decision making. Arms sales can either maintain or tilt regional balances, enhancing or destabilizing international security. In many of the liberal democracies, arms transfers have

Table 6-1 Top Ten Arms Exporters, 1984–1988 ($USMM Constant 1988)

ARMS EXPORTER	1984	1985	1986	1987	1988	As % All Exports (5-yr avg.)
World	58,960	50,450	49,090	56,060	48,640	2.2
U.S.S.R.	21,730	18,690	22,380	23,040	21,400	20.5
U.S.	12,040	12,130	9,803	14,770	14,300	4.8
France	4,615	5,575	4,582	2,789	1,890	3.1
UK	1,914	1,202	1,598	2,169	725	1.2
PRC	2,251	738	1,279	2,376	3,100	5.4
FRG	3,152	1,011	852	1,890	360	0.6
Czechoslovakia	1,069	1,640	1,385	1,240	850	5.6
Italy	1,126	1,011	613	372	390	0.7
Brazil	732	394	288	620	380	1.7
Israel	518	629	501	506	140	6.2

Source: U.S. Arms Control and Disarmament Agency.

been subject to intense political debate. The United States has undergone tremendous swings in arms sales policy, from promotion of such sales to general suppression. Similar shifts are visible in other countries. A series of scandals involving the Swedish arms manufacturer Bofors, for example, revolving around payoffs to officials in India, has led to greater scrutiny of arms exports in that country.

One problem with arms sales as a tool of foreign policy is that the arms tend to outlast the policies they were designed to advance. Given the durability of military hardware, contemporary systems can endure—if they are given proper maintenance—for a generation or more. Governments, in contrast, last a much shorter period of time, and regimes to which arms are sold may change quickly and violently. As will be discussed in greater detail below, the United States may have had sound foreign policy reasons for selling weapons to the shah of Iran during the early 1970s, but one downside of this policy became apparent when the shah was overthrown in 1978 and his arsenal fell into the hands of a government hostile to the United States. Arms sales are often made to serve immediate or short-term political objectives, but their legacy can endure for many years.

Why, then, do countries sell arms? A number of explanations can be offered. First and foremost, arms sales are made for reasons of foreign policy. In most cases, states sell weapons to friends and allies. Thus, most U.S. arms sales have been made to NATO countries, Japan, and middle eastern states (predominantly Israel, Egypt, and Saudi Arabia), while the Soviets delivered most of their weapons to Warsaw Pact nations and Cuba. In "periphery" countries, the story becomes more complex. Arms sales agreements may be struck primarily to support regimes of a particular type (i.e., "communist" or "noncommunist"), to maintain a regional balance of power, and/or to exercise influence over a recipient.

Second, countries sell weapons to make money; that is, the transactions are made for commercial purposes, with little regard for the systemic or regional consequences. Some of the new entrants, like Brazil, may be emblematic of this approach, though advanced states like France have often been accused of acting like arms mercenaries. From an economic perspective, the only countries in the world whose defense industries can survive on the basis of domestic procurement alone are the Soviet Union, China, and the United States. The domestic markets in all other countries are too small to support indigenous manufacturers of major weapons systems. In order to amortize the costs of research and development and weapons production, small-country firms must somehow lengthen production runs; in short, they must export in order to survive. To the degree that governments wish to maintain such industries (and the associated employment) on national soil, they have no choice but to support such weapons sales.[9]

The microeconomics of the defense industry are not the only rationale for promoting arms sales. From a macroeconomic perspective, arms sales will increase current account surpluses or will cut such deficits as may exist.

Aerospace sales, for example, constitute the largest category of U.S. manufacturing exports, and military aircraft sales have traditionally been a substantial proportion of the total. During the 1980s, when the United States suffered massive trade deficits, export promotion, including arms sales, assumed importance from a macroeconomic standpoint; similar stories can be told for France and Britain. Even though arms sales are generally marginal as a percentage of overall trade, margins are important, if only politically, during hard economic times.

Finally, and less obviously, bureaucratic interests within governments may promote arms sales. The ministry of defense in a country may have, for example, a pecuniary interest in such sales; the branch of the Pentagon that handles defense sales receives a fee for its services that would make any Wall Street investment firm envious. For their part, France and Britain have armies of defense trade officials associated with their embassies around the world, commercial attachés whose business it is to seek out market opportunities. To the extent that arms sales policies percolate from the bottom up in large government bureaucracies, of necessity they must have bureaucratic champions.[10]

These reasons for arms sales are not mutually exclusive. In considering such sales, governments naturally balance their competing objectives. The official arms transfer statement of the Reagan administration stated that:

> arms transfers can help deter aggression . . . project power in response to threats . . . foster regional and internal stability . . . help to enhance defense production capabilities and efficiency.[11]

But in attempting to balance competing objectives, it is easy to see how arms sales decisions can become politically volatile, both within governments and between governments and the citizenry.

THE UNITED STATES

In the United States, arms sales policy is set by the State Department; the actual sales are executed by the Department of Defense, which is responsible through its Defense Security Administration Agency (DSAA) for negotiating deals, shipping equipment, and coordinating training in the use of the new armaments. The legislative basis for arms exports is found in the Arms Export Control Act (AECA) of 1976, which was written in response to growing public concern over arms sales scandals (particularly, several well-publicized cases of U.S. defense firms bribing foreign officials) and exports to repressive regimes in Africa, Asia, and South America. Although the AECA vests the President with authority to establish arms export policy, the President must inform the Senate of any sale over 14 million dollars, and the Senate has veto power over such sales.[12]

Before World War II, arms sales were not major instruments of U.S. foreign policy. The United States was the world's third largest seller, after Great Britain and France, but its sales were mainly concentrated in South America. Only with the outbreak of the war in Europe did arms sales become significant from a policy

(British Aerospace)

The Tornado: This plane has been sold around the world by its European producers.

standpoint, especially with the revision of the Neutrality Act, which had prevented transfers to belligerents during wartime.[13]

During the war, the United States became a major weapons and materiel supplier to its allies. In March 1941, Congress passed the Lend-Lease Act, which provided the basis for wartime arms transfers. According to one study, "Under lend-lease, arms worth tens of billions of dollars were transferred to the Allies between 1941 and 1945."[14]

With the war's end, Congress acted quickly to end the Lend-Lease program. But growing concerns with the Soviet Union's global objectives after 1947 caused a reconsideration of U.S. policy. Most dramatically, the United States entered an "entangling alliance," the North Atlantic Treaty Organization (NATO). On April 5, 1949, the day after the North Atlantic Treaty was signed, the European members submitted a formal request for military and financial assistance to Washington. By 1954, "the value of military equipment shipped or planned by the United States for delivery to its European partners had reached about $15 billion."[15] At the same time, the United States instituted a program of "offshore" procurement under the Mutual Defense Assistance Program (MDAP). Under this program, the United States purchased materiel and weapons for its allies from European armament manufacturers. The objectives of the MDAP were to rebuild the European defense industries, to bolster the European economy, and in some cases to take advantage of lower production and/or transportation costs.

The expansion of the Soviet threat to other theaters caused the United States to increase its arms transfers to southeast Asia, Africa, and Latin America. Of interest, the United States, Britain, and France briefly attempted to control arms deliveries to the volatile middle east through the Tripartite Agreement, struck in 1950. This agreement, never enforced, marked a nascent effort at building a multilateral arms transfer regime. During the mid-1950s and early 1960s, the largest recipients of American arms were France, West Germany, Italy, Turkey, Taiwan, and South Korea.[16]

The Vietnam war and its aftermath brought about a sea change in U.S. arms transfer policy. With its defeat on the ground, and public opinion strongly opposed to military intervention in the third world, the United States adopted a policy of providing advanced weapons to friends and allies around the world. The "Nixon Doctrine," framed by President Richard Nixon and his Secretary of State Henry Kissinger, stated that the United States would "look to the nation directly threatened to assume the primary responsibility for providing the manpower for its defense." [17] Between 1966 and 1975, the number of recipients of American arms increased by 25 percent, growing to seventy-four nations.[18]

Another major turning point in postwar U.S. arms sales policy came with the downfall of the shah of Iran in 1978. During the 1970s, the United States had lavished modern weapons on the shah, who was viewed as a critical ally in a volatile region; Iran provided one of the great test cases of the Nixon Doctrine. Unlike any other developing country, Iran received cutting-edge weapons systems that were a part of the U.S. inventory. It was hoped that these weapons would deter external enemies and maintain internal stability.

In late 1978, U.S. policy collapsed with the revolution that ultimately forced the shah to abdicate his throne. The new regime of Ayatollah Khomeini captured a modern arsenal valued at billions of dollars. Owing to the abject failure of America's arms transfer policy, a period of intense reassessment occurred in Washington.

Indeed, even while campaigning for the presidency in 1976, Democratic candidate Jimmy Carter had made an issue of the arms sales policies of previous Republican administrations. At this time the United States was responsible for about one-half of the world's total arms exports, and of that amount the bulk of the sales went to three countries: Israel, Saudi Arabia, and Iran. Carter criticized America's policy as being irresponsible; the selling of advanced weaponry to unstable regions, he asserted, could only lead to more lethal conflicts.[19]

In May 1977, newly inaugurated President Carter announced sweeping changes in U.S. arms sales policy. He said that, henceforth, such sales would be an "exceptional" tool of foreign policy and that they would be limited both qualitatively *and* quantitatively; dollar ceilings were placed on the sales that would be approved in any single fiscal year. The Carter announcement provided six general guidelines for U.S. policy in this issue area:

1. The United States would not be the first country to introduce advanced weaponry into a region.
2. The United States would not sell weaponry that had not already been deployed with the U.S. armed forces.
3. The United States would not permit firms to modify or produce weapons solely for export.

4. The United States would not permit coproduction agreements for advanced weapons systems.

5. The United States would not allow recipients of American military hardware to transfer weapons to third parties without permission.

6. The United States would only permit arms sales on the basis of policy decisions first made by the Department of State, rather than in reaction to requests from defense manufacturers.[20]

Beyond these general provisions, Carter set dollar limits on the arms sales that would be approved in any fiscal year. For fiscal year 1978, Carter set a ceiling of 8.5 billion dollars, an 8 percent reduction from the fiscal year 1977 total. For fiscal year 1979, he made an additional 8 percent cut. In theory, these ceilings would force the Department of State to allocate arms sales to the most critical customers. In August, Carter went a step further, issuing the now infamous "leprosy letter" to U.S. embassies. The leprosy letter informed embassy officials that arms companies seeking foreign sales should not receive the traditional courtesies and forms of assistance accorded to American businesspeople who called from other industries; arms salespeople were to be treated as lepers.

In practice, the quantitative limits set by the President came with major loopholes. The most significant among these was that arms transfer agreements with "treaty allies" were not counted in the ceiling limits. As a result, U.S. arms transfers in fiscal years 1977 and 1978 totaled nearly 16 billion dollars—nearly twice the alleged limit—before dropping under 15 billion dollars in fiscal year 1979 and down to 13 billion dollars in fiscal year 1980.[21]

With the general prohibition against sales of advanced weaponry and with increasing competition for third world markets from European suppliers, American defense firms were left in a quandary by the Carter policy. Traditionally, American arms that were exported either came out of government inventories or were ordered by the government for foreign delivery. Although top-of- the-line equipment was sold only to a few countries, all weaponry offered was of the same type either presently or in the past used by the American armed services; there were no weapons designed solely for export purposes. In contrast, European firms designed their weapons at the outset with export markets in mind, since domestic procurement was too small to support production runs.

In January 1980, under intense pressure from arms manufacturers, President Carter announced a new "FX" policy. The President said that the development of a new lightweight fighter aircraft (FX), designed primarily for the export market, would be permitted under his administration's arms transfer regulations. While private firms were encouraged to build and sell such an aircraft, no government funds would be involved. The idea was to permit U.S. defense industries to compete with their European counterparts in offering to developing countries a new fighter, but one less capable than the most advanced American systems.[22]

This prospect was particularly tantalizing to Northrop, a prime contractor whose major weapons programs were winding down. The company thus launched a five-year, one-billion-dollar effort to build a lightweight fighter, the F-20 Tigershark. Although the plane would be built primarily for the export market, Northrop hoped that its low cost and design performance would persuade the U.S. Air Force to take it into inventory, thereby increasing production numbers and the plane's attractiveness to foreign buyers.

The F-20 project ended in disaster for Northrop, owing to corporate strategic failures on the one hand and government policy changes on the other. From the corporate perspective, the firm was overoptimistic about its ability to sell the airplane to the Air Force. Not only did the Air Force for budgetary reasons decide to upgrade its existing fleet of F-16s, rather than add yet another fighter aircraft to its inventory, but the F-20's operational performance was viewed as "dismal." [23]

As well, changes in government policy also took their toll. With the election of Ronald Reagan, arms transfer policy underwent a significant shift. The new administration permitted the sale of such front-line fighters as the F-16, leaving the FX program to history. The F-20 could not compete.

The Tigershark story provides an example of the changes in arms transfer policy and how these may affect defense industries. Paradoxically, it shows both the power of the defense firms and their weakness. Just as government policy can make a firm, so too it can break one. In the late 1970s, as a response to the new Carter arms policy, defense industries agitated for a program that could meet the export standards. Eventually, they got one. But by the time the plane was built, the policy had changed. Following the F-20 experience and other controversies at Northrop involving export markets, the company decided to withdraw completely from foreign sales. In 1990, the firm was relying completely on the B-2 bomber program and on subcontracts for its survival.

In the United States, arms transfer and procurement policies have been on separate tracks. This is because the domestic defense market absorbs most of the production of the prime contractors, leaving little for export. At most, export sales account for 20 percent of firm sales, and in most cases it is 10 percent or less. Such is not the case in western Europe, where one weapons program is, of economic necessity, designed to meet both domestic and foreign market requirements.

The Carter years represented a novel experiment in arms sales restraint. While critics found numerous contradictions with the President's policy, there is no doubt that it focused attention on the broader political, military-security, and ethical implications of arms sales, and that it encouraged public debate over an issue that had been the prerogative of the executive branch. Unfortunately, even if the United States policy had effectively limited the spread of advanced weaponry, Carter found it impossible to enlist the support of other arms-exporting nations in this ambitious endeavor.

In contrast to Jimmy Carter, Ronald Reagan had few qualms about arms sales as a tool of American foreign policy. Indeed, during the first years of his presidency, the budget for foreign military sales (FMS) increased by almost 50 percent, from a Carter-era low of 10 billion dollars in fiscal year 1980 to a Reagan-era high of 14.6 billion dollars in fiscal year 1983. Reagan rejected his predecessor's "exceptionalism" and instead argued that "the United States must . . . be prepared to help its friends and allies . . . through the transfer of conventional arms and other forms of security assistance." [24] The President also rescinded the leprosy letter, stating that arms salespeople should receive from U.S. embassies the "traditional courtesies." Concretely, the President demonstrated his resolve by approving the sale of advanced AWACS air surveillance aircraft to Saudi Arabia shortly after taking office, a request that Carter had rejected and one that catalyzed significant debate in Congress.

President Bush has continued the Reagan policy, and following the Iraqi invasion of Kuwait in August 1990, he proposed one of the largest arms sales of recent years—a 20 billion dollar package for Saudi Arabia which would include some of the most advanced weaponry in the U.S. arsenal. Since the fall of the shah, the Saudi regime had been the single biggest purchaser of American weaponry. But the 1990 deal was significant in a number of ways. First, despite traditional support for the Saudi regime, U.S. administrations have generally not sold top-of-the-line equipment to that country, owing to objections from Israel and domestic political concern with the Israeli lobby; recall that arms sales over 14 million dollars can be vetoed by the Senate. Indeed, to mute congressional opposition, the President broke down the 20 billion dollar sale into several different packages. Second, it appeared that the Saudis were diversifying their arms purchases away from the United States, turning most dramatically to Britain for the "arms sale of the century," the 9 billion dollar "Al Yamamah" purchase of Tornado strike aircraft, Hawk trainers, and other materiel.[25] The 1990 sale by the United States suggested possible Saudi dissatisfaction with the quality of British equipment and training. Finally, the timing of the deal was important for U.S. defense firms, which were facing significant reductions in orders owing to the decline in domestic procurement.

U.S. arms sales take two general forms: first, "security assistance," which encompasses the various American government programs to subsidize weapons sales; and second, "commercial sales," which are deals, mainly for smaller weapons and components, made directly between U.S. companies and foreign

Table 6-2 U.S. Foreign Military and Commercial Sales, 1980–1989 (dollars in millions)

	Commercial Export Deliveries	FMS Agreements	Total	Commercial as a Percent of Total
1980	1,968	12,431	14,400	13.67%
1981	2,198	6,409	8,608	25.54
1982	1,802	16,824	18,626	9.67
1983	918	14,560	15,478	5.93
1984	3,269	13,350	16,619	19.67
1985	5,256	10,678	15,934	32.99
1986	4,344	6,732	11,077	30.22
1987	5,319	6,834	12,153	43.77
1988	7,986	12,094	20,080	39.77
1989	4,369	10,864	15,233	28.68

Source: Department of Defense.

Figure 6-1 Foreign Military Sales, by Equipment Type, 1980–1989

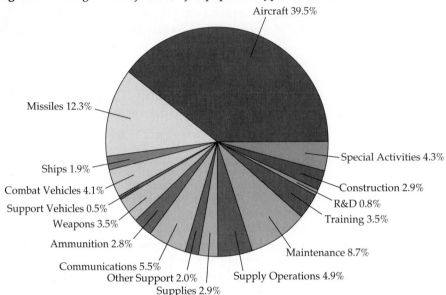

Source: Defense Security Administration Agency.

defense ministries (see Table 6-2). Commercial sales constitute the smaller share of arms exports, accounting for 29 percent of sales in 1989; this was down from a postwar peak of almost 44 percent, achieved in 1987.

Table 6-2 and Figure 6-1 provide data on foreign military sales (FMS) and commercial sales.[26] The figures reveal that aircraft are by far the largest export item, constituting about 40 percent of overall sales. Missiles come next, with 12 percent of sales. A variety of systems, along with training and maintenance, make up the remainder.

Security assistance comes in several forms, including the Foreign Military Sales program, which makes loans and grants for the purchase of American hardware; the Economic Support Fund, which basically provides financing for Egypt and Israel; and the International Military Education and Training program, which brings foreign military officers to the United States. The total value of these programs has run about 20 billion dollars per year during the 1980s, and about 8 billion dollars of this sum has gone to the middle east, principally Israel and Egypt. Other major beneficiaries of these programs include Pakistan, Turkey, and Greece. It is important to note that all grants and credits for military purchases are counted as part of U.S. foreign aid; there is no separate military aid account in the federal budget.

Commercial sales, in contrast, must be approved by the State Department, but the Senate can veto sales of over 14 million dollars. The Senate debate over arms sales to such countries as Saudi Arabia and Jordan has often become acrimonious, as protagonists lobby on behalf of various middle east regimes, arms suppliers, arms controllers, and so forth. By placing veto power in the hands of the Senate, Congress has increased its authority over the arms sales process.

Ironically, the United States has undermined its own position as an arms exporter owing to its role over the years as a vendor of defense-industrial capability (for more on this, see Chapter 7).[27] By engaging in coproduction and codevelopment of major weapons systems, in which armaments are produced jointly by American and one or more foreign firms, the United States diffused defense production capacity and technology to other countries. The beneficiaries of this policy have included not only the allies in western Europe and Japan, but many developing countries as well, including such prominent arms manufacturers as Israel, South Korea, Brazil, Taiwan, and India.[28]

The data on FMS agreements by purchaser are suggestive of the changing nature of the arms trade. As late as fiscal year 1984, NATO-Europe countries imported a substantial share of American armaments. Sales in the 1980s were in large part a reflection of the F-16 Fighting Falcon coproduction agreement with the European participating governments—the Netherlands, Denmark, Norway,

U.S. Troops in the Persian Gulf: Would they have fought here had arms sales to Iraq been halted earlier?

(AP/Wide World Photos)

and Belgium. But as the F-16 program ended, the United States discovered that it had no major replacement that the Europeans were willing to buy. The allies were increasingly "going it alone" in weapons design and development. As a result, U.S. arms sales shifted to the middle east.

At present, U.S. firms are nervous about the future of export markets for several reasons. First, many countries are "defecting" from American hardware, as competitors in Europe and the Soviet Union offer their wares at low prices. Such clients as Malaysia and Saudi Arabia, for example, have purchased an increasing amount of hardware from western Europe. Second, the United States has lost some important sales because buyers do not want to become embroiled in heated congressional debates over approval. Finally, the number of arms producers has increased dramatically in recent years, causing an overall decline in the size of the "off-the-shelf" market. Now, defense manufacturers must offer offsets or other coproduction or codevelopment incentives in order to secure a sale.[29] Mitigating these trends, however, was the exceptional performance of U.S. weapons during Operation Desert Storm.

At a time of a cyclical downturn in domestic defense spending, it is particularly troubling for U.S. firms to see the erosion of foreign markets. The largest military export item, aircraft, has steadily dropped from a 1987 foreign sales peak of 3.6 billion dollars to a 1990 level of 1.4 billion dollars. The Department of Defense projects foreign military sales of aircraft to total only 1.5 billion dollars in 1994 (in constant 1988 dollars), for near zero growth.[30] Defense executives hope that in the wake of the Gulf War, new market opportunities for their wares will arise.

Yet given the crisis in Iraq, the President will have a difficult time sustaining a policy of sending arms to middle east allies on the one hand, while seeking multilateral controls on the spread of weaponry on the other. The Tripartite Agreement of 1950 notwithstanding, previous efforts at multilateral control have had some effectiveness, especially in the area of nuclear technology. Attempts to control the proliferation of ballistic missile technology have also met with success, as the United States and its major allies have agreed to establish multilateral restrictions.[31] The United States has acted as the leader in creating any number of international regimes since the end of World War II, and it is certainly plausible to imagine that arms transfer policy will evolve in this direction as well.

OTHER COUNTRIES

As Table 6-1 suggests, the United States hardly dominates the arms trade. The Soviet Union, France, and Britain also have enjoyed substantial market share, and the industrial countries have been joined in recent years by such newcomers as Brazil, South Korea, and Israel. In this section we will examine the arms transfer policies of some of these other countries, by way of comparison with the American regime in this issue area.

It appears from the data that no country benefits more from arms sales than the Soviet Union. Sales have averaged over 21 billion dollars per year over the past five years and have constituted more than one-fifth of total Soviet exports. While a large portion of these sales are made on generous credit terms, with little hope of cash repayment, the hard-currency impact on the Soviet balance sheet should not be minimized. Sales to oil-exporting countries like Iraq, Libya, and Algeria have traditionally been made for cash, providing the Soviets with the dollars needed to purchase food and capital goods on world markets. The collapse of the Soviet domestic economy may even place more pressure on defense industries to seek export markets in the 1990s.

The Stockholm International Peace Research Institute argues that "the bulk of Soviet exports . . . are delivered to a very small group of clients." [32] In addition to the traditional postwar market in eastern Europe, the Soviets sell to about twenty clients in the developing world, among them Angola, India, Iraq, Libya, and Syria. The Soviet relationship with India is of particular interest since this is the only developing country that has been permitted to engage in coproduction of MiG aircraft. According to a 1989 report in *Time* magazine, Moscow has even considered codevelopment agreements with India, in which the two countries would jointly conduct weapons research and produce entirely new systems.[33]

Apparently, Moscow is less satisfied with many of its other client relationships, as the Kremlin accumulates unpaid credits from third world states. Some western analysts believe that the economic crisis in the Soviet Union will force that country to decrease arms sales on a credit basis and instead shift to cash sales. In the process of shifting to a "cash on the barrel" approach, the Soviets may even increase their marketing efforts in western countries, a development that would have been impossible to imagine even a few years ago.

Yet it will not be easy for the Soviets to make this shift. In fact, arms are not generally sold for cash; instead such sales are financed by some combination of firms and governments. Given the economic crisis in the Soviet Union, and the likelihood that it will become increasingly difficult for Moscow to obtain untied credits from western banks, defense salespeople may find it difficult to compete with such countries as the United States and France which still offer generous financing packages.

Whereas the Soviet Union, like the United States, has been motivated in the past largely by foreign policy rather than by economic considerations in its arms transfer policies, can the same be said of France? Analysts have frequently chastised France for its "irresponsibile" arms sales. After all, didn't France supply Iraq with a nuclear reactor and with a wide array of advanced weapons, including Mirage jet aircraft? Hasn't France exchanged arms for oil? Indeed, aren't French defense firms heavily dependent on export sales? The aerospace firm Dassault, for example, manufacturer of the famed Mirage aircraft, exported over 70 percent of its production in 1988, and 32 percent of total French defense production was exported that year.[34] Doesn't this dependence on foreign markets drive French arms transfer policy?

In fact, dispassionate analysis of the French case forces us to adopt a more nuanced view of its arms transfer policies. To begin with, even a superficial knowledge of history suggests that France, like other great powers, has used arms transfers as an active tool of foreign policy. Paris, for example, was Israel's major arms supplier from the 1950s up to the Six Day War of 1967 largely because France opposed Egyptian President Nasser's support of Algerian rebels. France also has consistently supplied arms to its former colonies in Africa, despite their frequent inability to pay cash. Thus, it is incorrect to assert that France has only been motivated by commercial considerations.

A careful student of French policy, Edward Kolodziej, suggests that "arms sales have served several masters." [35] To be sure, commercial considerations have influenced policy decisions. But when one examines "the amount, composition, and timing of arms transferred to a particular state—or the French refusal to respond to outside requests," [36] it becomes evident that broader policy considerations are at work. French arms sales in Africa, for instance, have served to bolster France's influence in the francophone region of that continent. Similarly, French sales in Saharan Africa appear dominated by foreign policy rather than mere economic considerations. [37]

What exactly are the "broader" foreign policy interests that France has pursued with its arms transfer agreements? Perhaps the most compelling, according to a former French defense official, has been to "offer a certain number of countries an alternative to the choice between the United States and the Soviet Union and thus to re-enforce our position in the world and our weight in certain regions." [38] Arms sales must be seen as part and parcel of France's larger "project" to become an independent pole in international politics.

During the 1970s, arms sales were also used to develop closer relations with Arab oil-exporting states. In 1974, for example, France signed its largest arms deals with Saudi Arabia and Iran—its major oil suppliers. According to Andrew Pierre, "Although arms-for-oil [was] never officially acknowledged as policy, the assurance of future supplies of oil [was] clearly an important motivation for French leaders." [39] It is significant, however, that France halted arms exports to Jordan and Iraq during the Persian Gulf crisis of 1990–1991, in line with the United Nations embargo; France had been one of Iraq's most important suppliers during its long war with Iran. Whereas, in the past, France may have attempted to act "au contraire" to the United States regarding middle east policy, in this case it signaled its commitment to the anti-Saddam coalition.

As in the case with France, many analysts have argued that Brazil entered the arms sales business solely for commercial reasons. During the 1980s, Brazil "hit the charts" as the tenth largest arms supplier, and between 1985 and 1989 it supplied the world with over 2 billion dollars of weaponry. The largest percentage of these sales went to Iraq and the pariah state of Libya. It appeared that Brazil had a particularly cynical approach to arms trafficking, selling without regard to how the weapons might be used.

But this view, as in the French case, overlooks the broader policy goal fashioned in Brasília during the 1970s. Specifically, Brazil has sought to become *primus inter pares* in the developing world and a regional hegemon in Latin America. Arms sales are a manifestation of Brazil's desire to become an independent force in world politics, a force that must be respected at the bilateral and multilateral levels. [40]

This is not meant to understate the commercialization of arms sales in Brazil. The Ministry of Foreign Affairs has played an active role in seeking opportunities for the country's defense industries, and diplomats have basically served as sales representatives. In negotiations with foreign defense ministries, the government has told potential buyers that, unlike the United States or the U.S.S.R., Brazil views arms sales as commercial transactions. A brochure from the defense firm Engesa expresses well the underlying philosophy: "Engesa as a true ally neither creates dependence nor imposes commitments."

While the Brazilian government has been criticized for its "no strings attached" arms policy, and while its declaratory policy is not to use exports as an instrument of foreign policy, all sales must be approved by a government body, PNEMEN. According to PNEMEN's guidelines, Brazil will not sell arms to guerrilla groups, to both sides of a conflict, to unstable governments, or to states on the brink of war. The rigor with which these guidelines are enforced remains an open question.

During the 1980s, Brazil exported weapons to some forty countries, with sales concentrated in the middle east. Unfortunately for the country's arms manufacturers, the end of the Iran-Iraq war and the lessening of tension in other regional conflicts (e.g., Angola) have sharply eroded their sales volume. In 1990, two major industries, Engesa and Avibras, filed for protection from creditors, in part owing to unpaid Iraqi war debts. During the boom years of the mid-1980s, however, arms exports were a major dollar earner for the country, and these dollars were vital to the country's economic health.

Today, the arms market is characterized by intense competition. As Anthony Jurkus writes, "Not only are more countries attempting their own [weapons] development and production, but marketing arrangements appear to favor the buyer." [41] Whereas in the past, weapons were generally sold "off-the-shelf," today an increasing percentage are being sold in terms of offset arrangements and coproduction deals. The influence of these changing terms of defense trade on international security remains to be seen, but it is hard to imagine how the proliferation of defense-industrial capability will promote regional stability. For some time now, the arms trade has been viewed as a genie that escaped the bottle, and there is little prospect of the genie's containment.

CONCLUSION

With the end of the cold war, the arms market began to cool at a time when the number of producers was higher than ever in postwar history. This situation must lead to market saturation, lower prices, and, ironically, the diffusion of even greater military capability around the world—if no controls are put into place. At the same time, the costs associated with arms production have been rising, and if states refuse to subsidize these industries, a large number of them must fail in the absence of foreign sales. The contraction of the international arms market will force defense officials to make difficult choices about industrial adjustment.

Until recently, talk of a multilateral regime to control the arms trade has been met with general skepticism. Following the Carter experiment in the United States, unilateral efforts to curb transfers have also been abandoned. In the 1990s, given the number of producers, along with the industry economics, arms sales would seem impossible to stop or even contain.

But Saddam Hussein's "wake-up call" has alerted the world to the immense dangers associated with arms trafficking. In light of the Persian Gulf crisis of 1990–1991, the United States may be expected to use its weight in world affairs to begin the long journey toward multilateralism in this issue area. Clearly, armaments represents one of the few sectors that the United States wishes to exempt from the liberal principles of free trade. An important question, however, is whether defense capabilities can be controlled in a world where industrial and technological processes are becoming truly global.

Selected Bibliography

Adams, James, *Engines of War: Merchants of Death and the Arms Race* (New York: Atlantic Monthly Press, 1990). This well-written account is by a journalist for the *Financial Times*.

Klare, Michael, *American Arms Supermarket* (Austin: University of Texas Press, 1984). Klare's book is a critical yet comprehensive account of U.S. arms transfer policies.

Pierre, Andrew, *The Global Politics of Arms Sales* (Princeton, N.J.: Princeton University Press, 1982). This is still the best introduction to the topic; one hopes that it will be updated.

U.S. Arms Control and Disarmament Agency, *World Military Expenditures and Arms Transfers* (published annually). This is the most reliable statistical source.

Notes

1. Eric Ambler, *Journey into Fear* (New York: Carroll & Graf, 1937), p. 114.
2. See, for example, *The New Republic*, December 3, 1990.
3. Cited in John Stanley and Maurice Pearton, *The International Trade in Arms* (New York: Praeger, 1972), pp. 3–4.
4. On the new entrants and the problem of defense-industrial proliferation, see James Adams, *Engines of War: Merchants of Death and the Arms Race* (New York: Atlantic Monthly Press, 1990).
5. Gowri Sundaram, "De Facto De-Regulation of the Arms Trade," *International Defense Review* 19, 4:4 (1986).

6. U.S. Arms Control and Disarmament Agency, *World Military Expenditures and Arms Transfers 1988* (Washington, D.C.: Government Printing Office, 1989).

7. *International Trade: 1986/87* (Geneva: General Agreement on Tariffs and Trade, 1987), p. 155.

8. Lisa Grobar, Robert Stern, and Alan Deardorff, "The Economic Effects of International Trade in Armaments in the Major Western Industrialized and Developing Countries," March 23, 1989, processed.

9. See Ulrich Albrecht, "The Federal Republic of Germany and Italy: New Strategies of Mid-Sized Weapons Exporters," *Journal of International Affairs* 40 (Summer 1986).

10. I am grateful to Dr. Todd Laporte of the Office of Technology Assessment, U.S. Congress, for this suggestion.

11. Richard V. Allen, "Conventional Arms Transfer Policy," the White House, July 8, 1981.

12. The best overviews of arms export policy remain Andrew Pierre, *The Global Politics of Arms Sales* (Princeton, N.J.: Princeton University Press, 1982), and Michael Klare, *American Arms Supermarket* (Austin: University of Texas Press, 1984).

13. See Roger Labrie et al., *U.S. Arms Sales Policy: Background and Issues* (Washington, D.C.: American Enterprise Institute, 1982), p. 13.

14. Ibid.

15. Lord Ismay, *NATO: The First Five Years* (Utrecht: Bosch, 1954), p. 125.

16. Labrie, *U.S. Arms Sales*, p. 8.

17. Ibid.

18. Ibid.; see also Paul Hammond et al., *The Reluctant Supplier* (Cambridge, Mass.: Oelgeschlager, Gunn & Hain, 1983).

19. See Lucy Wilson Benson, "Turning the Supertanker: Arms Transfer Restraint," *International Security* 3 (1978–1979): 3–17.

20. Adapted from Pierre, *Global Politics*, pp. 52–53.

21. Paul Ferrari et al., *U.S. Arms Exports* (Cambridge, Mass.: Ballinger, 1988), p. 42.

22. Anthony Jurkus, "Requiem for a Lightweight: The Northrop F-20 Strategic Initiative," *Strategic Management Journal* 2 (1990): 59–68.

23. Ibid.

24. Quoted in ibid., p. 53.

25. For an account of the sale, see John Newhouse, "Politics and Weapons Sales," *The New Yorker*, June 9, 1986, pp. 46–69.

26. Figures provided by the Defense Security Administration Agency, 1990.

27. See *Arming Our Allies* (Washington, D.C.: Office of Technology Assessment, 1990).

28. See Klare, *American Arms Supermarket*, and Adams, *Engines of War*.

29. See Richard Stevenson, "No Longer the Only Game in Town," *New York Times*, December 4, 1988, p. D1.

30. Interview with Department of Defense official, November 1990.

31. Arthur Manfredi et al., *Ballistic Missile Proliferation Potential of Non-Major Powers* (Washington, D.C.: Congressional Research Service), April 1987.

32. SIPRI, *SIPRI Yearbook: 1989* (Oxford: Oxford University Press, 1989), p. 200.

33. Ross Munro, "Superpower Rising," *Time*, April 3, 1989, pp. 10–17.

34. Dassault, *Annual Report 1989; French Defense Statistics, 1989* (Ministry of Defense, 1989).

35. Edward Kolodziej, *Making and Marketing Arms* (Princeton, N.J.: Princeton University Press, 1987), p. 391.

36. Ibid.

37. Ibid.

38. Henri Conze, "Avenir des Exportations d'Armement," Paris, processed, n.d.
39. Pierre, *Global Politics*, p. 84.
40. For a more detailed discussion of Brazil, see Ethan B. Kapstein, "The Brazilian Defense Industry and the International System," *Political Science Quarterly*, Winter 1990.
41. Jurkus, "Requiem for a Lightweight."

7

Economic Relations among Military Allies

"The Parties . . . will seek to eliminate conflict in their international economic policies and will encourage economic collaboration between any or all of them." ——Article II, North Atlantic Treaty, April 4, 1949
"The only thing common in NATO is the air in the tires." ——NATO Secretary General Lord Carrington, 1987

Military alliances are created when states do not possess sufficient power to maintain their national security on their own. The crucial tie that binds allies is fear of a common enemy, rather than a set of common values. The members of the coalition that opposed Iraq's invasion of Kuwait in August 1990, for example, were as diverse a group of nations as one could imagine. In the words of Hans Morgenthau, the creation of alliances is "not a matter of principle but of expediency." [1]

Since April 1949, the United States has been bound with western Europe in a military alliance and has had mutual security treaties with Japan and other states. The historic purpose of the North Atlantic Treaty Organization (NATO) (and other Western alliances) has been to deter Soviet aggression and, should deterrence fail, to defeat enemy forces.

The western alliance has been faced with a number of complex economic problems in carrying out its military mission. In this chapter, we will deal with three enduring issues: first, the long-standing effort of NATO to field an arsenal characterized by rationalization, standardization, and interoperability (RSI); second, the infamous burden-sharing debate; and third, the collective effort to control the export of technology to the Soviet bloc and other adversaries. Each of these has proved to be divisive within the alliance, and for nearly two generations a policy resolution has eluded statesmen. Indeed, alliance differences over

161

economic issues provide insights into the sharp strategic conflicts that have divided the member states since 1949, despite their common treaty obligations.[2]

Some readers may feel that these issues are now only of historical interest and no longer speak to contemporary concerns. This view would be incorrect on two counts. From a theoretical perspective, the three substantive issues that we treat here may be viewed in terms of the provision of collective goods in international organizations. Collective or public goods, it will be recalled, are goods characterized by two features: (1) nonexcludability and (2) nonrivalry of consumption. Once the collective good has been provided, all consumers may enjoy it, whether they have paid for it or not. Further, the consumption of the good by one does not diminish the enjoyment available to another.

As we will see in this chapter, a persistent issue within the alliance, and in international organizations more generally, has been the unilateral provision of collective goods by the United States (e.g., nuclear deterrence), with a consequent desire on the part of the United States to get other states to pay more of their "fair share." The broader questions are: If one state, motivated by its own national interests, is *willing* to provide public goods and to play the hegemon, why should other states volunteer to share the burden? and How can collective burdens be equitably shared? These are significant questions outside the NATO framework; indeed, they have been asked sharply with regard to the anti-Saddam coalition.

Second, beyond their theoretical interest, the issues discussed here are also of continuing policy-relevance. Regarding western armaments policy, it has been argued in recent years that the decline in defense budgets, combined with the rising costs associated with new weapons systems, will place greater pressure on nation-states to restructure their defense industries and engage in collaborative armaments production with friends and allies. In that the alliance experience provides useful lessons concerning arms collaboration, it is worthy of study, whether the alliance endures in its present form or not.

The issue of burden sharing pertains to every alliance and international organization, and it has been a prominent issue in the anti-Iraq coalition that formed in 1990. Senator Jim Sasser of Tennessee, for example, claimed that the "Bush Administration, preoccupied with forging international support for the use of American force in the Gulf, has given scant attention to the question of who will pay. It has . . . exerted minimal pressure on our allies to pay up."[3] In fact, the administration gave considerable thought to the question of "who will pay" (see Tables 7-1 and 7-2). But clearly, burden-sharing debates will not go away even if NATO does so.

Finally, the problem of export controls, which one might have expected to disappear with the end of the cold war, endures, as the industrial states debate how to cope with the proliferation of biological, chemical, and nuclear weapons in the developing world, along with the spread of ballistic missiles and other advanced weapons technologies. Again, the Iraqi crisis has placed renewed emphasis on the need for export controls on defense-related technologies.

Table 7-1 Gulf Crisis Financial Assistance (in billions of dollars as of March 1991)

Donor	Total Commitment	Egypt/ Turkey/ Jordan	Humanitarian	Other
Gulf States	$ 9.5	$ 6.1	$0.2	$3.2
European Community	2.7	2.4	0.1	0.2
Japan	2.1	2.0	0.1	0.0
Others	1.3	0.3	0.2	0.8
TOTAL	15.6	10.8	0.6	4.2

Source: U.S. Department of the Treasury.

RATIONALIZATION, STANDARDIZATION, AND INTEROPERABILITY

Since its inception, NATO has sought to transform its ragtag collection of troops and weapons into a united force capable of coalition warfare. In terms of weapons systems, this transformation has required that NATO seek to achieve rationalization, standardization, and interoperability. NATO leaders have long presumed that RSI would bring the alliance both economic and military benefits, as duplicative research and production were eliminated and as fielded systems reflected *alliance* rather than *national* requirements.

The terms by which RSI would be achieved, however, have been the subject of significant debate within NATO. In the early postwar years, RSI was easy to advance, as European countries depended on imports of U.S. weapons in order to equip their decimated armed forces. Indeed, on April 5, 1949, the day after the North Atlantic Treaty was signed in Washington, D.C., the European member states submitted a formal request for military and financial assistance to the

Table 7-2 Estimated Costs of Desert Shield/Desert Storm (in millions of dollars)

Contributor to U.S.	Commitments
Saudi Arabia	$16,800
Kuwait	16,000
UAE	3,000
Japan	10,700
Germany	6,600
Korea	385
Others	3
Sub-Total	53,488
Direct U.S. Costs	17,000
Direct Allied Costs	16,000
TOTAL COSTS	86,488

Sources: Author's estimates; U.S. Department of Defense.

(AP/Wide World Photos)

NATO Headquarters: Article 2 of the North Atlantic Treaty calls on the allies to collaborate on economic issues.

United States. By May 1954, the United States had shipped to Europe over 15 billion dollars' worth of defense equipment and materiel.[4]

At the same time, the United States instituted a program of "offshore" procurement under the Mutual Defense Assistance Program. Under this program, the United States purchased defense materiel for its allies from offshore (i.e., non-American) suppliers. The objectives of offshore procurement were to develop the European armaments industries, to bolster the European economy, and in some cases to take advantage of lower production and/or transportation costs buying weapons and materiel for American forces based in Europe.

The late 1950s and early 1960s brought about a change in U.S. policy toward RSI. Exports of American weapons to western Europe had been dropping precipitously, from a high-water mark in 1953 of 15 billion dollars to a level in 1962 of only 3 billion dollars. The Europeans had been successful in rebuilding their armaments capabilities and now had less need to import American systems.

In order to win sales in an increasingly competitive market, U.S. firms promised *coproduction* of weapons systems with their European counterparts; this meant that some of the assembly work on new weaponry would occur in European plants. As a result of America's willingness to coproduce weapons systems, U.S. dominance in the NATO weapons market was maintained, even as the United States was sharing technology and production techniques with potential competitors.[5]

A prominent example of these new arrangements and their competitive value for U.S. defense industries was the German decision to purchase the American Starfighter aircraft in the late 1950s over a competing design from the French manufacturer Dassault. Although the decision was embedded in broader security issues, the choice of the Lockheed design was made in part owing to the coproduction deal that the company offered. This included substantial technology transfer and German assembly of the aircraft from Lockheed blueprints. By the time the Starfighter program began to wind down in the mid-1960s, West Germany had developed the capacity to manufacture—though not yet to develop—advanced military aircraft.[6]

The growth in armaments capability in western Europe had both positive and negative elements. On the positive side, the creation of a defense-industrial infrastructure in Europe enlarged the mobilization capacity available to the alliance in case of war or crisis, and went a long way toward building a "second pillar" of western security. But, conversely, the overlap in weapons programs and the lack of RSI resulted in a tremendous waste of financial resources and military inefficiency that could prove fatal in combat. An influential report by Thomas Callaghan of the Center for Strategic and International Studies in Washington, published in 1974, asserted that NATO RSI could lead to alliance-wide acquisition savings of over 10 billion dollars per year, not to mention the increase in military effectiveness.[7]

The expansion of defense industries had another malign effect as well. Now, European countries were in a position to export advanced weapons to

The F-16: Selling this plane to western Europe was called the "deal of the century."

(Department of Defense)

third world states, not all of which were viewed as reliable security partners by the United States. NATO armaments policy thus began to entail a severe dilemma for the United States, as public officials had to trade off the gains provided by greater defense industrialization against the costs associated with the proliferation of equipment, decreased foreign sales for American firms, and increased exports to the third world by European producers.

Callaghan argued that NATO arms procurement should be based on the notion of a *two-way street*; that is, the United States should purchase weapons from Europe just as Europe had always relied on the United States. This would require the development of a "North Atlantic common defense market" in which European states would cooperate to build weapons, thereby combining their scattered resources and building in the process a united second pillar. A strong Europe could then compete with the United States to build advanced weapons, and the NATO armaments directors could determine which design best fit their military requirements.

In the summer of 1975, Secretary of Defense James Schlesinger articulated a new weapons policy for NATO that embodied the notion of the "two-way street." Schlesinger told Congress that the United States must work to develop a competitive market for defense hardware in the NATO orbit, and this meant that the United States must be willing to import European systems. According to Schlesinger, a two-way street would (1) promote NATO RSI, (2) develop American *and* European technological strength, (3) encourage the creation of independent, competitive national weapons programs, (4) increase U.S. purchases of European military hardware, and (5) increase European purchases of U.S. defense technology on the basis of coproduction. In July, Congress adopted the two-way street under the guise of the Culver-Nunn amendment, which "declared it to be national policy that weapons and equipment . . . shall be standardized or at least interoperable with the equipment of its NATO allies. . . ." [8] The United States would begin forthwith to increase its "side-by-side" testing of European and American hardware and would purchase foreign systems if proved superior.

At the same time as the two-way street was being declared official policy, the "deal of the century" was dramatically announced by the U.S. defense firm General Dynamics (GD). This entailed coproduction by four European participating governments (EPGs—Belgium, Denmark, the Netherlands, and Norway) of GD's F-16 lightweight fighter aircraft, which had recently been adopted by the U.S. Air Force. The F-16 program gave the EPGs access to advanced technology, the construction of two assembly lines in western Europe (in Belgium and the Netherlands), and a multitude of contracts for European aerospace suppliers. According to the GD official responsible for business development, the co-production deal led to "a number of innovative international business arrangements, which . . . include direct and indirect offsets, development of foreign suppliers, creation of joint ventures, and licensed production and co-development." [9]

The F-16 program effectively segmented NATO's jet aircraft market into three pieces: the EPGs that purchased the plane; the French, who remained autonomous in aircraft production; and the major allies (Britain, West Germany, and Italy) who had collaborated to codevelop and produce a multirole combat aircraft, named Tornado. Cynical European observers deemed that this is exactly what the United States sought to do: to divide and conquer the marketplace. By engaging at least some NATO countries in attractive coproduction deals, the United States could weaken major competitors and retain dominance over European industries.

On February 2, 1976, at least partly as a response to the F-16 deal, France joined the members of NATO-Europe in the creation of an *Independent European Programme Group* (IEPG). The objectives of IEPG were to strengthen European armaments industries, increase American purchases of European equipment, and promote standardization of weaponry *among the IEPG members*. The creation of the IEPG demonstrated a European commitment to the protection of domestic defense industries, in spite of competitive pressure from U.S. firms.[10]

With the formation of the IEPG, the United States government fully realized that NATO RSI would not be implemented unilaterally, but must be the product of joint efforts between American and European defense industries. In May 1985, Senator Sam Nunn of Georgia, the chairman of the Senate Armed Services Committee, introduced an amendment to the fiscal year 1986 Department of Defense Authorization Act, which called upon the United States and its NATO allies to build weapons *collaboratively*, from the initial stages of R&D up to production and procurement. The *Nunn amendment* set aside a pool of funds from the defense budget for such collaborative ventures, and at the same time the then senator from Indiana, Dan Quayle, added an amendment that would require the Department of Defense to conduct more *side-by-side testing* of U.S. and European weapons. The Nunn and Quayle amendments were designed to promote RSI while recognizing Europe's desire to maintain autonomous capabilities in defense.

In recent years, a number of collaborative approaches to western arms procurement have arisen. Underlying almost all collaborative approaches, however, is a desire on the part of each government involved to retain and enhance indigenous defense capabilities. Ironically, while collaboration has often been touted as a way to cut the costs associated with weapons development, the methods in practice today often result in higher overall expenses, since multinational projects maintain inefficient production in many countries (although the cost of the weapon *per country* may be less than if the country developed the system on its own). If the alliance had trade in weapons on the basis of comparative advantage rather than collaboration, more systems would be sold "off the shelf" rather than coproduced.

The debate over the costs and benefits associated with arms collaboration boiled over in 1989 during the U.S. government's consideration of a new jet fighter program with Japan. The FSX (fighter support/experimental) would be a modified version of the General Dynamics F-16 but would be codeveloped with Japan to incorporate new technology. Supporters of the program argued that in a competitive defense economy, General Dynamics had gotten the best deal it could from the Japanese. But critics said that the United States was giving away critical military and aviation technology that could help Japan develop its domestic aerospace industry.

Among the most common methods of arms collaboration found with the alliance today are *offsets, subsystem specialization, coproduction*, and *codevelopment*; one method that was heralded as having promise, but has seen few successes, is the *family-of-weapons* concept. Each is briefly described below.

Offsets "refers to a range of industrial or commercial compensation practices that are required as a condition of sale for military related exports." [11] Given the competitive nature of the contemporary arms market, buyers have been able to demand any number of services from sellers as part of a weapons package. Thus, a foreign government might demand that an American firm purchase components for an aircraft that it is buying from domestic suppliers, or build an assembly line in the country, or promise to use domestic subcontractors in future programs. These offsets have become one of the prominent costs associated with doing business abroad.[12]

Offsets have increasingly become a contentious political issue in the United States. It has been argued that owing to weapons sales based on offsets, U.S. subcontractors, or second- and third-tier suppliers to the primes, have lost their traditional markets. Owing to offset agreements, foreigners now have a lock on many inputs to the final defense product. Indeed, while the U.S. government has in the past refused to engage directly in offset negotiations, this is now changing, owing to domestic political pressure. The Commerce Department now has the authority to review memoranda of understanding that outline an arms sales package and to determine whether domestic firms are unduly harmed as a result. In one instance—a proposed McDonnell Douglas sale of the F/A-18 to South Korea—Congress actually placed quantitative restrictions on the offset package that would be permitted.

Subsystem specialization is an alternative form of international weapons agreement, and it holds the promise of being a more economically efficient approach to arms collaboration. It requires the partners in a weapons program to divide the work among themselves and then specialize in the production of a particular component. As Shannon Hurley correctly observes, "The extent of the savings realized depends on the extent to which the location of the production line is chosen by virtue of technical skill, location, or other qualification." [13]

Coproduction and codevelopment have already been described. Coproduction refers to arrangements, like the F-16 program, whereby foreign countries have the right to produce a weapons system under license from the prime contractor. Codevelopment refers to Nunn amendment and similar programs, whereby two or more countries agree to develop a weapon jointly, from the earliest stages of R&D through to production.

As noted above, yet another approach to NATO arms procurement that came in with a bang but appears to be fading with a whimper is the family-of-weapons concept. A weapons family refers to a number of weapons that are strategically linked. For example, a family of missiles would include ground-to-air and air-to-air variants, or missiles that serve antipersonnel, antiarmor, and antiaircraft functions. Under this concept, a group of countries would agree to produce the entire family, with each country specializing in one system and buying the others from their collaborators. While the family concept appears to offer advantages to participants on paper—for example, technology sharing, division of burdens, assured markets—in practice few successful cases exist.

In the early 1990s, the future of alliance arms collaboration and RSI appears to be no clearer than that of the alliance itself. NATO and what remains of the Warsaw Pact are currently engaged in wide-ranging talks concerning conventional forces in Europe, and the outcome of these negotiations will have important implications for defense procurement. Important categories of weapons systems, such as tanks and fighter aircraft, will be greatly reduced in numbers. As the cold war recedes into memory, it is likely that the political pressure on NATO members to engage in RSI will diminish. Further, as the FSX controversy suggests, there is a growing sentiment in the U.S. Congress that arms collaboration may benefit economic competitors more than it strengthens alliance relations.[14]

Ironically, however, economic pressures are pushing in the opposite direction. After a generation of coproduction and codevelopment deals, multinational defense firms have created complex linkages that cannot readily be interrupted. These linkages run the gamut from the modest sourcing of foreign components to shared research and development. Thus, while the Nunn amendment promise of collaborative NATO weapons may go largely unfulfilled, it is probable that industry-to-industry cooperation will endure. Further, the economics of military production, including the rising "up-front" costs associated with R&D, the high cost of capital to the industry, and the comparative advantage of certain countries in the production of weapons-related components, make it essential for those states that are determined to maintain indigenous arms industries to form partnerships in order to lower costs, to spread technical and financial risks, and to access advanced technology.

In sum, NATO may be moving toward the formation of an integrated defense industry that produces collaborative products. To be sure, this structure is less efficient than one characterized by an alliance division of labor based on comparative advantage, and it reflects what may be called a "second-best" world in which politics no less than economics makes industrial decisions. But in the second-best world of defense production, collaboration among multinational industries is preferable to wasteful competition by nation-states and the complete closure of domestic markets to foreign firms.

BURDEN SHARING

No economic question has dominated NATO since 1949 more than *burden sharing*, or the allocation of collective defense spending on an equitable basis. During the early 1980s, with growing perceptions of American decline, the issue became particularly contentious in the United States. In 1983, Senator Sam Nunn of Georgia, chairman of the Senate Armed Services Committee, proposed an amendment to the Department of Defense budget that would have cut U.S. troop levels in Europe unless the allies increased their defense spending.

With the end of the cold war and the changing security order in Europe, it might be thought that burden sharing had become of only historical interest. But to the contrary, burden-sharing disputes are at the heart of every international organization, and have been central, for example, to the economic disputes among the members of the anti-Saddam Hussein coalition that formed in 1990. Senator Jim Sasser, for example, has argued that "every nation with a definable interest in the Persian Gulf should make a contribution that is commensurate with its interest." [15] But how does one assign a dollar amount of contribution to a given amount of national interest? On what basis should charges be assessed? These questions have never been answered, nor are they answered here. Instead, this section seeks to provide a conceptual framework for understanding the burden-sharing debate, using NATO as a case study.

The issue of how NATO should divide the costs associated with collective security was given intensive consideration at the earliest ministerial meetings held in 1950. While it was quickly agreed in theory that the alliance must devise a system akin to progressive taxation, in practice this proved difficult to establish. To begin with, at that time no accurate measures existed for comparing the GNPs of different countries; indeed, this remains an important problem for economists. Crude figures based on, for example, dollar exchange rates were clearly inadequate given the situation in postwar Europe. Further, since many European countries were still devoting a considerable percentage of their defense budget to colonial matters, a debate was raised about whether these funds should be included in the figures of collective security.[16]

In 1951, NATO convened a group of "wise men" (Averell Harriman of the United States, Jean Monnet of France, and Edwin Plowden of the UK) to study the economic problems that faced NATO. These problems had been brought into sharp relief by the North Korean invasion in June 1950 and the fear that an all-out communist offensive against western interests had begun. The wise men presented their report to the alliance leaders who were holding a summit meeting in Lisbon in 1952, and their recommendations provided a new framework for viewing the burden-sharing problem. Since it proved too difficult to establish a common analytical framework for determining adequacy of effort, the NATO leaders instead decided to focus on national contributions based on a division of labor. Thus, the United States would provide the alliance with air power, a nuclear shield, and naval forces; the UK would provide additional naval forces; and the western Europeans would be responsible for the bulk of ground troops. Indeed, at this time western Europe had been contemplating the establishment of a European Defense Community; its ultimate demise, and the failure of the Europeans to agree on troop levels, led the United States to shoulder more of this burden than it had originally intended.[17]

Since the Lisbon meeting, the effort to erect a formal burden-sharing formula has not been repeated. According to Jon Pincus, "After 1952 the adequacy of national defense efforts was examined by NATO annual reviews. It is significant that during the course of these reviews, formal recommendations for increased national defense budgets were never made." [18]

Despite cajoling by the United States for higher defense expenditures from its allies in the ensuing years, NATO-Europe never appeared to deliver the level of effort that was asked of it, or, more important, that was deemed sufficient to achieve the goal of collective security. The failure of NATO to provide sufficient funds to meet its requirements posed a puzzle for policymakers and scholars alike; after all, if member states shared a common interest in security, why didn't they all contribute to it?

In a seminal article published in 1966, economists Mancur Olson and Richard Zeckhauser offered an explanation; indeed, their explanation has provided the conceptual framework for viewing the burden-sharing debate ever since.[19] Building on Olson's 1965 treatise *The Logic of Collective Action*, the economists showed why actors with a common interest mght fail to contribute to the provision of a collective good. The problem, they said, was inherent in the nature of collective goods; once the good is provided (like a lighthouse or nuclear deterrence), nobody can be denied its benefits, whether or not they paid for it.

International organizations, Olson and Zeckhauser said, existed to provide member states with collective goods. However, in the absence of coercive agreements, each state will seek a "free ride" on the goods provided by others; this is why—to give domestic examples—union members are coerced into paying dues and citizens are coerced into paying taxes. In NATO, European states have been able to free-ride on the United States because American defense expenditures are so large on an absolute and relative scale; the marginal value of Luxembourg's defense spending to collective security is small. Since each state views its contribution to the collective defense as insignificant in comparison with the contribution made by the United States, each state has an incentive to provide as little as possible. As the statistics in Table 7-3 show, the United States has consistently been NATO's big spender.

It is important to point out that the central hypothesis generated by Olson and Zeckhauser was that a positive correlation existed between defense expenditure and gross domestic product; in short, larger countries spent more on defense. Since that article was written, however, many scholars have come to question that correlation. As Table 7-3 suggests, relatively small economies like Portugal have spent as much as or more than Germany and Italy as a percentage of gross domestic product. During the 1960s, for example, Portugal was engaged in a costly colonial war in Angola. On the basis of this research, scholars began to emphasize the role of *strategy* rather than *size* in the determination of defense budgets and alliance burdens.[20]

From an alternative perspective, the disproportionate defense spending of the United States reflects not economic size but rather *dominant strategy*—that is, a strategy that will be maintained *no matter what the allies do*. Japan and NATO-Europe do not free-ride on the American defense budget, but rather on American strategy. Since the end of World War II, the United States has been committed to the defense of Japan and western Europe. So long as that commitment is credible, the Japanese and Europeans are given an incentive to free-ride and underspend. Conversely, should the American strategic commitment come into question, one

Table 7-3 NATO Defense Expenditures as a Percentage of
Gross Domestic Product (average for each period)

Country	1970–1974	1975–1979	1980–1984
Belgium	2.9	3.2	3.4
Denmark	2.4	2.4	2.5
France	3.9	3.9	4.1
Germany	3.5	3.4	3.3
Greece	4.7	6.7	6.6
Italy	2.7	2.4	2.6
Luxembourg	0.8	1.0	1.2
Netherlands	3.1	3.2	3.2
Norway	3.3	3.1	2.9
Portugal	6.9	3.9	3.4
Turkey	4.4	5.7	4.8
United Kingdom	5.1	4.9	5.3
Canada	2.1	2.0	2.1
United States	6.6	5.2	6.0

Source: NATO Review 35 (February 1987).

would predict greater European and Japanese efforts to maintain a credible
defense on their own.

Looked at from the perspective of dominant strategy, the burden-sharing
debate becomes a trivial congressional exercise in letting off steam. Threats to
remove troops from western Europe, or other types of sanctions, are bluffs that
will not work unless and until the Europeans believe that the United States no
longer has a strategic interest in maintaining a free European continent. Should
the United States change its strategy with the diminution of the cold war, then the
Europeans and Japanese (who rationally have acted as free riders until now)
would rightfully become anxious about their ability to depend on Washington's
continued largesse.

As an economic problem, however, burden sharing is not without interest;
again, consider the debate that arose during the Gulf War of 1991. The question of
equity of effort in international organizations remains an enduring problem, and
economists still have not come up with formulas that allow us to determine
appropriate contributions. To be sure, even if such calculations were made, the
problem of enforcing contributions would remain. In sum, equity issues are
likely to become more problematic in NATO and other international organizations should the United States withdraw from the leadership position it has
assumed since the end of World War II.

CONTROLLING TRADE

Controls on foreign trade in general, and east-west trade in particular, are of
more than historical interest for three reasons. First, they suggest the dilemmas
posed by the globalization of economic activity on the one hand and the

enduring concern with national security on the other. Second, they elucidate the conflicting national interests that have divided the allies ever since 1949, despite their collective interest in Soviet containment. By exposing these differences, export controls have pointed toward contrasting methods for dealing with the Soviet Union, prominently the contrast between "economic denial" (the preferred U.S. approach) and "co-optation" (the European method). Third, export controls on defense-related technology remain important in the post-cold war environment, as Saddam Hussein reminded all those who might have forgotten.

Two scholars have summarized the conflict in alliance relations over east-west trade as follows: "The problem of Western collaboration on East-West trade," they write, "has its roots in the tension between the principles of free trade (in which all parties benefit), and the principles of international politics (in which each state tries to increase its own benefits from interaction, and thus its own power over others)." [21] Since the end of World War II, the United States has promoted liberal economic values, but until recently their spread was bounded by the "free world." Outside that world lay the communist bloc, which was denied participation in the new international economic order. In short, the United States used economic policy to reward friends and punish adversaries.

Given its reliance on American foreign aid at the war's end, Europe had little choice but to reorient its trade and investment patterns to suit Washington's preferences. But this meant a dramatic shift in commercial relations. Before World War II, the European continent exemplified economic interdependence, as the west shipped capital goods to the east in exchange for agricultural products, raw materials, and energy resources (Romania was a large supplier of petroleum; Poland, an important source of coal). With the emergence of the cold war, politics overtook economics, and Europe turned away from its brothers in the east to its cousin across the Atlantic.

American efforts to win west European support of export controls began in 1948. At this time, the United States developed a list of products that had "strategic significance" and thus should be denied to Soviet bloc countries. Washington urged the Europeans (some would argue that the Europeans were coerced rather than urged) to adopt a similar list, and in November 1949 the allies joined to create the *Coordinating Committee*, known by its acronym, Cocom. [22]

Before proceeding with the history of Cocom, a brief theoretical diversion is in order. As we know from our previous discussion of burden sharing, international organizations exist to provide collective goods. The provision of those goods, however, tends to fall disproportionately on the organization's leader, which places a high value on such goods. Further, there is a tendency of such organizations to provide fewer of such goods than the members would like to consume. In the case of NATO and CoCom, the objective of each has been to provide the west with security; the leader in each case has been the United States.

Oligopoly and cartel theory provides further insights into the behavior of such organizations. As we know, there is a tendency for small states to cheat on agreements that they have struck. Thus, while the allies might agree to boost their defense spending, in fact they don't do it; and while they might agree to withhold strategic goods from the Soviet Union, they sell such goods anyway. To take another prominent example of cartel management, when OPEC members agree on oil quotas at their meetings in Vienna, they usually begin to cheat on the agreements even before they return home.

What explains such behavior? The theory of collective action provides us with some insights. Since each state in an organization views itself as small, it believes that it contributes little to the common good being sought; at the same time, it benefits from any common good that is provided. In the absence of coercion, therefore, the state has an incentive to maximize its private benefit (cheating) while free-riding on the public benefits that are provided by the organization as a whole.

In point of fact, cheating has been a problem for CoCom since its creation.[23] The only goods that the organization has effectively controlled are those whose production is monopolized by firms based in the United States. Not surprisingly, as European and Japanese technological capabilities have increased, the number of items on the export control list have been reduced.[24]

Export controls have been sources of tension not only between east and west, but within the western alliance itself and, to descend a level of analysis, within the western member states. It is worth describing these tensions at the systemic, alliance, and state levels in more detail.

At the level of east-west relations, export controls are an element of what David Baldwin has called *economic statecraft*: the manipulation of commerce by the state to advance political objectives. As tools of economic statecraft, export controls have been used by the United States both as a carrot and as a stick. As a carrot, the United States has promised to expand economic ties with the Soviet Union as a reward for "good behavior," such as allowing Jews to emigrate. As a stick, it has been a tool for punishing the Soviets, as exemplified by President Jimmy Carter's grain embargo in response to the invasion of Afghanistan in 1979. It has also been used to deny the Soviets goods and services that might be used by their military-industrial complex.[25]

At the alliance level, tensions have arisen over the nature of the Soviet threat and the best way to contain Soviet aggression. European and Japanese leaders have long held the view that economic interdependence would lessen rather than increase tensions so long as mutually beneficial exchanges occurred. For Japan, economic ties have also been seen as a useful element in trying to secure a favorable World War II peace treaty; the two parties never came to terms after surrender. The Japanese and Europeans also saw the U.S.S.R. as a huge, untapped market that could generate profits for national firms. For the United States, economic growth in the Soviet Union meant that the Kremlin could devote more resources to defense, and thus it was not in the west's strategic interest to bolster Moscow's industrial strength (and from the perspective of American firms, the Soviet market was, with few exceptions, inconsequential as a source of profits).

Within states, export controls have also created controversy. First, and most obviously, such controls hurt particular interests, especially banks and exporters; more on this below. But second, other societal groups have *linked* export controls to their narrow political concerns. Trade with the Soviet Union, for example, has been linked by the U.S. Congress with emigration of Jews. These linkage strategies have opened the floodgates to domestic political debate over the appropriate use of foreign policy and national security controls on trade. The executive branch and Congress have frequently been at loggerheads over such policy linkage.

Differing perspectives on the costs and benefits associated with east-west trade have been a constant source of alliance dispute, and among the most publicized of these was the western crisis in the early 1980s over Europe's role in building a natural gas pipeline from Siberia to the Czech border with West Germany. It is worth exploring this crisis in some detail since it provides unique insights into the politics of export control.[26]

The Soviet Union began to consider development of a pipeline between Siberia and western Europe in 1978. The Urengoi gas field targeted for exploitation was the largest in the world, containing 20 percent of Soviet, and 7 percent of world, gas reserves. In June 1980, Moscow and Bonn signed an agreement concerning pipeline construction and gas purchases, which the French and Italian gas utilities later joined.

A consortium of German banks agreed to finance the project at below-market interest rates, with the Soviets granted a credit line of nearly 2 billion dollars. The French also offered attractive credit arrangements. These credits would be used to purchase technology and pipe from western European firms. For European governments, mired in the worst recession since the 1930s, the scale and scope of the pipeline proved a godsend.

The American government of Jimmy Carter initially withheld judgment on the project. After all, Carter's CIA had taken the unprecedented step of publicly issuing a report that foretold declining energy resources and a potential scramble for supplies. Development of Soviet energy reserves seemed prudent under these conditions.

But upon coming to power in 1981, the Reagan administration expressed a different view, and several arguments were made against pipeline development. First, the administration held that the gas deal would make Europe overly dependent on Soviet energy supplies; this, incidentally, had been a consistent concern of the United States since the end of World War II, when an energy-starved Europe sought to import more Polish coal, to which the United States objected. Second, the Pentagon expressed the view that the Soviets would use the cheap credits and cash receipts on gas sales to continue their military buildup. Finally, others in the administration believed that the Soviets would be given access to advanced energy and computer technology in the process of importing American and European equipment for pipeline construction.

The imposition of martial law in Poland in December 1981 provided President Reagan with an opportunity to act on his negative assessment of the pipeline project. Using *foreign policy controls* on trade to punish the Soviets for their meddling in Poland, Reagan prevented the American firm General Electric from exporting turbine technology that would be used to push gas through the pipe. Since GE had a monopoly on this particular technology, the turbines could only be supplied by the firm or its licensees in western Europe.

Within the United States, these sanctions created a furor. The U.S. Chamber of Commerce and other trade groups pleaded for Reagan to reverse himself. At a time of record-high unemployment, firms were lobbying for all the export business they could get. Clearly, export controls stood in their way.

But Reagan refused to budge. Indeed, in the summer of 1982 he extended his ban not only to all U.S. firms working on the project, but to their licensees as well. Since many of these licensees were subsidiaries that also operated under the laws of the countries where they were based, such as France and Britain, the firms quite literally found themselves between a rock and a hard place. British Prime Minister Margaret Thatcher and French President Mitterrand ordered the firms to keep their contractual arrangements with Moscow; Reagan ordered them not to export.

Ultimately, the allies worked out a compromise. They agreed to limit their imports of Soviet gas to no more than 30 percent of overall gas consumption. At the same time, they agreed not to build a second pipeline, which was then under discussion with Moscow. In late 1983, the Soviets began shipping gas from Urengoi to the west, and at the same time the allies began sending hard currency east.

The pipeline episode illustrates several points concerning east-west trade. First, the allies have clearly had differing perceptions regarding the strategic value of such trade; the United States has viewed such trade as largely negative from a security perspective, while the allies have taken a more positive view. Ironically, the bastion of free trade, the United States, has adopted a neo-mercantilist position, while our neo-mercantilist allies have been more liberal. The cynic might argue that this is because the allies can afford to be more liberal, since the United States guarantees their security. Second, in a world of multinational corporations, export controls have become more difficult to enforce. Such firms lack a clear national identity, and they operate under differing jurisdictions. This gives them the ability to "arbitrage" their regulatory position and to adopt policies that maximize corporate profits. Finally, domestic actors pay costs for export controls, and effective policies are difficult to maintain without political support.

As the cold war unwinds, it has been argued that the United States will place less emphasis on strategic trade controls. If these controls ever served a purpose, their value is now in doubt as the allies attempt to encourage Moscow's efforts to promote glasnost and perestroika. But the emergence of new threats in the developing world and the proliferation of ballistic missiles and biological, chemical, and nuclear warfare materials mean that export controls will retain their strategic value. The challenge for the United States and other CoCom members is to adapt these controls to the changing times, rather than to abandon them altogether.

CONCLUSION

Alliances are formed when states face a common security threat. In the process of fashioning an appropriate military response, the allies will confront complex economic problems. In order to succeed in its mission, an alliance will have to develop economic policies that provide the combined military forces with sufficient human and natural resources, and with the weapons and materiel necessary to do battle. At the same time, the alliance will seek to weaken its enemy economically.

Since its inception, the western alliance has struggled to resolve three critical economic problems: rationalization of its weapons inventory; sharing the burden of military expenditure; and control on trade with adversaries. The inability of the allies to reach enduring agreements in these issue-areas suggest not only collective action problems in the presence of a hegemonic leader—a leader who provides allies with "public goods"—but also the continuing clash between national and alliance interests. The desire to maintain an indigenous defense industry, for example, may provide a single alliance member state with a greater sense of security, but for the alliance as a whole it could be viewed as a waste of scarce resources that could be better employed elsewhere.

Both as a theoretical and empirical problem, the economics of international organizations will continue to attract the interest of statesmen and scholars. Indeed, with the end of the Cold War and the development of a "New World Order" that places renewed emphasis on the United Nations, these problems can be expected to be at the center of continuing debate. For the United States, the question will be how to exercise international political leadership without footing the bill. At a time of growing responsibilities abroad and diminishing resources at home, this is certain to be one of the critical issues of the 1990s.

Selected Bibliography

Gordon, Lincoln, "Economic Aspects of NATO," *International Organization 10* (Autumn 1956): 529–543. Lincoln's article provides an early and perceptive statement of the economic problems confronting alliance members.

Hartley, Keith, *NATO Arms Cooperation* (London: George Allen & Unwin, 1983). This book provides a good introduction to the politics and economics of NATO RSI.

National Academy of Sciences, *Balancing the National Interest* (Washington, D.C.: NAS Press, 1987). This is a comprehensive report on the costs and benefits of export controls.

Olson, Mancur, Jr., and Richard Zeckhauser, "An Economic Theory of Alliances," *Review of Economics and Statistics 48* (August 1966): 266–279. This classic article continues to influence the way we analyze the economics of international organizations.

Pincus, Jon, *Economic Aid and International Cost Sharing* (Santa Monica, Calif.: RAND Corporation, 1965). This is an excellent overview of the burden-sharing problems associated with international collective action.

Notes

1. Hans Morgenthau, "Alliances in Theory and Practice," in Arnold Wolfers, ed., *Alliance Policy in the Cold War* (Baltimore: Johns Hopkins University Press, 1959), p. 185.
2. For further elaboration of this point, see Ethan B. Kapstein, *The Insecure Alliance: Energy Crises and Western Politics since 1944* (New York: Oxford University Press, 1990).
3. Jim Sasser, "Is Uncle Sam Getting Stiffed?" *New York Times*, December 19, 1990, p. A25.
4. Lord Ismay, *NATO: The First Five Years* (Utrecht: Bosch, 1954), p. 125.
5. See Keith Hartley, *NATO Arms Cooperation* (London: George Allen & Unwin, 1983).
6. Jonathan Tucker, "Shifting Advantage," Ph.D. dissertation, Massachusetts Institute of Technology, Cambridge, Mass., 1989.
7. Thomas Callaghan, *U.S./European Economic Cooperation in Military and Civil Technologies* (Washington, D.C.: Center for Strategic and International Studies, August 1974).
8. See Gardiner Tucker, *Toward Rationalizing Allied Weapons Production* (Paris: Atlantic Institute, 1976); and Thomas Callaghan, "Pooling Allied and American Resources to Produce a Credible, Collective Conventional Deterrent," a report prepared for the U.S. Department of Defense, August 1988.
9. R. H. Trice, "International Cooperation in Military Aircraft Programs," Working Paper OIWP-90-002, John M. Olin Institute for Strategic Studies, Harvard University, Cambridge, Mass., November 1989.
10. On IEPG see Paul Hammond et al., *The Reluctant Supplier* (Cambridge, Mass.: Oelgeschlager, Gunn & Hain, 1983); Edward Kolodziej, *Making and Marketing Arms* (Princeton, N.J.: Princeton University Press, 1987); and Andrew Moravcsik, "1992 and the Future of the European Armaments Industry," Working Paper OIWP-90-001, John M. Olin Institute for Strategic Studies, Harvard University, Cambridge, Mass., November 1989.
11. Shannon M. L. Hurley, "Arms for the Alliance: Armaments Cooperation in NATO," *Comparative Strategy* 7 (1989): 377–398.
12. The definitive study on offsets is Grant Hammond, *Countertrade, Offsets and Barter in International Political Economy* (New York: St. Martin's, 1990).
13. Ibid.
14. See the Office of Technology Assessment report, *Arming Our Allies* (Washington, D.C.: Government Printing Office, 1990).
15. Sasser, "Is Uncle Sam Getting Stiffed?"
16. See Lincoln Gordon, "Economic Aspects of NATO," *International Organization* 10 (Autumn 1956): 529–543.
17. See John Oneal and Mark Elrod, "NATO Burden Sharing and the Forces of Change," *International Studies Quarterly* 33 (December 1989): 435–456.
18. Jon Pincus, *Economic Aid and International Cost Sharing* (Santa Monica, Calif.: RAND Corporation, 1965), p. 106.
19. Mancur Olson, Jr., and Richard Zeckhauser, "An Economic Theory of Alliances," *Review of Economics and Statistics* 48 (August 1966): 266–279.
20. See Todd Sandler, "Sharing Burdens in NATO," *Challenge* (March–April 1988): 29–35; Oneal and Elrod, "NATO Burden Sharing"; Brian Field, "Economic Theory, Burden Sharing and the NATO Alliance," *NATO Review* 36 (December 1988): 11–15; and Bruce Russett, *What Price Vigilance?* (New Haven, Conn.: Yale University Press, 1970).

21. Beverly Crawford and Stefanie Lenway, "Decision Modes and International Regime Change: Western Collaboration on East- West Trade," *World Politics 37* (April 1985): 375–402.
22. Michael Mastanduno, "Trade as a Strategic Weapon: American and Alliance Export Control Policy in the Early Postwar Period," *International Organization 42* (Winter 1988): 121–150.
23. See Crawford and Lenway, "Decision Modes."
24. See Henry Nau and Kevin Quigley, eds., *The Allies and East-West Economic Relations: Past Conflicts and Present Choices* (New York: Carnegie Council, 1989).
25. For a comprehensive study of export controls, see National Academy of Sciences, *Balancing the National Interest* (Washington, D.C.: NAS Press, 1987).
26. On the pipeline crisis see, *inter alia*, Jonathan Stern, *East European Energy and East-West Trade* (London: Policy Studies Institute, 1982); Angela Stent, *Soviet Energy and Western Europe* (New York: Praeger, 1982); and Jonathan Stein, *The Soviet Bloc, Energy and Western Security* (Lexington, Mass.: Lexington Books, 1983).

8

National Security and the Global Economy

"To an extent far greater than in the past, governments confront
a globalization trend in technology, markets and industrial
structure. With that trend, governments find themselves
increasingly obliged to reach beyond their own borders in order
to mobilize the critical ingredients for their basic defense
programs." ——*Raymond Vernon*[1]

In an anarchic international environment, states are responsible to their citizens for the provision of military security and social welfare. But in that same international environment, finance, commerce, culture, science, technology, and—increasingly—people are flowing freely. To be sure, the globalization of production provides opportunities for states that are seeking both growth and security. However, it also poses policy dilemmas.

This chapter explores the contemporary disjunction between nationalistic conceptions of security and the globalization of the economy. The tensions produced by this disjunction, of course, are not new. As stated throughout this book, states have rarely achieved an autarkic defense economy. Reliance on far-flung supplies of raw materials and energy has been a traditional concern of policymakers in the industrial world, and countries have frequently turned to foreign suppliers for defense-related technology.

Nonetheless, until recently, the United States and the Soviet Union achieved an admirable degree of autarky in their defense economies. For the United States, autarky is no longer a viable strategy, and as the country turns increasingly to the international economy for goods and services, officials responsible for national security planning have been forced to rethink their strategies for procuring materiel. In the Soviet Union, the enormous costs associated with a "fortress" strategy have become all too apparent; Moscow is currently trying to formulate an economic strategy that bolsters civilian production while maintaining defense-industrial capabilities.[2]

In exploring contemporary issues at the interface of national security and the global economy, it will prove useful to begin with a discussion of the concepts of "dependence" and "interdependence." These terms are often used in the current national security debate over the risks associated with globalization, yet they mean different things to different people. The chapter then turns to "case studies," examining raw materials, energy, and technology. In each example, the central policy dilemmas facing public officials are outlined and discussed.

DEPENDENCE AND INTERDEPENDENCE

In essence, contemporary concerns over reliance on foreign technology, energy, or capital for defense and prosperity are really about dependence. Dependence means a state of being determined or significantly affected by external forces. In economic parlance, dependence may be thought of in terms of the "opportunity costs" of severing an ongoing relationship; opportunity costs are the costs associated with forgoing other options that may be available to an economic agent. The higher the costs, the greater the dependency.[3]

For most of its postwar history, the United States has viewed itself as independent or self-sufficient when it came to needed goods and services. But a sea-change began in October 1973 where the Organization of Arab Petroleum Exporting Countries (OAPEC) embargoed the sale of oil to America, in response to U.S. support for Israel during the Yom Kippur War. In short order, oil prices quadrupled, gasoline shortages occurred, and the American economy reeled from stagflation. The oil embargo brought home to public officials and scholars alike the fact that America, like other advanced industrial countries, was dependent on foreign energy supplies for its economic well-being.

Of course, there are even stronger examples of economic dependency than that associated with the oil embargo. During the 1930s, for example, Nazi Germany proved adept at purposefully structuring economic dependency relations with the countries of eastern Europe, a region that after World War I had been a stronghold of British and French influence. The Germans engaged in preemptive purchasing of eastern European agricultural products, and they gave eastern European countries favorable tariff rates. In turn, they sold industrial goods to those countries at below-market prices. This was an example of a strategic economic policy; it was Germany's express aim to envelop eastern Europe in its sphere of influence even before war erupted in 1939. The Japanese followed similar policies in east Asia before the war, as they created a Co-Prosperity Sphere with Tokyo at the hub.[4]

Examples of one-sided dependence are rare in international politics. More often, states are concerned with *interdependence,* or mutual dependence. To be sure, the United States is dependent on foreign nations for oil supplies, but these trading partners rely on the United States for dollars, military equipment, and foodstuffs. Interdependence does not imply that the relationship between trading partners is always equal, but it does suggest that the partners cannot be indifferent to one another's actions. Indeed, actors are likely to seek "asymmetries" in their economic relationships, and to exploit these for political gain.

Despite the liberal idea that trade and investment flows promote international security, interdependence is not necessarily about peaceful relations among states. As discussed in the introduction to this book, it has been a peculiarly Anglo-Saxon idea that interdependence is a positive-sum game, while the search for independence and autarky must lead to conflict. The historical record, in fact, suggests a more ambivalent picture. Economically, the European states were highly interdependent before 1914, but this did not prevent the outbreak of World War I. In contrast, the United States and the Soviet Union have had a trivial economic relationship since 1945, but despite a cold war the superpowers have never engaged in hostilities. We must be careful to specify the effects that flow from a particular set of economic relationships and to state why we believe one outcome is more likely than another.

Robert Keohane and Joseph Nye suggest that interdependence has two distinct attributes: *sensitivity* and *vulnerability*.[5] Sensitivity interdependence refers to the immediate costs suffered in country B as a result of unilateral decisions in country A. The unilateral decision to boost oil prices had immediate effects on consuming countries.

Over time, however, countries can initiate policies to mitigate such harmful effects. The ability of countries to formulate an acceptable policy response will determine their vulnerability to external shocks. Again to take the case of the oil embargo, if country B could easily shift its source of supply from Saudi Arabia to Mexico, it would be less vulnerable than a country that relied completely on the Saudis. Alternatively, if a country held large stockpiles of oil which could be released during a shortage, it would be less vulnerable to blackmail or the direct effects of a supply disruption. In fact, diversification of suppliers, the development of alternative resources, and the building of stockpiles are the time-honored methods of dealing with the problem of vulnerability (think of Joseph's effort to stockpile grain against the seven lean years in Eqypt!).

To take another example, imagine that Japan suddenly declared an embargo on the sale of semiconductor chips, perhaps as part of a strategy to raise their price. Over the short term, consumers of semiconductor chips would suffer. Over the longer term, however, alternative supplies would develop. These supplies would come from countries that had the capability of producing semiconductor chips at the higher prices now found in the world economy. Consumers may have been sensitive to the effects of the embargo, but their vulnerability decreased as new suppliers came on stream.

The concept of vulnerability interdependence suggest the limits on those states that would seek to blackmail the world economy. But in the short term, states must be concerned with sensitivity interdependence—with the immediate costs of a supply disruption. During the Yom Kippur War of 1973, for example, Israel quickly exhausted its domestic supplies of war materiel. It needed military equipment in a hurry, and the United States agreed to provide the needed supplies. Had the United States refused to act, Israel would have needed time and money to find alternative suppliers. This costly lag may have spelled the difference between victory and defeat.

In thinking about dependence and interdependence, therefore, it is useful to have some relevant time frame in mind. From a policy perspective, this is critical, since public officials always take risks when they depend on the world economy for needed goods and services. By accepting the logic of the international division of labor, states forgo domestic production for imports, thus making the country sensitive to trade disruptions. For defense officials in the United States, who recognize that autarky no longer provides a viable defense-industrial policy, this question of dependence on foreign sources for materiel has risen high on the contemporary policy agenda.

Of course, for certain defense-related inputs, dependence has been of long-standing concern to most nation-states. Specifically, few countries in the modern age have possessed the necessary energy and raw materials required to wage total war. In the next section we explore the problem of access to energy and raw materials and look at how worries over supply have changed in recent years. After that, we take up the problem of technology dependence.

ENERGY AND RAW MATERIALS

One of the lessons that statesmen drew from the First and Second World Wars was that the alliance with the greatest supplies of energy and raw materials at its disposal emerged victorious. In 1918 Britain's Lord Curzon said that the Allies had "floated to victory on a tide of oil," and similar sentiments were expressed in 1945. In both cases, the defeated powers had been ground to a halt by adversaries with superior resources.

Accordingly, by the end of World War II all the major powers sought secure energy and raw material supplies for both economic and security reasons. By 1947 the United States had become, for the first time in its history, a net oil importer, creating anxiety among public officials like Defense Secretary James Forrestal, who thought this growing dependence would undercut its leadership role. Indeed, a major focus of U.S. foreign policy at the war's end was to avoid an energy "scramble" by the wartime allies for concessions in the Arab world.[6]

The potential for a scramble in the developing world was also seen in the area of raw materials. At the war's end the United States was importing tungsten from China, copper from Chile, graphite from Madagascar, and mica from India.[7] It was also importing minerals from several colonies of European countries, and indeed recipients of Marshall Plan aid pledged to make raw materials available to the United States. Out of a growing concern over America's mineral dependence, Congress in 1946 passed the Strategic and Critical Materials Stockpiling Act, which "created a program that mandated the purchase and stockpiling of certain materials as well as research and development into ways to extend supplies and find substitutes."[8] The act defined strategic and critical materials as those that "a) would be needed to supply the military, industrial, and essential civilian needs of the United States during a national emergency, and b) are not found or produced in the United States in sufficient quantities to meet such need."[9]

In fact, policies for managing the stockpiles of raw materials have been beset by contradictions. According to the National Defense Stockpile Policy proposed by President Reagan in 1985, the national stockpile of strategic minerals was to have been enhanced to meet the military, industrial, and essential civilian needs for a three-year conventional military conflict.[10] At the same time this was being proposed, however, Reagan authorized the sale of large quantities of these minerals in order to meet his budget goals, providing a nice example of trade-offs between economic and security objectives. A career intelligence analyst concluded that Reagan "found it difficult to maintain a consistent policy" owing to the "competing and often contradictory demands of multiple public interests."[11] Ironically, despite strong public support for the military buildup, the Reagan administration balked when it came to funding for energy and raw materials stockpiles. In the words of one official, "In the absence of immediate national security problems . . . the marketplace and the private sector must take the lead. . . ."[12]

Energy and raw material dependence creates a classic guns-versus-butter trade-off for public officials. Many countries, in fact, could be relatively self-sufficient for their resources if they devoted adequate funds to the development of alternative fuels and raw material substitutes. The problem with such a strategy is simply that it would be extremely costly; it would prevent society from allocating scarce financial resources to other objectives. Policymakers must balance dependence against national security requirements, and adopt strategies that meet both civilian and military needs.

In terms of markets for energy, raw materials, and most other military goods, policymakers can intervene in any one of three ways: they can act to influence supplies; they can act to influence demand; and they can act directly to control prices. Supplies can be increased through the diversification of supplying countries, by the increase in production by a particular supplying nation, and by the creation of substitutes. Demand can be influenced through various restraint measures that curb usage of particular commodities. Prices can be influenced through direct and indirect controls and by moral suasion.

An example of how governments may use these three policy instruments is offered by the energy policy of the United States in the wake of the Suez crisis of 1956. Since the end of World War II, increasing energy imports had been a national security concern of government officials (and Texas oilmen), but imported fuels were cheaper than domestic products. Three postwar energy crises, however, suggested that a "security premium" must be attached to the cost of imported energy. The Israeli war of independence in 1948 had led Arab states to cut oil pipelines leading to the Mediterranean, while the nationalization of British Petroleum by Iran in 1951, and the subsequent turmoil in that country, caused the closure of the world's largest refinery at Abadan. The most severe crisis, however, emanated from the nationalization of the Suez Canal by Egypt's

President Nasser, and the aborted invasion of the canal launched by Britain and France in November 1956.[13]

At the time of the Suez crisis, the United States imported 1.4 million barrels per day (MBD) of petroleum, or 16 percent of domestic demand. Despite the small volume, domestic producers were becoming concerned by what they viewed as a trend toward higher import levels. The Suez-induced energy shortages played right into their hands, providing them with a ready-made "national security" argument to stem the import flow.

Following the crisis, President Eisenhower appointed a Special Committee to Investigate Oil Imports, with the task of clarifying the national security risks associated with dependence on the middle east. The committee recommended that imports be reduced to 12 percent of domestic demand. By 1959, Eisenhower had placed quotas on imported oil, using the national security provisions of the Trade Agreements Act of 1954, which authorized the chief executive to control imports and exports when the nation's defense and security efforts were threatened.

The impact of the import quotas was far-reaching. This energy policy severed the United States from the world market, permitting domestic oilmen to keep high-cost production in service. At the same time, it lowered American demand for foreign crude, leading to global price reductions, with positive effects on consumers, negative ones on producers. Indeed, in 1960 representatives from the leading oil-producing countries met and agreed to establish the Organization of Petroleum Exporting Countries (OPEC), with the objective of winning higher prices for oil products.

Many recent analysts of the oil import program have been critical of Eisenhower's quota policy, viewing it as a major blunder. Political scientist Robert Keohane has argued that special interests (i.e., Texas oilmen) "drained America first" and "prevented the implementation of a farsighted strategic policy of conservation."[14] But it can be argued that a "free market" for petroleum would have "flooded America first." The resulting imports would have limited domestic production that could not have been readily restored in the event of a national emergency. This does not mean that a quota was the most efficient or equitable way to maintain domestic oil production, but that the strategic rationale should not be dismissed.

Over time, however, the flow of oil imports could not be halted. As domestic oil prices rose in the late 1960s, and as environmental regulations prevented offshore drilling and the use of such alternative fuels as coal and nuclear power, the United States increased its imports. By 1970, the United States was importing 165 million tons of petroleum, up from a 1967 level of 95 million tons. The growing demand for foreign oil on the part of the United States led to widespread anxiety in consumer countries, which feared that the balance of market power was now tipping to the producers.

On October 6, 1973, Egypt and Syria launched a coordinated attack on Israel. The attack placed the Israeli armed forces on the defensive, causing them to deplete their existing inventories at a rapid rate. Prime Minister Golda Meir placed an urgent request with President Richard Nixon for emergency supplies, to which he agreed. On October 14, Nixon began the shipments to Israel.

Allegedly in response to this emergency aid, the Arab oil-exporting countries decided on October 16 to raise crude prices unilaterally, from 3 dollars to over 5 dollars per barrel. The following day, the Gulf oilmen agreed to cut their production by 5 percent. The Arabs said that states that supported Israel would be embargoed totally, while states friendly to the Arab cause would continue to receive supplies on a normal basis.

The Arab oil embargo of 1973 caused immediate panic in energy markets and severe alliance conflict; over the longer term the price hikes triggered economic recession throughout the industrial world. Energy dependence became the gravest concern of statesmen in all the western states, and efforts were made to curry favor with Arab leaders on the one hand while developing alternative sources and suppliers on the other. In the United States, a new cabinet-level department was created, the Department of Energy, and it would put billions of dollars into research and development over the next decade in an effort to develop substitutes for imported fuel. In France, a crash program led to the widespread use of nuclear power for electricity generation. In Britain, Holland, and Norway, the oil and gas fields of the North Sea region were exploited. The industrial countries also built up large oil stockpiles, both as a deterrent against a future embargo and as a source of supply should another embargo or unilateral price hike take place.

Following the Iranian revolution of 1978–1979, at which time oil prices again hit record-high levels, a new round of energy policy measures were emplaced in the industrial countries. These included, *inter alia,* conservation, tax credits for investment in energy-saving technologies, and mandatory mile-per-gallon standards for automobiles. At the same time, with the election of conservative governments in Britain and the United States, more market-oriented energy strategies were launched, including an end to price controls, supply allocations, and the like.

These measures have helped to erode the dominant position held by OPEC in the oil marketplace of the 1970s. Over the longer term, however, the free-market approach may have ironic consequences. The Arab countries remain the low-cost producers of oil, and imports of middle east oil by the industrial countries are expected to rise during the 1990s. In energy, the appropriate balance between market- and security-oriented policies has yet to be found.

This was painfully demonstrated in August 1990 when Iraq invaded Kuwait, laying claim to one-fifth of the world's proven oil reserves, and 8 percent of current world production. In the aftermath of the invasion, President Bush called upon the United Nations to embargo and boycott Iraq and its conquered territory. Overnight, oil prices climbed by over 50 percent, and fears of a new energy crisis were widespread. But by the late autumn, prices began to drop toward pre-crisis levels, and confidence in energy markets was restored. What had occurred to effect this change?

During the early stages of the Persian Gulf crisis, the Bush administration acted to influence supply, demand (though weakly), and prices. It called upon oil

(Jacques Langevin/Sygma)

Saudi Oil: Is the middle east a reliable energy source?

suppliers, particularly Saudi Arabia, to increase output and make up for the loss of Iraqi and Kuwaiti oil. By the late autumn, millions of barrels of additional production came on-stream. Regarding demand, the administration made rather weak calls for conservation, although increased prices certainly had some effect on consumer usage. Finally, in the area of price, the President requested that the oil companies not pass on all their additional costs to consumers, moderating the price shock.

Of interest, the President did not make extensive use of the national stockpile of oil, known as the strategic petroleum reserve (SPR). Five million barrels were released as part of a "test" of the system (the SPR contains 600 million barrels) six weeks into the Persian Gulf crisis, but the President decided to save the oil in the event a shooting war occurred, rather than use it as a tool for oil price stability. This decision was second-guessed by many economists, who thought that a more active reserve policy would have moderated the oil price shocks of August and September.[15]

To conclude, dependence on foreign sources of energy and raw materials has been an enduring problem for the great powers since the dawn of the industrial age. Public officials have found it difficult, however, to fashion energy and mineral security policies that could be sustained during prolonged periods of peace. Stockpiling, research and development, and the use of alternative fuels have always been expensive propositions, and they have been difficult to justify after hostilities or threats cease.

Yet few states have been willing to adopt a laissez faire approach to energy and minerals policy either. Such a diverse group of countries as Britain, France, Germany, Japan, and the United States have all combined some measure of liberalism and neo-mercantilism in this issue area. To be sure, the diversity of policies adopted by these countries is suggestive of the role that domestic political interests play in the policy formulation process, but the similarities speak to a common set of concerns with the anarchic international environment.[16]

TECHNOLOGY DEPENDENCE

In recent years, anxiety over access to technology has taken the place of resource dependence that dominated policy agendas during the 1970s. In the 1990s, public officials in the industrial and developing worlds alike worry about whether they will be able to obtain the technology they need for economic development and national security. This anxiety is not necessarily misplaced. As Theodore Moran has written, "A survey of post-World War II experience suggests that external domination of technology, goods, and services may well lead to persistent attempts at meddling, manipulation, and harassment in the recipients' sovereign affairs even in peacetime relations among allies."[17]

Examples of technology manipulation and control are not difficult to come by. The United States, for example, has prevented the sale of such technologies as supercomputers to countries like Brazil for fear they will use the computers to help build nuclear weapons. Indeed, the United States withheld the sale of computer technology to France during the 1960s to inhibit the French drive for a nuclear arsenal.[18] It has been alleged that during the Vietnam war, Japan refused to sell to the United States some critical technologies used by the armed forces.[19]

As Raymond Vernon suggests, there are even more subtle forms of technological dependence that are beginning to concern policymakers. Building on the case of the supercomputers discussed above, imagine that the United States does, in fact, license the export of such end-items to country X. The leaders of country X may now presume that they control the technology and can use it as they like. But one day the computer breaks down and is in need of repair. While country X has been clever in demanding that a local engineering firm learn how to repair the machine, in the case at hand that firm may have to rely on advice and information stored in the mainframe computer of the foreign manufacturer, or in the minds of its engineers. In order to get the computer repaired, the local engineering firm is dependent on the vendor to make the proper diagnosis.[20]

Since the end of World War II, the center of technological development and application has been the United States. But in recent years, new challengers have assailed that dominant position, notably Japan. Beyond the emergence of new technological centers, however, is the globalization of the world economy, which has led multinational firms to engage in research, development, and production in a myriad of corporate centers, from New York to Hong Kong. Thus, even if U.S. firms continued to lead in technology development, policymakers would have to be concerned about where the research and the production were actually taking place.

The contemporary debate over technological access in the United States and many other countries revolves around three questions: First, what is the appropriate role of government in stimulating technological development? Second, what is the appropriate role of government in protecting domestic industries that produce technologies deemed critical for national security? Third, what role should government play in attracting or blocking foreign investment in defense-related industries? Each of these questions is addressed below.

In the literature of classical economics, one finds surprising support for the thesis that governments have a role to play in support for basic research and development. Economists would argue that R&D generates positive externalities that provide widespread benefits to society. Since no single firm that conducts R&D can capture all those benefits, the firm will tend to underinvest; that is, firms will invest less than the socially optimal amount. Given the existence of market failure, there is justification for government intervention.

In all the industrial countries, of course, there is a considerable history of government support for defense-related technology. In the United States, the modern effort has its roots in the Office of Scientific Research and Development (OSRD) established by President Franklin Roosevelt in 1940. The head of the OSRD, Vannevar Bush of MIT, brought together "a special committee of scientists from outside the . . . government who would direct research on weapons for immediate use in the war."[21] This partnership between government, industry, and universities for the creation of defense-related R&D, forged in the early days of World War II, remains central to the American approach to science and technology policy.[22]

During the early postwar years, an awesome scientific establishment was built in the United States, guided by such organizations as the Atomic Energy Commission, the National Science Foundation, the National Institutes of Health, the National Aeronautics and Space Administration, and the Defense Advanced Research Projects Agency. These agencies of government, which brought together the research talents of scientists and engineers from the academy and industry, led in the development of a vast array of technologies that supported the armed forces, including the tremendous advances in aerospace, electronics, and computation. At a time when laissez faire ideology informs many governments, it is important to recall the prominent role played by the state in postwar science and technology.

Yet government support for R&D once rested on the belief that the social benefits generated as a result remained on national soil; that is, the benefits were captured by national firms. If the United States subsidized R&D in the aerospace industry, it could be sure that American companies—and the U.S. military—would be the main beneficiaries. Today, this assumption can no longer be made.

As argued above, technological developments that occur in country A are now quickly diffused to countries B, C, and D. As Raymond Vernon points out, "The implications of the fact that technology cannot easily be locked onto any single national turf have not yet been fully assimilated in the minds of science policymakers anywhere in the world."[23] Indeed, once policymakers grasp this point, "they may be tempted to conclude that the government should withdraw its support from efforts to stimulate research and development."[24] Vernon suggests that, in a global economy where states cannot hope to capture all the national security and economic benefits that accrue from R&D support, "there is a case for encouraging joint national programs . . . rather than unilateral national efforts. . . ."[25] Within the European Community, such programs are already apparent in a number of sectors, including aviation and semiconductors. But in a world of nation-states where security is defined by *relative position* in the international system rather than by absolute gain, the prospects for joint programs that may lead to advanced military technologies remain limited.

The process by which technologies are diffused around the globe is still subject to intense academic debate, and no single covering explanation has withstood close scrutiny. Perhaps the most well-known theory is that of the "product life cycle" (PLC). This theory, developed in the 1960s by Raymond Vernon and his associates at the Harvard Business School, offers a powerful analysis of technological trade.[26] In summary, the PLC argues that product innovation begins at home. After a time, the product is exported to foreign markets. Later, the product is manufactured in those same countries. The cycle is completed as foreign countries ultimately export the product they now manufacture to the original, innovating country. A useful test of the PLC is provided by color television sets. Color TVs were invented and marketed in the United States. In the 1960s, U.S. firms began to export the sets globally. By the late 1960s and early 1970s, color TVs were manufactured in many countries, including Japan. By the 1980s, most of the color televisions purchased in America were built in east Asia.

Other explanations of technological innovation focus on the education process. There are two variants of this argument, which are by no means mutually exclusive. One variant stresses the improvements in education that have occurred around the world since the end of World War II. The technical education that students obtain in such countries as France, Germany, and Japan is particularly notable. Graduates of these programs, armed with their technical skills, then go to work for local corporations that encourage innovation. The success of non-American firms in high technology competition speaks to the educational attainment of the firm's employees.

The other variant stresses the fact that large numbers of foreign students are educated in American colleges and universities. By the 1980s, foreigners formed the majority of students in many science and engineering programs at such leading research institutions as Harvard, Stanford, and MIT. Indeed, European universities experienced a similar phenomenon, educating large numbers of foreigners. When (and if) these foreign students return to their homelands, they bring with them tremendous technical knowledge.[27]

It is difficult to test the proposition that technology has become more diffuse using any single statistical measure. But one useful proxy is provided by patents, particularly patents granted to foreigners. Foreigners will seek patents in different countries in order "to ensure that others do not appropriate and apply the inventions . . . that the inventors hope to exploit."[28] According to Raymond Vernon, "By the 1970s, most European countries were issuing a majority of their patents to foreigners; even in the United States, about one-third of the patents were going to foreign inventors."[29]

From a security standpoint, the eroding of technological superiority has troubling implications. If pools of advanced, defense-related technology are located beyond a state's borders, it means that countries may not be able to access the technologies in a timely fashion, and that potential adversaries will be fishing in the same technological pond. The issue is whether the state should and can respond by promoting the development of technologies on national soil that it deems to be essential to its defense requirements.

In the United States, these concerns have been shaped into a "Critical Technologies Plan," which was released by the Department of Defense in 1990.[30] The plan identifies twenty critical technologies that the Pentagon plans to promote through an "investment strategy" (see Table 8-1). The technologies were selected on the basis of their ability to enhance the performance of existing weapons systems, provide new weapons capabilities, contribute to weapons system affordability, and strengthen the industrial base.

But despite such an ambitious plan, there is reason for skepticism that a government can act on the microeconomic level to ensure national superiority.

Table 8-1 Twenty Critical Technologies

Semiconductor materials and microelectronic circuits
Computer software
Parallel computer architectures
Machine intelligence and robotics
Simulation and modeling

Photonics
Sensitive radars
Passive sensors
Signal processing
Signature control

Weapons system environment
Data fusion
Computational fluid dynamics
Air-breathing propulsion
Pulsed power

Hypervelocity projectiles
High energy density materials
Composite materials
Superconductivity
Biotechnology materials and processes

Source: U.S. Department of Defense.

As business strategist Michael Porter has pointed out, technologies are "nested" within a broader set of economic activities. In the absence of an appropriate infrastructure that supports a given sector, it would appear difficult for that sector to thrive.[31]

In general, it is widely accepted that one of the most promising approaches that governments can take to ensure technological competitiveness is to support education, and perhaps to offer incentives to citizens who engage in advanced study in areas that are deemed critical to national security. Further, the liberal argument that superiority begins in the establishment of a macroeconomic climate that encourages investment and innovation has substantial merit, and it is here where public policy should place its focus.

What about protection of domestic industries? Should firms that are important to the Pentagon be kept in business by government largesse? Or should they be subject to the same market forces as the mom-and-pop grocery store at the corner?

Protection, which is often carried out in the name of national security (take our oil import example, cited above), in fact poses serious problems for contemporary Pentagon officials. Protection of domestic industries is costly: it leads to higher prices, less production, and perhaps less advanced technology than the Pentagon could access from overseas suppliers. Given scarce defense dollars, it is by no means obvious that defense officials (as opposed to members of the House and Senate) would offer protection to all defense-related industries.

Prominent cases where the protectionist impulse has come into play include the steel, machine tool, and semiconductor industries, all of which have been subject to severe foreign competition and all of which have been viewed by defense officials as critical to the nation's defense-industrial base. In each case, an array of protectionist policies has been employed by government, including import quotas, "voluntary" export restraints, tariffs, bilateral agreements, subsidies, and the like. Since the semiconductor case has occupied such a central role in the national security and industrial competitiveness debates, and since government intervention has been so critical to the industry's development, a closer study of it is warranted.

In the eyes of some analysts, the health of the U.S. semiconductor industry is nothing less than a manifestation of America's position as an economic and military power. Whereas in 1978 American firms controlled over three-quarters the world share of semiconductor production, by 1986 their share had slipped to 44 percent, while that of Japanese firms had climbed to 45 percent. At the same time, the Japanese were engaged in a major semiconductor investment boom, plowing more than 9 billion dollars into the industry between 1980 and 1986.[32] The evidence seemed to be clear: the semiconductor industry, and hence the United States, was suffering relative decline (see Table 8-2).

Fears for America's economic and military health were fueled in early 1987 when the Defense Science Board—a committee of outside scientists and engineers who advise the secretary of defense—stated that the condition of the semiconductor industry had become a national security issue, since advanced electronics were at the heart of the U.S. high-technology arsenal. It recom-

Table 8-2 Leading Semiconductor Producers, 1989

Company	Home Base	Market Share
NEC	Japan	8.9%
Toshiba	Japan	8.8
Hitachi	Japan	7.0
Motorola	U.S.	5.9
Fujitsu	Japan	5.3
Texas Instruments	U.S.	5.0
Mitsubishi	Japan	4.7
Intel	U.S.	4.4
Matsushita	Japan	NA
Philips	Netherlands	3.0

Source: David Sanger, "Contrasts on Chips," *New York Times,* January 18, 1990, p. D1.

mended that the Pentagon increase its R&D support for the industry, and that government and industry join together to form a semiconductor manufacturing consortium that would develop production methods rivaling those of America's industrial competitors, especially Japan. In the absence of drastic measures, the United States would find that technological leadership in this industry was residing overseas (it should be noted that already in 1986 the United States had struck a bilateral agreement with Japan which forced the Japanese to raise prices on and limit exports of many of their semiconductor products).[33]

Within weeks of the DSB report, fourteen U.S. companies agreed to join a government-sponsored consortium called *Sematech* (for semiconductor manufacturing technology). Sematech was given an annual budget of 250 million dollars, half of which was provided by the Pentagon, with the rest supplied by the industrial participants. Charles Sporck, president of National Semiconductor Corporation, one of the nation's oldest and largest "chip" manufacturers, was chosen president, and Austin, Texas, was selected as the site. Sematech was given the task of conducting R&D in manufacturing technology; it was not to make or sell chips for the commercial market.[34]

Despite widespread political support for Sematech, economists and business strategists have expressed reservations about the project. According to one technology consultant, Sematech's objective of getting the United States back into "commodity" chip manufacturing is wrong-headed; instead, the U.S. government should be investing in the development of next-generation "smart" chips. Just as the United States has forgone industrial production in many consumer electronics, from color TVs to VCRs, so too it should allow the product life cycle to work in semiconductors.[35]

From a business perspective, doubts have been raised about the ability of U.S. firms to engage in "cooperative" R&D, given the cultural and legal bias toward competition; in this regard, the economic and business climate in the United States is very different from that found in western Europe or Japan, where consortium agreements among industrial firms are commonplace. Again the problem is of the collective goods variety. If, for example, firm A comes up with a better way to build a mousetrap, why should it share that knowledge with firm B? It would prefer to capture the benefits for itself. In a consortium, firms always run up against the problem of which company will benefit the most from the cooperative research programs—the public goods—that are being conducted.

A further problem derives from technological diffusion. Even if Sematech was able to generate new production technologies, could the participating firms really capture the benefits and become more profitable and efficient as a result? Or would the new technologies simply leak abroad, where they would be incorporated by foreign competitors? The issue is one of concern to the president of Sematech, who says that new technologies diffuse overseas within "six months to a year. . . ."[36]

The impediments to corporate cooperation were made painfully clear with the demise in early 1990 of another highly touted consortium, *U.S. Memories* (USM), only six months after its creation.[37] Unlike Sematech, U.S. Memories was a for-profit venture that was to have challenged Japanese firms in the production and marketing of memory chips. But the participating companies were unable to

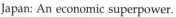

Japan: An economic superpower.

(J. P. Laffont/Sygma)

agree on financing for the project, nor did the large chip users (e.g., IBM) make a firm commitment to purchase USM's output. Observing USM's demise, Japanese executives said that it only demonstrated the short-term horizon of American industry, its unwillingness to make new investments in manufacturing, and the need for larger American semiconductor firms (American semiconductor firms like Intel are generally much smaller than Japanese companies like Toshiba and Hitachi which manufacture chips).[38]

Given the difficulties that American high-technology firms face in the international economy, given the globalization of the technology base, and given the importance of high tech to national security, what role should the U.S. government play in protecting national firms? These questions have risen high on the policy agenda. Indeed, in 1989 the U.S. government designated twenty-two technologies as critical to national security and "the long-term qualitative superiority of U.S. weapons systems."[39] Further, the government suggested that these are technologies in which "self-sufficiency" should be maintained. The technologies include microelectronic circuitry, software design, parallel processing for computers, robotics, and fiber optics. But the question remains: What should government do?

At the macroeconomic level, there is widespread agreement among economists and political scientists that the United States should reduce the budget deficit, encourage savings, improve education, and so forth. As a nation, the United States suffers from a relatively high cost of capital (caused in large measure by the budget deficit), and for much of the 1980s the dollar was overvalued, bringing exports to a halt. Further, the educational attainment of American children, especially in math and science, is far below that found in the nation's economic competitors. Microeconomic intervention will be to little avail if the macroenvironment is not supportive of industrial growth.

In any event, there is substantial disagreement about government policy at the micro level. Georgetown's Theodore Moran argues that "trade protectionism is a measure defense industrial strategists will want to avoid" as they ponder the alternatives.[40] But even Moran has an exception to his rule: In cases where the United States is dependent on a concentrated, external supplier for a critical item, a "national security tariff" might be appropriate to maintain domestic industries.

In contrast, a growing school of *strategic trade theorists* argues that governments *should* protect and promote industries critical to national security. This "school" supports government targeting of industries, import restrictions, and export promotion. Proponents of a positive role for government include such public officials as Senator Jeff Bingaman, chairman of the Armed Services Subcommittee on Defense Industries, who argued that the United States must "think strategically about how we spend billions of research dollars every year. . . ."[41] Bingaman played a key congressional role in the founding of Sematech.

Advocates of industrial policy cite, of course, Japan as their role model. It is said that Japan's Ministry of International Trade and Investment has demonstrated that industrial targeting works, and can be used to hasten investment in strategic sectors. At the same time, trade policy can be manipulated to ensure protected markets for domestically made goods. In this way, states can create "added value."

To the extent that the Japanese state has outsmarted the market (and there is substantial academic debate concerning business-government relations in Japan),[42] the lessons for the United States and other envious countries remain unclear. Historical analysis suggests that the ability of countries to adopt the policy approaches of their rivals is constrained by both cultural and political factors. On a cultural level, it appears that some states may find it easier than others to reach a domestic consensus over the direction and goals of economic policy. On a political level, the ability of central governments to execute various options depends heavily on the legal and legislative frameworks established over the history of the state. Thus, even if Japan, or any other state, did provide a role model for industrial policy, the question of "what next?" would still remain.

But as defense spending declines and the process of globalization proceeds, the debate over the role of government in industrial protection and technology stimulation will likely become more heated. Increasingly, Americans view economic competitiveness as a national security problem, and they worry about the health of the nation's manufacturing base. This will likely place pressures on members of Congress to "do something" to promote industrial growth. In the absence of sound macroeconomic management, however, microeconomic interventions will not produce lasting results.

Yet there is one further issue of concern that must be addressed in this section on technology dependence, and that is the question of foreign direct investment (FDI), particularly in defense-related industries. The top five foreign investors in the United States—Britain (102 billion dollars), Japan (53 billion dollars), the Netherlands (49 billion dollars), Canada (27 billion dollars), and Germany (24 billion dollars)—in 1990 held over 250 billion dollars in assets, including oil companies, real estate, and—increasingly—defense-related industries (see Table 8-3). In a recent opinion poll, 69 percent of the Americans questioned said that there was "too much" Japanese investment in the United States.[43]

Although concerns over foreign direct investment have economic, political, and military roots, we will focus only on the latter in the discussion that follows.[44] From a military perspective, the issues arising from foreign direct investment are threefold: (1) Do the armed forces have unrestricted access to the production of the foreign-owned plant? (2) Do foreign owners respect U.S. export controls? (3) Do foreigners use domestic operations to carry out industrial espionage or to gain access to classified research? Each of these raises difficult questions for public officials.

These questions came into sharp focus in 1987 when Japan's Fujitsu Corporation announced its plan to purchase troubled Fairchild Semiconductor of California, a unit of the French giant Schlumberger. Fairchild was an "also-ran" semiconductor firm that had been suffering huge losses for several years and was thus unable to make the fresh investments needed to remain competitive in a rapidly evolving industry. Despite a search for domestic buyers,

Table 8-3 Foreign Acquisitions, by Country

Country	Number of U.S. Companies Purchased	
	Past 10 Years	1987
1. United Kingdom	640	78
2. Canada	435	28
3. Germany	150	15
4. France	113	19
5. Japan	94	15
6. Switzerland	86	9
7. Netherlands	81	9
8. Australia	68	17
9. Sweden	63	9
10. Italy	31	6

Source: Eric Rosengren, "Is the United States for Sale? Foreign Acquisitions of U.S. Companies," New England Economic Review (November/December 1988): 50.

Fairchild's investment bankers came up empty-handed. Finally, in an effort to establish a toehold in the American market, Fujitsu made an offer to purchase 80 percent of the firm for 400 million dollars.[45]

In most cases, this would have been a happy ending. But the purchase of a semiconductor firm by a Japanese electronics company catalyzed a backlash of protectionist sentiment. Fears were stated that the Japanese would gain access to advanced U.S. technology, enabling them to put even more pressure on the American firms still battling to survive in this highly competitive market. Senator James Exon wrote to President Reagan, arguing that he block the takeover. "It is imperative," he wrote, "for our national defense and overall security that we maintain our existing advantages. . . ."[46] Somehow, none of the protagonists cared to remind the President that Fairchild was already owned by a foreign firm, albeit a French one.[47] Ultimately, the Pentagon vetoed the Fairchild sale; in late 1987 the firm was bought by an American company, National Semiconductor, for 120 million dollars, or 280 million dollars less than Fujitsu had offered!

The Fairchild case demonstrated how national security concerns had entered the debate over foreign direct investment in the United States. By 1988, the Pentagon was investigating any number of proposed acquisitions, and in several cases it had recommended that purchases not go forward. As Pentagon official Robert McCormack suggested, "We could become the ultimate takeover defense."[48]

In the United States, foreign acquisition of American assets is reviewed by an interagency group called the Committee on Foreign Investment in the United States (CFIUS). Under the Exon-Florio amendment to the 1989 federal trade bill, introduced following the Fairchild case, the Department of Defense is empowered to review and in some cases block foreign investment for national security reasons.[49] The power of the amendment was demonstrated in early 1990 when President Bush vetoed the sale of an American manufacturer of airplane parts to a firm owned by the Chinese government. Bush determined that the Chinese "might be seeking technology in the United States that is restricted for export or might be put to military use."[50]

And yet the Pentagon recognizes that there are real benefits that accrue from foreign direct investment. In many cases, foreigners bring newer technology, more efficient production techniques, and higher levels of support for R&D than American firms. As Department of Defense official Robert McCormack has remarked, "Anything that strengthens the industrial base in the U.S. is beneficial."[51] Thus, the Pentagon finds itself in the difficult position of attracting foreign investment with one hand while pushing it away with the other.

Despite a general American presumption in favor of free investment flows, "the problems associated with foreign direct investment are likely to increase in frequency rather than diminish."[52] Until the United States bolsters its savings and investment rates and reduces the budget and trade deficits, a large pool of foreign savings will continue to enter the country in search of "cheap" assets. Although efforts to restrict foreign investment are unwise in most cases, there will certainly be a political temptation to interfere with international business transactions.

CONCLUSION

Dependence on foreign countries for vital resources and technologies is naturally unsettling for public officials charged with national security. Laissez faire economics aside, not all the arguments in favor of protectionism and trade restrictions can be dismissed out of hand. As this review has shown, countries *have* used asymmetric dependencies to win political advantage; oil embargoes, technology transfer controls, and unilateral price hikes have all been used by states to advance their interests in an anarchic international system.

The costs of government intervention in the economy to advance national security, however, may outweigh the benefits that accrue. The Pentagon's tacit blockage of the Fairchild sale to Fujitsu cost Fairchild shareholders 280 million dollars, with questionable benefits in terms of America's technology base. Government efforts to produce alternative energy fuels during the 1970s were an economic disaster. The ability of the U.S.—or any other—government to "target" high-technology industries for future growth remains to be seen; the experience of such countries as Japan, France, and the United States has produced decidedly mixed results.

Further, the presumption that technologies can be captured for national gain is becoming increasingly questionable. As multinational enterprises continue to spread globally, governments cannot be sure where defense-related R&D is being conducted, by whom it is being conducted, and where the various components going into military end-items are being produced. In such an environment, protection becomes an inefficient solution to the defense problem, even if it were desirable.

One "solution" to this problem of globalization may be the creation of international joint ventures. It may be less distressing for Pentagon planners to buy from a joint venture between Chrysler and Mitsubishi than from Mitsubishi alone. Joint ventures and corporate alliances allow countries to maintain the myth of "domestic" industries while accessing technology and capital from abroad.

The problem of national security in a global economy is bound to become more complex in the coming decades. States remain responsible for the provision of defense and social welfare, but they cannot provide these goods without entering the world economy. Throughout the postwar era, the industrial states have accepted the risks associated with the division of labor, so long as some defense-related production remained safely grounded on national soil and critical raw materials were stockpiled for emergency needs. Today, these traditional efforts to reduce vulnerability are less likely to prove effective during a crisis.

As a beginning, the most useful policy measures that states can take are at the macroeconomic level. If the government does not provide a climate conducive to investment and entrepreneurial activity, microeconomic interventions will have little effect. Beyond that, of course, governments can play a positive role in supporting basic research and development and in supporting education at all levels. Industrial targeting, protectionism, and other such efforts at the micro level will inevitably occur on a case-by-case basis, but as general policy approaches to the promotion of defense-related industries they are probably best avoided.

Selected Bibliography

Hirschman, Albert, *National Power and the Structure of Foreign Trade* (Berkeley: University of California Press, 1945). This powerful account details Nazi Germany's successful effort at turning eastern Europe into an economically dependent region.

Keohane, Robert, and Joseph Nye, *Power and Interdependence* (Boston: Little, Brown, 1977). This text has had a major influence on international relations scholarship, challenging traditional realist notions with the paradigm of "complex interdependence."

Lipschutz, Ronnie, *When Nations Clash* (Cambridge, Mass.: Ballinger, 1989). This is a penetrating study of international conflict over energy and raw materials.

Moran, Theodore, "The Globalization of America's Defense Industries," *International Security* (Summer 1990). This theoretically sophisticated article makes a set of policy recommendations regarding the problem of foreign dependence in defense-related industries. See also Moran, "International Economics and National Security," *Foreign Affairs* (Winter 1990/1991).

National Academy of Engineering, *Technology and Global Industry* (Washington, D.C.: National Academy Press, 1987). This edited volume contains several excellent articles that introduce the policy problems associated with technological diffusion.

Notes

1. Raymond Vernon, "National Needs, Global Resources," unpublished manuscript, Economics and National Security Program, Harvard University, Cambridge, Mass., 1990.
2. See Christopher Davis, "Soviet National Security Strategy and Foreign Economic Relations," unpublished manuscript, Economics and National Security Program, Harvard University, Cambridge, Mass., July 1990.
3. See Robert Keohane and Joseph Nye, *Power and Interdependence* (Boston: Little, Brown, 1977).
4. See Albert Hirschman, *National Security and the Structure of Foreign Trade* (Berkeley: University of California Press, 1944).
5. Ibid., p. 12.
6. For a detailed study, see Ethan B. Kapstein, *The Insecure Alliance: Energy Crises and Western Politics since 1944* (New York: Oxford University Press, 1990).
7. Edward Mason, "American Security and Access to Raw Materials," *World Politics 1* (January 1949): 148–160.
8. Ronnie Lipschutz, *When Nations Clash* (Cambridge, Mass.: Ballinger, 1989), p. 101.
9. Kenneth Kessel, *Strategic Minerals: U.S. Alternatives* (Washington, D.C.: National Defense University Press, 1990), p. 14.
10. The White House, "National Defense Stockpile Policy," July 8, 1985, press release.
11. Kessel, *Strategic Minerals*, p. 92.
12. Robert Wilson, "Natural Resources: Dependency and Vulnerability," in Uri Ra'anan and Charles Perry, eds., *Strategic Minerals and International Security* (Cambridge, Mass.: Institute for Foreign Policy Analysis, 1985), p. 29.
13. For details, see Kapstein, *The Insecure Alliance.*
14. Robert Keohane, "Hegemonic Leadership and U.S. Foreign Economic Policy in the Long Decade of the 1950s," in William P. Avery and David P. Rapkin, eds., *America in a Changing World Political Economy* (New York: Longman, 1982), pp. 70–71.
15. See Matthew Wald, "A Little Oil Means a Lot," *New York Times*, August 27, 1990, p. 1.
16. For more on this, see Peter Katzenstein, ed., *Between Power and Plenty* (Madison: University of Wisconsin Press, 1978).
17. Theodore Moran, "New Sources of Insecurity in the 1990s" (prepared for the Aspen Strategy Group, 1990); and Moran, "International Economics and National Security," *Foreign Affairs* (Winter 1990/1991).
18. Ibid.
19. Interview, U.S. Department of Defense, 1990.
20. Raymond Vernon, "National Needs, Global Resources," unpublished manuscript, Economics and National Security Program, Harvard University, Cambridge, Mass., 1990.

21. See A. Hunter Dupree, "National Security and the Post-War Science Establishment in the United States," *Nature 323* (1988): 214.
22. Ibid., pp. 213–216.
23. Raymond Vernon, "Coping with Technological Change: U.S. Problems and Prospects," in National Academy of Engineering, *Technology and Global Industry* (Washington, D.C.: National Academy Press, 1987), p. 173.
24. Ibid.
25. Ibid.
26. See Raymond Vernon, "International Investment and International Trade in the Product Cycle," *Quarterly Journal of Economics 80* (May 1966): 190–207.
27. Raymond Vernon, *Exploring the Global Economy* (Lanham, Md.: University Press of America), p. 32.
28. Ibid.
29. Ibid.
30. *Critical Technologies Plan* (Washington, D.C.: Department of Defense, March 18, 1990).
31. Michael Porter, *The Competitive Advantage of Nations* (New York: Free Press, 1990).
32. See Samuel P. Huntington, "The U.S.—Decline or Renewal?" *Foreign Affairs* (Winter 1988/1989): 76–96.
33. Office of the Undersecretary of Defense for Acquisition, *Report of the Defense Science Board Task Force on Semiconductor Dependency* (Washington, D.C., March 1987).
34. See "Sematech: United We Stand?" *Electronic Business:* 30–37.
35. Andrew Rappaport, "Wrong Way to Save Chip Industry," *Wall Street Journal,* December 15, 1989, p. A14.
36. "Sematech: United We Stand?"
37. For an early view, see George Melloan, "Chipping Away at Good Old-Fashioned Competition," *Wall Street Journal,* July 11, 1989, p. A21.
38. David Sanger, "Contrasts on Chips," *New York Times,* January 18, 1990, p. D1.
39. Martin Tolchin, "Critical Technologies: 22 Make the U.S. List," *New York Times,* March 16, 1989, p. D1.
40. Theodore Moran, "The Globalization of America's Defense Industries," *International Security* (Summer 1990).
41. Cited in Tolchin, "Critical Technologies."
42. See, for example, Thomas Hout and Ira Magaziner, *Japanese Industrial Policy* (Berkeley, Calif.: Institute for International Studies, 1981); and Chalmers Johnson, *MITI and the Japanese Miracle* (Stanford, Calif.: Stanford University Press, 1982).
43. Urban Lehner and Alan Murray, "Strained Alliance," *Wall Street Journal,* June 19, 1990, p. A1.
44. But for a review, see Raymond Vernon, "Foreign Owned Enterprise in the United States: Threat or Opportunity?" (Center for Business and Government, Kennedy School of Government, Harvard University, Cambridge, Mass., June 20, 1988).
45. For the background, see Michael Malone, "Fear and Xenophobia in Silicon Valley," *Wall Street Journal,* February 23, 1987, p. 1.
46. Ibid.
47. Ibid.
48. Andy Pasztor and Eduardo Lachica, "Pentagon Is Handed Growing New Defense Role: Policing U.S. Corporate Takeovers from Abroad," *Wall Street Journal,* March 8, 1989, p. A16.
49. For a review of CFIUS and Exon-Florio, see Jeffrey Bialos, "The Review of Foreign Acquisitions on National Security Grounds" (Washington, D.C.: Weil, Gotshal and Manges, 1989).

50. Andrew Rosenthal, "Bush, Citing Security Law, Voids Sale of Aviation Concern to China," *New York Times*, February 3, 1990, p. A1.
51. Cynthia Mitchell, "Buying American," *Wall Street Journal*, April 28, 1988, p. A1.
52. Vernon, "Foreign Owned Enterprise," p. 23.

9

Conclusions

"The frequency of war is in itself the best argument against accepting the idea of its abnormality." ——*Alan S. Milward*[1]

The end of the cold war notwithstanding, the political economy of national security will remain a prominent policy issue in every nation-state. The spread of defense industries and advanced weaponry around the globe, the diffusion of defense-related technologies, and the hard choices over force structure, procurement, and deployment that must be made as defense budgets decline will test the ability of our public officials everywhere to make wise normative decisions. Indeed, the problem of national security in a global economy poses one of the great management problems of our times.

This concluding chapter has three objectives: first, it draws out some of the policy implications of the issues that the book has addressed thus far. Second, it raises questions about the capacity of nation-states to cope with the rapidly changing economic and security environments. Finally, it provides some suggestions for future research.

POLICY ISSUES

At the outset it must be emphasized that the distinguishing characteristic of the international system of the early 1990s is *uncertainty*. The Manichaean cold war is apparently giving way to a new order, but what that order will look like remains unclear. Some analysts believe that we are entering a multipolar era, although the definition of the poles is contested. Many scholars believe that world politics will revolve around the poles of Japan, western Europe, and the United States. Others believe that western Europe itself will revert to a pre-World War I geopolitical environment in which Germany, France, Britain, and the Soviet Union vie for supremacy. Others believe that, despite relative Soviet decline, bipolarity will endure, given the overwhelming nuclear arsenals possessed by

Moscow and Washington. And still others hold that the world has entered a new, unipolar age, in which the United States is the only great power capable of exercising both economic *and* military power.[2]

The security environment that emerges from this period of uncertainty will naturally influence the decisions about force structure that each country must make. But more decisively than in the past, the economic environment will also play a role in the decision-making process. While public officials in various capitals grapple with the shape of the future as they determine such critical issues as the integration of the European Community, the shift from centrally planned to market-based economies, and the establishment of free trade zones in North America and elsewhere, business executives have already sought global solutions to corporate problems.

Indeed, the territories that states occupy have little to do with the space in which multinational firms operate. Just as the international security environment has always "pressed down" on decision makers, focusing their choices, so too the economic environment is "pressing down," providing states with new sets of opportunities and constraints. As defense officials ponder the future of their armed forces, they must also take into account the location of industries that provide weapons and materiel. Thus, the defense economy is firmly embedded in the international economy, with profound policy implications. How should public officials respond?

In terms of the political economy of national security, state policies should be examined along their macroeconomic, microeconomic, and international economic dimensions. In terms of macroeconomics, the most important contemporary issues have to do with managing the decline in defense spending and maintaining (or, in the case of the United States, creating) a macroenvironment that encourages savings and investment. Each of these will be discussed in turn.

Recalling the macroeconomic identity that $Y = C + I + G + (X - M)$, it will be seen that defense spending (part of G) remains a significant contributor to GNP; in the United States in recent years defense has been responsible for 5–7 percent of gross national product, and in some countries (notably the Soviet Union and those of the Middle East) it is much higher. A cut in defense spending of 25 percent or more would thus have a measurable impact on GNP, with potentially severe consequences for industrial output and employment.

The objectives of public policy during a downturn in defense spending should thus be to stimulate demand and to facilitate the transfer of resources from the military to commercial sectors. In most industrial countries—including the United States—there is legislation that requires governments to pursue full-employment policies (e.g., the Employment Act of 1946 and the Trade Adjustment Act). Policies to maintain economic growth and investment include five general instruments: (1) tax policy, particularly tax credits and tax cuts, (2) monetary policy, especially lowering interest rates, (3) increased government purchases of nondefense products and services, (4) increased transfer payments and adjustment assistance to displaced workers and industries, and (5) export promotion policies.

The importance of establishing a sound macroeconomic environment for savings and investment cannot be understated. While American analysts, for example, tend to focus on the success of such countries as Japan and South Korea in "targeting" high-technology industries for growth, one of the greatest accomplishments of these countries has been in the macroeconomic and not the microeconomic realm. The newly industrializing countries of Asia, along with Germany and—more recently—France, have committed themselves to a macroeconomy that encourages (in the Asian case many would say coerces) savings and, consequently, investment. In that investment is the source of innovation and economic growth, it is critical to national security. It is notable that in recent years Japan, an economy that is only 40 percent the size of the American economy, has invested more in *absolute terms.* The lack of investment in the United States does not bode well for the nation's future.

Despite—or perhaps because of—the persistent failure of public officials to deliver sound macroeconomic policies, at the level of the microeconomy states will continue to intervene to protect and promote specific industries and to finance research and development. Normally, these interventions will be justified for reasons of national security, but often they are simply a political response to special-interest groups. What guidelines may be suggested at the micro level to help direct public policy?

As stated in Chapter 8, there is a well-established literature in support of the proposition that governments have a positive role to play in funding basic research and development. Different countries, however, have adopted different strategies in this area, and these are worth our notice. The Japanese, for example, have targeted their research and development on the manufacturing and production end of business enterprise, rather than the development of new products. Economic efficiency, cost control, and the commercialization of products are among Japan's R&D goals—goals that stand in sharp contrast to those pursued in the United States.[3]

In the United States, R&D has been the province of the military-industrial complex for much of the postwar period; indeed, more than 70 percent of R&D in the United States is directed toward defense and aerospace. As a result, American firms have spent the bulk of their research dollars meeting the needs of the Pentagon rather than the consumer marketplace. This has led to the production of high-performance weapons systems and to impressive advances in systems integration, but it has led to relatively few spin-offs in the areas of production technology and the commercial economy.

So long as America had few economic competitors, this strategy could be pursued with little downside. But in recent years the malign consequences of an R&D policy focused on defense have become clear, as American inventions are all too often put into production not by U.S. firms, but by the Japanese, the Germans, and others. There is widespread consensus among industry executives that policy changes are desperately needed if the nation is to remain competitive in high-technology products.[4]

Among those changes, one idea has become especially prominent, and that is the promotion of *dual-use* technology, that is, technology that has both military and civil applications (e.g., computers and jet engines). To date, Department of Defense regulations have largely forced U.S. firms to separate their defense and nondefense activities, reducing the diffusion of technology between the two sectors. However, with pressure being placed on the Pentagon to "do more" for the civilian economy, a number of innovative programs have been established, including *MANTECH*, which focuses on manufacturing technology, and *CIM*— computer integrated manufacturing. In spite of these promising developments, "technology base R&D has amounted to only about 10 percent of the total military R&D budget. . . ."[5]

The dual-use technology issue is likely to claim increasing attention in the coming years, as public officials seek a way to maintain both national security *and* economic competitiveness. But stringent security controls will continue to hinder firms that seek to commercialize technology that was initially developed for the military. Ironically, as economic competition replaces the cold war as a national security issue, and as officials become increasingly preoccupied by threats in the developing world, technology and trade controls may become even more cumbersome. Such controls, of course, will continue to stand in opposition to the general free trade ideas that most industrial states accept, in principle if not in practice.

Beyond its role in support of R&D, the state will also continue to intervene in the marketplace to protect and maintain defense-related industries. But with growing pressure on the federal budget in general, and on the defense budget in particular, policymakers will have to be more discerning in choosing who will survive and who will be allowed to die. Again, some decision rules will be needed.

The most sophisticated set of rules yet to emerge have come from Georgetown professor Theodore Moran.[6] Borrowing from microeconomic and antitrust theory, Moran has suggested that the Pentagon adopt the "4/50" rule in its deliberations over protection. The 4/50 rule stipulates that when a market is controlled by four firms having over 50 percent of the market, there is justification for government intervention on antitrust, antimonopoly grounds. Since the Pentagon's primary concern, Moran argues, should be access to needed goods and services, it should focus its attention on the number of suppliers in a market. So long as there are more than four suppliers—foreign or domestic—the Pentagon has no business protecting manufacturers.

At the microeconomic level there are also a number of seemingly more mundane changes that the Pentagon could make to assist industry. For example, the Department of Defense in recent years has placed increasing pressure on defense firms to make "up-front" investments in R&D and prototypes, and it has shifted toward fixed-price contracting (contracts in which the price is set before all the program requirements are known and understood). There is a case to be made for making the Pentagon take on more of the up-front risk, so that defense firms are not forced into "betting the company" with each new program. This is not to say that all existing defense firms should be kept in business; clearly some mergers and acquisitions—and failures—will occur over the next decade. But the Pentagon should not use its monopsony power to destroy the industry, either.

With regard to the international economy, there are a number of contemporary national security concerns, including export controls, foreign direct investment, and foreign sourcing of defense-related technology. Let us treat each of these in turn.

Export controls have always been a controversial instrument of national security policy. While most American executives would agree that controls should be placed on weapons sales and sales of highly sensitive technology, there is little support for the cumbersome set of controls that now licenses export sales of over 150 billion dollars annually. By one estimate, these controls cost the U.S. economy nearly 10 billion dollars per year in lost sales, administrative costs, and so forth.[7]

Beyond the economic costs, export controls have led to significant political controversy among the members of the western alliance, and within the United States itself. For example, when the Reagan administration used such controls to block the sale of technology to the Soviet Union for the Urengoi natural gas pipeline project (as punishment for the declaration of martial law in Poland in December 1981), there was a tremendous outcry from business groups and members of Congress, especially since the controls were being used at a time when the American economy was mired in its worst postwar recession. When the President subsequently extended the controls to the licensees of American firms overseas, a major alliance conflict erupted. The lesson is not that the President was wrong to use export controls; it is that their efficacy depends in large measure on public and alliance support and on the number of states that control a given technology.

As the cold war unwinds, many analysts have expected the export control regime to weaken. There are signs that this may already be happening. The CoCom list is getting shorter, as the allies rush to do business in the Soviet Union and eastern Europe. Indeed, one wonders if CoCom can survive the end of the cold war.

But the need for some export controls will remain, and even new controls may be applied. For example, in 1987 the industrial countries agreed to voluntarily limit the export of ballistic missile technology to the third world. Further, as countries such as Iraq and Libya pursue the production of nuclear and chemical weapons, the need for country-specific controls will remain. And changes in the Soviet Union aside, there is still a place for east-west technology controls.

What about *import controls*, specifically controls on foreign direct investment in the United States? As stated in Chapter 8, the gap in domestic savings and investment has attracted foreigners to this country, where they have purchased both financial and real assets. Among the real assets are a growing number of high-technology firms, including firms that pursue defense-related research, development, and production. Should the Pentagon prevent such investment, as it did with the Fairchild-Fujitsu case? Or should foreigners be allowed into the United States on equal terms as domestic investors, as befits our historical tradition in this issue area?

To begin the discussion, it must be emphasized that foreign direct investment largely reflects America's macroeconomic imbalances. Given the shortage of domestic savings, there is a need for foreign capital to provide for the investment that is in demand. In the best of all possible worlds, more domestic savings would be encouraged, but foreign savings at the margin are certainly preferable to no inflows at all.

With this as our starting point, it may be stated that, with very few exceptions, the government does not have much of a role to play in preventing foreign direct investment. Fortunately, this is the tack that the United States has taken to date. To be sure, the American government has the right to force foreign owners to segment their defense activities and to implement American security procedures (foreign owners must do this if they wish for their subsidiaries to maintain security clearances). But in few cases will government be justified in blocking the investment altogether. In the Fairchild case, the government failed to make the case that the benefits of denial outweighed the costs.

What about import restrictions on foreign-made defense goods and services that compete with American industry? Again, unless the foreign supplier is a monopolist, there is little case to be made for import restrictions on security grounds. American firms have petitioned for relief under Section 232 of the Trade Act, which allows the government to prevent imports when the national security is threatened, and in recent years the machine tool, bearings, and plastic injection molding machinery industries have won relief. But "import restrictions are generally considered to be ineffective in helping U.S. industry gain its competitive edge."[8] Indeed, over the long run, the Pentagon may be hindered rather than helped by import restrictions, as it comes to depend on high-cost, inefficient, and less advanced manufacturers of needed goods and services.

In short, as governments ponder their national security role in the global economy, the focus of attention should be placed squarely on macroeconomic policy. Microeconomic interventions and protectionism will rarely benefit either the domestic economy or the national defense. In contrast, the establishment of a climate that fosters fresh investment will do both.

THE CAPACITY OF GOVERNMENTS

The problem of maintaining national security in a global economy will tax governments everywhere. A critical variable in determining how well governments handle the challenges they must face is their institutional capacity to filter information and make appropriate decisions. In most countries, defense and economic policy have occupied separate worlds, with only ad hoc coordination by interagency committees on such issues as export controls, foreign direct investment, and the arms trade. One may rightly wonder about the ability of our traditional governmental institutions to respond to the complexities of the modern world.

In the United States, for example, the institution responsible for coordinating economic and defense policy at the highest level is the National Security Council (NSC). But the NSC itself is broken up into divisions that are responsible for defense and economics, and these divisions tend to be run not by broadly trained strategists, but by regional or functional specialists. Further, few national security advisers have possessed the tools necessary for integrating economic and security concerns. Henry Kissinger, for example, who served as Richard Nixon's national security adviser and secretary of state, now admits that he was woefully unprepared to cope with the economic challenges that faced him, such as the Arab oil embargo of 1973–1974.

The reader of this book has undoubtedly already become aware of an alphabet soup of institutions that have some economic and some security responsibilities, including the CIA, CFIUS, CoCom, NSC, NSA, and so forth. And over the coming decade, it is expected that the traditional security- and intelligence-oriented institutions will become more geared toward economic issues. The National Security Agency, for example, "is debating plans to shift its global electronic eavesdropping network to other activities, including spying on world trade and financial transactions. . . ."[9]

It is already apparent that governments are becoming preoccupied with a wide range of issues at the interface of economics and national security. In examining those issues, however, there is room for skepticism concerning the ability of contemporary institutions to handle the problems they will face. In the 1950s, the United States had a National Security Resources Board, an Office of Trade and Security, and other organizations dedicated to problems in the realm of defense economics. These institutions, run by officials with broad experience and training in both economic and security questions, attempted to meet the mobilization and defense-industrial problems of their day. Should such organizations be resurrected?

Concern about the capacity of the federal government to mediate issues in the area of defense economics (or, in current Washington parlance, "economic security," which has a broader connotation) has recently been expressed by Senators Jake Garn and John Heinz, who have presented a bill to Congress— Senate bill S.1796—that would create a new Office of Strategic Trade and Technology (OSTT) in the White House. The OSTT would be responsible for implementing export control and technology transfer policies, and its director would also sit on such existing committees as CFIUS, the Competitiveness Policy Council, and the Trade Policy Council. According to Garn and Heinz, the director would have important responsibilities for "ensuring the economic security of the United States."

Without commenting on the specifics of the Garn-Heinz proposal, the concept of establishing a point person or agency responsible for issues at the interface of economics and security is very much in the Washington tradition of creating new bureaucracies to solve every emerging problem. On the one hand, the idea of creating a new organization must seem tempting. As controversies like that which pitted the Commerce Department against the Defense Department over the coproduction of a jet fighter with Japan—the FSX—demonstrate, there is a powerful need for integrative institutions in Washington. Without such institutional capabilities, the government will find itself unable to respond in a timely fashion to the critical issues of the day.

But on the other hand, it would appear that intermediate steps are available that could be usefully followed before many new institutions are created. Prominently, the United States and other governments make extensive use of interagency committees in their deliberations of complex issues, but scholars have done little investigation into the workings of such groups. Is the interagency process successful, or does it have inherent failings? Could it be improved, or is there a role for new organizational forms? In-depth research would be useful before yet other bureaucracies are created.

The question of the capacity of governments is not simply an institutional one. On another level, fundamental questions must be raised concerning state-society relations in an increasingly global economy. How have domestic politics changed with economic globalization? Do states have the same ability to execute their preferred national security policies as they may have possessed in the past? Or does the global economy pose a fundamental constraint on state action? These are basic questions to ask, but they have been little explored by political scientists. If there has been a transformation of relations between governments and the societies they manage, this has important consequences for national security no less than economic policymaking.[10]

FUTURE RESEARCH

This book will have fulfilled a large part of its task if it has stimulated the reader to pursue research in the political economy of national security. Given that the field has been left largely untouched for nearly a generation, there is no shortage of topics that would contribute to our understanding of the modern defense economy. Beyond that, however, research in this area can illuminate broader questions concerning the international economic and security environments.

Without any attempt at providing an exhaustive list, a few of the questions worthy of further study, listed in terms of "macro," "micro," and "international" issues, are:

I. Macro Questions

1. What, if any, macroeconomic policies will be needed during the 1990s to offset the decline in defense spending? What can be learned from the lessons of the past concerning the economic effects of sharp declines in defense spending?
2. How are defense budgets set in different countries? How are trade-offs made between guns and butter in the budget process, if they are made at all?
3. What, if any, institutional changes might states adopt in order to integrate issues at the interface of economics and national security?

II. Micro Questions

4. How are states and industries managing the decline in defense spending that is now under way? What microeconomic policies are being adopted? What are the prospects for conversion of military enterprise?
5. What policy actions are states taking to promote technological development in defense-related areas? What policies should they adopt?
6. What, if any, incentives should be provided to industry to continue defense work, given the downturn in spending?

III. International Questions

7. How will changes in the international security environment affect the international economic environment? Will economic tensions become more widespread as the cold war military competition recedes? Will international economic relations become more competitive, or might they remain cooperative? Are there useful historical analogies that could be studied?
8. How are national security officials in different countries responding to the globalization of the world economy? Are pressures increasing for protectionism in certain industrial countries? Are governments spending more for research and development? For stockpiles of imported goods?
9. From a security standpoint, what is the appropriate role of the United States and its allies in the economic rehabilitation of eastern Europe? Of the Soviet Union? Should foreign aid be provided outright? Or should it be contingent on political change? Should private-sector investment in the east be regulated by the allies? Does the western alliance—NATO—have a specific economic role to play in world politics?
10. What have been the policies of the advanced industrial countries toward the proliferation of defense-related industries and technologies? What policies are likely to emerge in the future regarding the proliferation of defense industries and technologies? What are the prospects for a multilateral regime to control the spread of armaments and defense production technology?

CONCLUSION

In the past, textbook writers have treated the defense economy as a closed system. Even as states entered the international economy and accepted the logic of comparative advantage, scholars fenced off the defense sector, giving it an appearance of autarky. But self-sufficiency has been a historical aberration in the defense sector, existing briefly if imperfectly in the United States and Soviet Union after World War II. For most of history, states have depended upon the global economy for labor, money, and materiel. A fundamental tension has thus existed between national security and the international economy, a tension that is reemerging in the United States and the Soviet Union as the costs of self-sufficiency grow in each country.

The internationalization of the defense economy has proceeded partly owing to market forces and partly owing to state-directed forces. International collaborative arrangements for the production of armaments, arms sales, industrial espionage, and technology diffusion have all contributed to the globalization of defense-related industries. Interdependence in the defense sector poses a new set of challenges for those public officials raised on autarky. It also poses fresh challenges for defense industry executives, who in the 1990s must cope both with globalization and with declines in procurement spending.

The myriad changes in the defense economy are occurring at a time when the international security environment is also in tremendous flux and uncertainty. With the end of the cold war, fundamental questions are being asked in every state about security policy, force structure, and defense budgeting. The answers to those questions will naturally shape the future of defense spending, procurement decisions, and technology policy.

As the changes in the economic and security environments play themselves out, we may well find that the traditional nation-state is ill-equipped to respond to the many demands being placed upon it. Already, a wide variety of economic and political issues are requiring international policy coordination. It has been argued here that many prominent issues in the defense economy, such as control over arms transfers, will also require multilateral agreements.

But so long as the international system remains anarchic, states will have to depend on their own wherewithal for survival. The self-help nature of the international system means that the search for security and prosperity will endure. Should American hegemonic power decline and the international economy break down, that search could become more challenging than at any time in postwar history.

Surveying the anarchic environment, the great strategist Clausewitz said that war was "state policy by other means." Surveying the international economy, Benjamin Franklin said that "no nation was ever ruined by trade." Contemporary defense economics recognizes these two truths, but still seeks their reconciliation. If this book advances that process, its mission has been largely accomplished.

Notes

1. Alan S. Milward, *War, Economy and Society* (Berkeley: University of California Press, 1979), p. 2.
2. See Joseph Nye, *Bound to Lead* (New York: Basic Books, 1990), who makes an articulate case for American leadership. See also Henry Nau, *The Myth of America's Decline* (New York: Oxford University Press, 1990).
3. See Jean-Claude Derian, *America's Struggle for Leadership in Technology* (Cambridge, Mass.: MIT Press, 1990).
4. Alan Murray and Urban Lehner, "What U.S. Scientists Discover, the Japanese Convert—into Profit," *Wall Street Journal*, June 25, 1990, p. A1.

5. Alexander Flax, "Interdiffusion of Military and Civil Technologies in the United States of America," in Philip Gummett and Judith Reppy, eds., *The Relations between Defense and Civil Technologies* (Boston: Kluwer, 1988), p. 134.

6. Theodore Moran, "The Globalization of America's Defense Industries," *International Security* (Summer 1990).

7. National Academy of Sciences, *Balancing the National Interest* (Washington, D.C.: NAS Press, 1987).

8. *Foreign Vulnerability of Critical Industries* (Arlington, Va.: TASC, 1990).

9. Michael Wines, "Security Agency Debates New Role: Economic Spying," *New York Times,* June 18, 1990, p. A1.

10. One scholar beginning to examine these issues is Michael Barnett of the University of Wisconsin. See Barnett, "High Politics Is Low Politics: The Domestic and Systemic Sources of Israeli Security Policy, 1967–1977," *World Politics* 42 (July 1990): 529–562. See also Edward Morse, *Modernization and the Transformation of International Relations* (New York: Free Press, 1976). On domestic politics in a global economy, see Helen Milner, *Resisting Protectionism* (Princeton, N.J.: Princeton University Press, 1988).

Bibliography

GOVERNMENT AND OFFICIAL DOCUMENTS

Critical Technologies Plan (Washington, D.C.: Department of Defense, 1990).
Defense Management: Report to the President (Washington, D.C.: Department of Defense, June 12, 1989).
French Defense Statistics (Paris: Ministry of Defense, 1990).
International Trade (Geneva: General Agreement on Tariffs and Trade, annual).
Militarily Significant Western Technology: An Update (Washington, D.C.: Department of Defense, September 1985).
U.S. Arms Control and Disarmament Agency, *World Military Expenditures and Arms Transfers* (Washington, D.C.: Government Printing Office, annual).
U.S. Central Intelligence Agency, *A Guide to Monetary Measures of Soviet Defense Activities,* November 1987.
———, *Dollar Costing of Foreign Defense Activities: A Primer on Methodology and Use of the Data,* July 1988.
U.S. Congress, *Ballistic Missile Proliferation Potential of Non-Major Military Powers* (Washington, D.C.: Congressional Research Service, 1987).
———, *Defense Spending and the Economy* (Washington, D.C.: Congressional Budget Office, February 1983).
———, Joint Economic Committee, *Economic Effects of Vietnam Spending* (Washington, D.C.: Government Printing Office, 1967).
———, Office of Technology Assessment, *Holding the Edge* (Washington, D.C.: Government Printing Office, 1988).
———, Office of Technology Assessment, *Arming Our Allies* (Washington, D.C.: Government Printing Office, 1990).
U.S. Department of Defense, *Annual Report to Congress* (Washington, D.C.: Government Printing Office, annual).

———, *Bolstering Defense Industrial Competitiveness* (Washington, D.C.: Government Printing Office, 1988).

———, *Report of the Defense Science Board on Semiconductor Dependence* (Washington, D.C.: Defense Science Board, March 1987).

———, *Soviet Military Power: 1989* (Washington, D.C.: Government Printing Office, 1989).

U.S. Office of the President, *Conventional Arms Transfer Policy* (Washington, D.C.: The White House, July 1981).

———, *National Defense Stockpile Policy* (Washington, D.C., White House press release, July 8, 1985).

———, President's Blue Ribbon Commission on Defense Management (Packard Commission), *A Formula for Action: A Report to the President on Defense Acquisition* (Washington, D.C., April 1986).

BOOKS, ARTICLES, AND DISSERTATIONS

Adams, Gordon, *The Iron Triangle: The Politics of Defense Contracting* (New York: Council on Economic Priorities, 1981).

——— and David Gold, *Defense Spending and the Economy: Does the Defense Dollar Make a Difference?* (Washington, D.C.: Defense Budget Project, 1987).

Adams, James, *Merchants of Death and the Arms Race* (New York: Atlantic Monthly Press, 1990).

Albrecht, Ulrich, "The Federal Republic of Germany and Italy: New Strategies for Mid-Sized Weapons Exporters," *Journal of International Affairs 40* (1986).

Alexander, Barbara, "Prime Contract Competition Regimes and Subcontracting among Military Aircraft Manufacturers," Ph.D. dissertation, Harvard University, Cambridge, Mass., 1990.

Ambler, Eric, *Journey into Fear* (New York: Carroll and Graf, 1937).

America's Next Crisis (Arlington, Va.: Aerospace Education Foundation, September 1989).

Art, Robert J., *The TFX Decision: McNamara and the Military* (Boston: Little, Brown, 1968).

———, "Why We Overspend and Underaccomplish: Weapons Procurement and the Military-Industrial Complex," in Steven Rosen, ed., *Testing the Theory of the Military-Industrial Complex* (Lexington, Mass.: Lexington Books, 1973).

———, "The Pentagon: The Case for Biennial Budgeting," *Political Science Quarterly 104* (1989).

Augustine, Norman, *Augustine's Laws* (New York: Viking, 1986).

Azar, Edward, and Chung-In Moon, *National Security in the Third World* (London: Elgar, 1988).

Backman, Jules, et al., *War and Defense Economics* (New York: Rinehart and Co., 1952).

Baer, Werner, *Industrialization and Economic Development in Brazil* (Homewood, Ill.: Richard D. Irwin, 1965).

Baldwin, David, *Economic Statecraft* (Princeton, N.J.: Princeton University Press, 1985).

——— and Helen Milner, *The Political Economy of National Security: An Annotated Bibliography* (Boulder, Colo.: Westview Press, 1990).

Ball, Nicole, *Security and Economy in the Third World* (Princeton, N.J.: Princeton University Press, 1988).

Barnett, Michael, "High Politics Is Low Politics: The Domestic and Systemic Sources of Israeli Security Policy, 1967–1977," *World Politics 42* (July 1990).

Barnhart, Michael, *Japan Prepares for Total War* (Ithaca, N.Y.: Cornell University Press, 1987).

Benoit, Emile, *Defense and Economic Growth in Developing Countries* (Lexington, Mass.: Lexington Books, 1973).

Benson, Lucy Wilson, "Turning the Supertanker: Arms Transfer Restraint," *International Security* 3 (1978–1979).

Bolton, Roger, ed., *Defense and Disarmament* (Englewood Cliffs, N.J.: Prentice-Hall, 1966).

Bracken, Paul, "Mobilization in the Nuclear Age," *International Security* 3 (1978–1979).

Braudel, Fernand, *The Mediterranean and the Mediterranean World in the Age of Philip II* (New York: Harper & Row, 1973).

Brewer, John, *The Sinews of Power* (New York: Knopf, 1989).

Brodie, Bernard, *Seapower in the Machine Age* (Princeton, N.J.: Princeton University Press, 1941).

——, *How Much Is Enough? Guns vs. Butter Revisited* (Santa Monica, Calif.: RAND Corporation, 1975).

Brzoska, Michael, and Thomas Olson, eds., *Arms Production in the Third World* (Philadelphia: Taylor & Francis, 1986).

Burnett, William, and William Kovacic, "Reform of United States Weapons Acquisition Policy," *Yale Journal of Regulation* 6 (Summer 1989).

Callaghan, Thomas, *U.S./European Economic Cooperation in Military and Civil Technologies* (Washington, D.C.: Center for Strategic and International Studies, 1974).

——, *Pooling Allied and American Resources to Produce a Credible, Collective Conventional Deterrent* (report prepared for the U.S. Department of Defense, August 1988).

Calleo, David, *Beyond American Hegemony: The Future of the Western Alliance* (New York: Basic Books, 1987).

Caves, Richard, and Ronald Jones, *World Trade and Payments* (Boston: Little, Brown, 1981).

Center for Strategic and International Studies, *Deterrence in Decay: The Future of the U.S. Defense Industrial Base* (Washington, D.C.: Center for Strategic and International Studies, 1989).

Chan, Steve, "The Impact of Defense Spending on Economic Performance: A Survey of Evidence and Problems," *Orbis* (Summer 1985).

——, "Defense Burden and Economic Growth: Unravelling the Taiwan Enigma," *American Political Science Review* 82 (1988).

Chandler, Lester, and Donald Wallace, *Economic Mobilization and Stabilization* (New York: Henry Holt and Co., 1951).

Chardonnet, Jean, *L'Economie Française* (Paris: Dalloz, 1970).

Cole, Charles, *Colbert and a Century of French Mercantilism* (New York: Columbia University Press, 1939).

Conway, Hugh, ed., *Defense Economic Issues* (Washington, D.C.: National Defense University Press, 1990).

Coulam, Robert F., *Illusions of Choice: The F-111 and the Problem of Weapons Acquisition Reform* (Princeton, N.J.: Princeton University Press, 1977).

Cowen, Regina, *Defense Procurement in the Federal Republic of Germany* (Boulder, Colo.: Westview Press, 1986).

Crawford, Beverly, and Stefanie Lenway, "Decision Modes and International Regime Change: Western Collaboration on East-West Trade," *World Politics* 37 (April 1985).

Crowl, Philip, "Alfred Thayer Mahan: The Naval Historian," in Peter Paret, ed., *Makers of Modern Strategy* (Princeton, N.J.: Princeton University Press, 1986).

Davis, Christopher, "Economic and Political Aspects of the Military Industrial Complex in the USSR," in Hans Hohmann, ed., *Economics and Politics in the USSR* (Boulder, Colo.: Westview Press, 1986).

DeGrasse, Robert, *Military Expansion, Economic Decline* (Armonk, N.Y.: M. E. Sharpe, 1983).

Denoon, David B., ed., *Constraints on Strategy* (McLean, Va.: Pergamon-Brassey, 1986).

Derian, Jean-Claude, *America's Struggle for Leadership in Technology* (Cambridge, Mass.: MIT Press, 1990).

Domke, William, Richard Eichenberg, and Catherine Kelleher, "The Illusion of Choice: Defense and Welfare in Advanced Industrial Democracies, 1948–1978," *American Political Science Review 77* (March 1983).

DuBoff, Richard, "What Military Spending Really Costs," *Challenge* (September/October 1989).

Dumas, Lloyd, "National Security and Economic Delusion," *Challenge* (March/April 1987).

Dupree, A. Hunter, *Science in the Federal Government* (Cambridge, Mass.: Harvard University Press, 1957).

———, "National Security and the Postwar Science Establishment in the United States," *Nature 323* (1988).

Earle, Edward Mead, "Adam Smith, Alexander Hamilton, Friedrich List: The Economic Foundations of Military Power," in Peter Paret, ed., *Makers of Modern Strategy* (Princeton, N.J.: Princeton University Press, 1986).

Edmonds, M., *International Arms Procurement* (New York: Praeger, 1986).

Epstein, David, "The Economic Costs of Soviet Security and Empire," *Working Papers in International Studies* (Stanford, Calif.: Hoover Institution, December 1988).

Etzold, Thomas, "National Security and Mobilization: Emerging Issues for the 1990s," *Naval War College Review* (Winter 1990).

Evangelista, Matthew, *Innovation and the Arms Race: How the United States and the Soviet Union Develop New Military Technology* (Ithaca, N.Y.: Cornell University Press, 1988).

Faramazyan, D., *Disarmament and the Economy* (Moscow: Progress Publishers, 1981).

Ferrari, Paul, *U.S. Arms Exports* (Cambridge, Mass.: Ballinger, 1988).

Field, Brian, "Economic Theory, Burden Sharing and the NATO Alliance," *NATO Review 36* (1988).

Flax, Alexander, "Interdiffusion of Military and Civil Technologies in the United States of America," in Judith Reppy and Philip Gummett, eds., *The Relations between Defense and Civil Technology* (Boston: Kluwer, 1988).

Foreign Vulnerability of Critical Industries (Arlington, Va.: TASC, 1990).

Fox, Ronald, *The Defense Management Challenge* (Boston: Harvard Business School Press, 1988).

Friedberg, Aaron, *The Weary Titan* (Princeton, N.J.: Princeton University Press, 1988).

———, "The Political Economy of American Strategy," *World Politics 41* (April 1989).

Galbraith, John Kenneth, *A Theory of Price Controls* (Cambridge, Mass.: Harvard University Press, 1951).

Gansler, Jacques, *The Defense Industry* (Cambridge, Mass.: MIT Press, 1980).

———, "Integrating Civilian and Military Industry," *Issues in Science and Technology 5* (1988).

———, *Affording Defense* (Cambridge, Mass.: MIT Press, 1989).

Gerschenkron, Alexander, *Economic Backwardness in Historical Perspective* (Cambridge, Mass.: Harvard University Press, 1962).

Gilbert, Felix, "Machiavelli: The Renaissance of the Art of War," in Peter Paret, ed., *Makers of Modern Strategy* (Princeton, N.J.: Princeton University Press, 1986).

Gilpin, Robert, *U.S. Power and the Multinational Corporation* (New York: Basic Books, 1975).

——, *The Political Economy of International Relations* (Princeton, N.J.: Princeton University Press, 1987).

Golstein, Joshua S., *Long Cycles* (New Haven, Conn.: Yale University Press, 1988).

Gordon, Lincoln, "Economic Aspects of NATO," *International Organization 10* (Autumn 1956).

Granirer, Dan, "Multinational Corporate Power in Inter-State Conflict: The Toshiba Case," senior honors thesis, Harvard College, Cambridge, Mass., March 1989.

Gregory, William, *The Defense Procurement Mess* (Lexington, Mass.: Lexington Books, 1989).

Grieco, Joseph, "Anarchy and the Limits of Cooperation," *International Organization 42* (Summer 1988).

——, *Cooperation among Nations* (Ithaca, N.Y.: Cornell University Press, 1990).

Hammond, Grant, *Countertrade, Offsets and Barter in International Political Economy* (New York: St. Martin's, 1990).

Hammond, Paul, et al., *The Reluctant Supplier* (Cambridge, Mass.: Oelgeschlager, Gunn and Hain, 1983).

Hampson, Fen, *Unguided Missiles* (New York: Norton, 1989).

Hartley, Keith, *NATO Armaments Collaboration* (London: George Allen and Unwin, 1983).

Hayward, Keith, *The UK Defense Industrial Base* (London: Brassey's, 1989).

Heckscher, Eli F., *Mercantilism* (New York: Macmillan, 1955).

Heilbroner, Robert, *Marxism: For and Against* (New York: Norton, 1980).

Hiller, John, and Judith Larrabee, *Production for Defense* (Washington, D.C.: National Defense University Press, 1980).

Hirschman, Albert, *National Power and the Structure of Foreign Trade* (Berkeley: University of California Press, 1945).

Hitch, Ronald, and Charles McKean, *The Economics of Defense in the Nuclear Age* (Cambridge, Mass.: Harvard University Press, 1960).

Hobkirk, Michael, *The Politics of Defense Budgeting* (Washington, D.C.: National Defense University Press, 1983).

Holzman, Franklyn, "Politics and Guesswork: CIA and DIA Estimates of Soviet Defense Spending," *International Security 14* (Fall 1989).

Hout, Thomas, and Ira Magaziner, *Japanese Industrial Policy* (Berkeley: Institute for International Studies, 1981).

Howard, Michael, *War in European History* (Oxford: Oxford University Press, 1976).

Hull, Cordell, *Memoirs* (New York: Macmillan, 1948).

Huntington, Samuel, "The U.S.—Decline or Renewal?" *Foreign Affairs* (Winter 1988/1989).

Hurley, Shannon, "Arms for the Alliance: Armaments Cooperation in NATO," *Comparative Strategy 7* (1989).

Intrilligator, Michael D., "On the Nature and Scope of Defense Economics," *Defense Economics 1* (1990).

Ismay, Lord, *NATO: The First Five Years* (Utrecht: Bosch, 1954).

Johnson, Chalmers, *MITI and the Japanese Miracle* (Stanford, Calif.: Stanford University Press, 1982).

Jurkus, Anthony, "Requiem for a Lightweight: The Northrop F-20 Strategic Initiative," *Strategic Management Review 2* (1990).

Kapstein, Ethan B., "The Improvement of the West Highlands Fisheries, 1785–1800," *The Mariner's Mirror: Journal of the Royal Maritime Society* (May 1980).

——, "Economic Development and National Security," in E. Azar and Chung-In Moon, eds., *National Security in the Third World* (London: Elgar, 1988).

——, "Economics and Military Power," *Naval War College Review* (Summer 1989).

——, "Corporate Alliances and Military Alliances: The Political Economy of NATO Arms Collaboration," *John M. Olin Institute Working Papers* (November 1989).

——, "From Guns to Butter in the USSR," *Challenge* (September/October 1989).

——, "Losing Control: National Security and the Global Economy," *The National Interest* (Winter 1989/1990).

——, *The Insecure Alliance: Energy Crises and Western Politics since 1944* (New York: Oxford University Press, 1990).

——, "The Political Economy of National Security," *Political Science Teacher* (Spring 1990).

——, "The Brazilian Defense Industry and the International System," *Political Science Quarterly* (Winter 1990/1991).

Katz, James Everett, ed., *Arms Production in Developing Countries* (Lexington, Mass.: Lexington Books, 1984).

——, *The Implications of Third World Military Industrialization* (Lexington, Mass.: Lexington Books, 1986).

Katzenstein, Peter, *Between Power and Plenty* (Madison: University of Wisconsin Press, 1978).

Kaufman, Richard, "Causes of the Slowdown in Soviet Defense," *Soviet Economics 1* (January 1985).

Kennedy, Gavin, *Defense Economics* (New York: St. Martin's Press, 1983).

Keohane, Robert, "Hegemonic Leadership and U.S. Foreign Economic Policy in the Long Decade of the 1950s," in William P. Avery and David P. Rapkin, eds., *America in a Changing World Political Economy* (New York: Longman, 1982).

——, *After Hegemony* (Princeton, N.J.: Princeton University Press, 1984).

—— and Joseph Nye, *Power and Interdependence* (Boston: Little, Brown, 1977).

Kessel, Kenneth, *Strategic Minerals: U.S. Alternatives* (Washington, D.C.: National Defense University Press, 1990).

Keynes, John Maynard, *The Economic Consequences of the Peace* (New York: Harcourt, Brace and Howe, 1920).

Kindleberger, Charles P., *The World in Depression: 1929–1939* (Berkeley: University of California Press, 1973).

Klare, Michael, *American Arms Supermarket* (Austin: University of Texas Press, 1984).

Klein, Burton, *Germany's Economic Preparations for War* (Cambridge, Mass.: Harvard University Press, 1959).

Knorr, Klaus, *The War Potential of Nations* (Princeton, N.J.: Princeton University Press, 1956).

—— and Frank Trager, eds., *Economic Issues and National Security* (Lawrence: Regents Press of Kansas, 1977).

Kolodziej, Edward, *Making and Marketing Arms* (Princeton, N.J.: Princeton University Press, 1987).

—— and Robert Harkavy, eds., *Security Policies of Developing Countries* (Lexington, Mass.: Lexington Books, 1982).

Krasner, Stephen D., *Defending the National Interest* (Princeton, N.J.: Princeton University Press, 1978).

Kupchan, Charles, "Defense Spending and Economic Performance," *Survival* (Autumn 1989).

Kurth, James, "The Military-Industrial Complex Revisited," in Joseph Kurzel, ed., *American Defense Annual* (Lexington, Mass.: Lexington Books, 1989).

Labrie, Roger, et al., *U.S. Arms Sales Policy: Background and Issues* (Washington, D.C.: American Enterprise Institute, 1982).

Lenin, Vladimir Ilyich, *Imperialism: The Highest Stage of Capitalism* (New York: International Publishers, 1939).

Levi, Margaret, *Of Rule and Revenue* (Berkeley: University of California Press, 1988).

Libicki, Martin, *What Makes Industries Strategic* (Washington, D.C.: National Defense University Press, 1989).

Lifeline in Danger (Arlington, Va.: Aerospace Education Foundation, September 1988).

Lincoln, George, *Economics of National Security* (Englewood Cliffs, N.J.: Prentice-Hall, 1954).

Lipschutz, Ronnie, *When Nations Clash* (Cambridge, Mass.: Ballinger, 1989).

Luckham, R., "Of Arms and Culture," *Current Research on Peace and Violence 7* (1984).

Lynch, John, ed., *Economic Adjustment and Conversion of Defense Industries* (Boulder, Colo.: Westview Press, 1987).

Mack, Andrew, and Paul Keal, eds., *Security and Arms Control in the North Pacific* (Boston: Allen & Unwin, 1988).

Mahan, Alfred Thayer, *The Influence of Sea Power upon History, 1660–1789* (New York: Hill and Wang, 1957).

March, Artemis, "The Future of the U.S. Aircraft Industry," *Technology Review* (January 1990).

Mason, Edward, "American Security and Access to Raw Materials," *World Politics 1* (January 1949).

Mastanduno, Michael, "Trade as a Strategic Weapon: American and Alliance Export Control Policy in the Early Postwar Period," *International Organization 42* (Winter 1988).

Mayer, Kenneth, "The Politics and Economics of Defense Contracting," Ph.D. dissertation, Yale University, New Haven, Conn., 1988.

McNaugher, Thomas, *New Weapons, Old Politics: America's Military Procurement Muddle* (Washington, D.C.: Brookings Institution, 1989).

McNeill, William, *The Pursuit of Power* (Chicago: University of Chicago Press, 1982).

Medlicott, W. N., *The Economic Blockade*, 2 vols. (London: HMSO, 1952, 1959).

Meehan, Robert P., *Plans, Programs and the Defense Budget* (Washington, D.C.: National Defense University Press, 1985).

Melman, Seymour, *The Permanent War Economy* (New York: Simon and Schuster, 1985).

Mendershausen, Horst, *The Economics of War* (New York: Prentice-Hall, 1943).

Merritt, Hardy, and Luther Carter, *Mobilization and the National Defense* (Washington, D.C.: National Defense University Press, 1985).

Milner, Helen, *Resisting Protectionism* (Princeton, N.J.: Princeton University Press, 1988).

Milward, Alan S., *War, Economy and Society* (Berkeley: University of California Press, 1977).

Minowitz, Peter, "Invisible Hand, Invisible Death: Adam Smith on War and Socio-Economic Development," *Journal of Political and Military Sociology 17* (Winter 1989).

Moran, Theodore, "The Globalization of America's Defense Industries," *International Security* (Summer 1990).

———, "International Economics and National Security," *Foreign Affairs* (Winter 1990/1991).

Moravcsik, Andrew, "The Future of the European Armaments Industry," *Survival* (Spring 1990).

Morgenthau, Hans, "Alliances in Theory and Practice," in Arnold Wolfers, ed., *Alliance Politics in the Cold War* (Baltimore, Md.: Johns Hopkins University Press, 1959).

———, *Politics among Nations* (New York: Knopf, 1968).

Morse, Edward, *Modernization and the Transformation of International Relations* (New York: Free Press, 1976).

National Academy of Sciences, *Balancing the National Interest* (Washington, D.C.: National Academy Press, 1987).

Nau, Henry, *The Myth of America's Decline* (New York: Oxford University Press, 1990).

——— and Kevin Quigley, *The Allies and East-West Economic Relations: Past Conflicts and Present Choices* (New York: Carnegie Council, 1989).

Newhouse, John, "Politics and Weapons Sales," *The New Yorker,* June 9, 1986.

Nye, Joseph, *Bound to Lead* (New York: Basic Books, 1990).

Olson, Mancur, *The Logic of Collective Action* (Cambridge, Mass.: Harvard University Press, 1965).

——— and Richard Zeckhauser, "An Economic Theory of Alliances," *Review of Economics and Statistics 48* (1965).

Olvey, Lee, et al., *The Economics of National Security* (Garden City, N.Y.: Avery, 1984).

Oneal, John, and Mark Elrod, "NATO Burden-Sharing and the Forces of Change," *International Studies Quarterly 33* (1989).

Parenti, Michael, *The Sword and the Dollar* (New York: St. Martin's, 1989).

Pierre, Andrew, *The Global Politics of Arms Sales* (Princeton, N.J.: Princeton University Press, 1982).

Pincus, John, *Economic Aid and International Cost Sharing* (Santa Monica, Calif.: RAND Corporation, 1965).

Polanyi, Karl, *The Great Transformation* (Boston: Beacon Press, 1944).

Price, Don, *The Scientific Estate* (Cambridge, Mass.: Harvard University Press, 1965).

Ra'anan, Uri, et al., *Arms Transfers in the Third World* (Boulder, Colo.: Westview Press, 1978).

——— and Charles Perry, *Strategic Minerals and International Security* (Cambridge, Mass.: Institute for Foreign Policy Analysis, 1985).

Rasler, Karen, and William Thompson, "Defense Burdens, Capital Formation and Economic Growth," *Journal of Conflict Resolution 32* (1988).

Reppy, Judith, and Philip Gummett, eds., *The Relations between Defense and Civil Technologies* (Boston: Kluwer, 1988).

Rosen, Steven, ed., *Testing the Theory of the Military-Industrial Complex* (Lexington, Mass.: Lexington Books, 1973).

Rosengren, Eric, "Is the United States for Sale? Foreign Acquisition of U.S. Companies," *New England Economic Review* (November/December 1988).

Rothenberg, Gunther, "Maurice of Nassau, Gustavus Adolphus, Raimondon Montecuccoli, and the Military Revolution of the 17th Century," in Peter Paret, ed., *Makers of Modern Strategy* (Princeton, N.J.: Princeton University Press, 1986).

Rothschild, Kurt W., "Military Expenditures, Exports and Growth," *Kyklos 26* (1973).

Rowen, Henry, and Charles Wolf, eds., *The Impoverished Superpower* (San Francisco: Institute for Contemporary Studies, 1990).

Russett, Bruce, *What Price Vigilance? The Burdens of National Defense* (New Haven, Conn.: Yale University Press, 1970).

———, "Defense Expenditures and National Well-Being," *American Political Science Review 76* (1982).

Samuels, Richard, and Benjamin Whipple, "Defense Production and Industrial Development," in Chalmers Johnson, ed., *Politics and Productivity* (Cambridge, Mass.: Ballinger, 1989).

Sandler, Todd, "Sharing Burdens in NATO," *Challenge* (March/April 1988).

Sapolsky, Harvey, *The Polaris System Development* (Cambridge, Mass.: Harvard University Press, 1972).

Schelling, Thomas, *International Economics* (Boston: Allyn and Bacon, 1958).

Schlesinger, James, *The Political Economy of National Security* (New York: Praeger, 1960).

Schultze, Charles, ed., *Setting National Priorities: The 1971 Budget* (Washington, D.C.: Brookings Institution).

Shelton, Judy, *The Coming Soviet Crash* (New York: Free Press, 1989).

Smith, Adam, *An Inquiry into the Nature and Causes of the Wealth of Nations* (Chicago: University of Chicago Press, 1976).

Smith, Ron, "Military Expenditures and Investment in OECD Countries, 1954–73," *Journal of Comparative Economics 4* (1980).

Spykman, N. J., *America's Strategy in World Politics* (New York: Harcourt, Brace, 1942).

Stanley, John, and Maurice Pearton, *The International Trade in Arms* (New York: Praeger, 1972).

Stein, Jonathan, *The Soviet Bloc's Energy and Western Security* (Lexington, Mass.: Lexington Books, 1983).

Stent, Angela, *Soviet Energy and Western Europe* (New York: Praeger, 1982).

Stern, Jonathan, *East European Energy and East-West Trade* (London: Policy Studies Institute, 1982).

Stiglitz, Joseph, *Economics of the Public Sector* (New York: Norton, 1986).

Stockholm International Peace Research Institute, *SIPRI Yearbook: 1989* (Oxford: Oxford University Press, 1989).

Stockman, David, *The Triumph of Politics* (New York: Harper & Row, 1986).

Trice, Robert H., *International Cooperation in Military Aircraft Programs* (Cambridge, Mass.: John M. Olin Institute for Strategic Studies, 1989).

Tucker, Jonathan, "Shifting Advantage," Ph.D. dissertation, Massachusetts Institute of Technology, Cambridge, Mass., 1989.

The U.S. Aerospace Industry and the Trend toward Internationalization (Washington, D.C.: Aerospace Industries Association of America, March 1988).

van Creveld, Martin, *Supplying War: Logistics from Wallenstein to Patton* (London: Cambridge University Press, 1977).

———, *Technology and War* (New York: Free Press, 1989).

Vernon, Raymond, "International Investment and International Trade in the Product Cycle," *Quarterly Journal of Economics 80* (May 1966).

———, *Sovereignty at Bay* (New York: Basic Books, 1971).

———, *Exploring the Global Economy* (Lanham, Md.: University Press of America, 1985).

———, *Foreign Owned Enterprise in the United States: Threat or Opportunity?* (Cambridge, Mass.: Kennedy School of Government, 1988).

Walker, William, and Philip Gummett, "Britain and the European Armaments Market," *International Affairs 65* (Summer 1989).

Weidenbaum, Murray, *Military Spending and the Myth of Global Overstretch* (Washington, D.C.: CSIS, 1989).

Weinberger, Caspar, "Strategy: The Driving Force behind the Defense Budget," *Defense 87* (March/April 1987).

White, Gerald, *Billions for Defense* (University: University of Alabama Press, 1980).

Wirth, John, *The Politics of Brazilian Development, 1930–1954* (Stanford, Calif.: Stanford University Press, 1954).

Wolfers, Arnold, ed., *Alliance Policy in the Cold War* (Baltimore, Md.: Johns Hopkins University Press, 1959).

Woods, Stan, "Weapons Acquisition in the Soviet Union," *Aberdeen Studies in Defense Economics* 24 (Summer 1982).

Index

Note: Page numbers in *italic* refer to tables and figures; page numbers in **boldface** refer to illustrations.